Culture, Mind,

MW00831886

The Book Series of the Society for Psychological Anthropology

The Society for Psychological Anthropology—a section of the American Anthropology Association—and Palgrave Macmillan are dedicated to publishing innovative research that illuminates the workings of the human mind within the social, cultural, and political contexts that shape thought, emotion, and experience. As anthropologists seek to bridge gaps between ideation and emotion or agency and structure and as psychologists, psychiatrists, and medical anthropologists search for ways to engage with cultural meaning and difference, this interdisciplinary terrain is more active than ever.

Possessing Spirits and Healing Selves

EMBODIMENT AND TRANSFORMATION IN AN AFRO-BRAZILIAN RELIGION

Rebecca Seligman

palgrave
macmillan

POSSESSING SPIRITS AND HEALING SELVES
Copyright © Rebecca Seligman, 2014.

Softcover reprint of the hardcover 1st edition 2014 978-1-137-40959-1

All rights reserved.

First published in 2014 by
PALGRAVE MACMILLAN®
in the United States—a division of St. Martin's Press LLC,
175 Fifth Avenue, New York, NY 10010.

Where this book is distributed in the UK, Europe and the rest of the world,
this is by Palgrave Macmillan, a division of Macmillan Publishers Limited,
registered in England, company number 785998, of Houndmills,
Basingstoke, Hampshire RG21 6XS.

Palgrave Macmillan is the global academic imprint of the above companies
and has companies and representatives throughout the world.

Palgrave® and Macmillan® are registered trademarks in the United States,
the United Kingdom, Europe and other countries.

ISBN 978-1-349-48875-9   ISBN 978-1-137-40960-7 (eBook)
DOI 10.1057/9781137409607

Library of Congress Cataloging-in-Publication Data

Seligman, Rebecca.
    Possessing spirits and healing selves : embodiment and
transformation in an Afro-Brazilian religion / Rebecca Seligman.
        pages cm
    Summary: "Spirit possession involves the displacement of a human's
conscious self by that of a powerful other – a spirit, god, or demon –
who temporarily occupies the human's body. To many, spirit possession
is quintessentially exotic, a novelty, an example of the ways in which
"others" are fundamentally different. In this book, Seligman shows
that, far from being exotic and "other," spirit possession mediumship
represents a privileged site for understanding a number of fundamental
aspects of human experience – especially those involved with
interactions among meaning, embodiment, and subjectivity. Using a
diverse set of ethnographic, psychological, and biological data gathered
during fieldwork among spirit possession mediums of the Candomble;
religion in Northeastern Brazil, she explores how everyday and religious
practices and meanings shape and interact with the bodily experiences
and psychophysiological states of Candomble; mediums, both before
and after their initiations, and how such interactions shape their
experiences of selfhood"— Provided by publisher.

    1. Candomblé (Religion)—Brazil. 2. Blacks—Brazil—Religion. 3. Spirit
possession—Brazil. 4. Spiritual healing—Brazil. 5. Healing—Brazil.
6. Ethnology—Brazil. 7. Ethnobiology—Brazil. 8. Brazil—Religious life
and customs. I. Title.

BL2592.C35.S44 2014
299.6'730981—dc23   2014009195

A catalogue record of the book is available from the British Library.

Design by Newgen Knowledge Works (P) Ltd., Chennai, India.

First edition: September 2014

10 9 8 7 6 5 4 3 2 1

For Thom, Nate, and Imogen

Contents

Tables

Series Preface

Psychological anthropologists study a wide spectrum of human activity: child development, illness and healing, ritual and religion, selfhood and personality, political and economic systems, to name just a few. In fact, as a discipline that seeks to draw the lines connecting persons and culture, it would be difficult to come up with examples of human behavior that fall outside the purview of psychological anthropology. Yet beneath this substantive diversity lies a common commitment. The practitioners of psychological anthropology—and in particular the authors in this series—seek to answer broad questions about how peoples' inner worlds are interwoven with their outer ones. And while psychological anthropologists may focus on emotions or human biology, on language or art or dreams, they rarely stray far from the attempt to understand the mental and physical possibilities and limitations that ground human experience.

Professor Rebecca Seligman's study of possession—of how believers in the Candomblé religion come to be inhabited, taken over by spirits—takes us deep into the heart of one of the enduring mysteries about human beings, the relationship between the mind and the body. Seligman gets to know believers on a personal level, to understand their lives and their concerns, and she also studies their health perceptions and physiology. By combining these diverse forms of evidence, she is able to synthesize a powerful account of the ways in which experiences of possession help believers not only to reframe their emotional and physical conditions in less disruptive ways, but also fundamentally reshape their bodily experiences. This profound account of healing has wide-ranging implications for our understanding both of religion and therapeutic processes, and indeed for our very conception of the relationship between the body and the mind.

Acknowledgments

I owe thanks to a great many people for their contributions large and small, direct and indirect, to the writing of this book. To begin at the very beginning, I thank my parents for instilling in me an intellectual curiosity, sense of reflexivity, and great love and respect for words. I thank my sisters for their unconditional love and support, especially Leah who has always always been there when I need her. I owe a great deal of thanks to my dissertation committee, Carol Worthman, Robert Paul, William Dressler, and Drew Westen, for helping to shape the barest seed of an idea into a dissertation project, which became a dissertation, and finally, a book. I am grateful to each of them for their wisdom and intellectual generosity in mentoring me. I owe special thanks to both Carol and Bill for their ongoing mentoring and friendship. Thank you to Laurence Kirmayer for his wonderful mentorship and for teaching me how to think critically about psychopathology while still taking seriously peoples' suffering. I am also grateful to Laurence for printing my very first article about this research in *Transcultural Psychiatry*. Parts of that article appear by permission in chapter 3 of the book. Parts of chapter 5 first appeared in the journal *Ethos*, and I am grateful for the opportunity to expand upon both articles here.

I thank all of my colleagues at Northwestern University for providing such a supportive and dynamic place to work, especially members of the Department of Anthropology and the Institute for Policy Research (IPR). Scholarly and financial support from IPR have been instrumental in facilitating my work on this book. Special thanks are due to Jessica Winegar and Mark Hauser for their invaluable feedback on an earlier draft of one of these chapters. I owe an enormous debt of gratitude to Megan Crowley-Matoka for being my one-woman writing group during the most intense period of the book's development. Without her smart, thoughtful, and always gentle critiques, this book would probably be unreadable.

Many thanks to Rebecca Lester for her unflagging support, for genuinely wanting this manuscript for the Culture, Mind, and Society Series, and for her insightful feedback in the early stages of writing. I am eternally indebted to Peter Stromberg for his hand-holding, careful and thoughtful editing, dynamic scholarly feedback, and most especially, for his wonderful friendship since the moment we met many years ago. I owe thanks to the graduate students and undergraduates in my medical and psychological anthropology seminars at Northwestern and to the students and faculty involved in the Clinical Ethnography Workshop at the University of Chicago, for feedback on my articles and earlier chapter drafts that have influenced the shape of this book. I am grateful to the National Institutes of Health (fellowship number F31AT00065–01) and the National Science Foundation (BCS-0075796) for funding the field research that was the basis of this work.

I am deeply indebted to my "Brazil husband," Heather Shirey, for her companionship, knowledge, and support in the fieldwork adventure and her thoughtful insights into Candomblé belief and practice—especially for drawing my attention to the aesthetic aspects of the religion. I am extremely grateful to her for sharing her wonderful photographs of Candomblé objects, one of which graces the cover of the book. Most of all, I am thankful for her deep and abiding friendship. The most voluminous thanks are owed to my husband Thom, for his support, encouragement, and patience throughout the writing process. He deserves thanks both for his feedback as a colleague in the field of anthropology—over the years every idea in this book has probably been bounced off of him at some point—and for his efforts to smooth the way for my writing in myriad practical ways. He has picked up the slack at home as I scrambled to complete this manuscript, by being a spectacular, present, and loving father to our children. I gave birth to this book and my second child almost simultaneously, and although it has been challenging, I like to think that balancing the demands of my writing with caring for an infant has enriched both projects. Both of my children inspire me everyday and keep me firmly tied to reality. To use the terminology of the book, they have made me a "whole self"—infusing my life with the kind of joy, humor, and frustration that make life worth living.

I cannot adequately thank Mae Tiana and Pai João for opening their *terrieros* to me, and for their mentoring and spiritual guidance. Finally, my deepest gratitude goes to the *filhas* and *filhos de santo* who shared their stories and their friendship with me. I have tried to do justice to both.

Chapter 1

Introduction: Stepping into the "Supernatural World" of Candomblé

On a blistering hot day early in my year of fieldwork in Salvador, Brazil, I set out to have a ritual divination performed on my behalf. I had come to Brazil to study spirit possession mediumship in the African-derived religion Candomblé, and motivated by curiosity and the desire to make connections within this spiritual community, I had made arrangements to have a spiritual leader[1] perform a divination for me that would reveal to which of the Candomblé deities, known as *orixás*, I belonged. In Candomblé, every human being belongs to, or is the *filho* (child) of, a pair of orixás. These two deities share responsibility for both the personality characteristics and the destinies of the humans who belong to them. In order to discover who one's orixás are, a divination, which involves throwing a set of cowry shells and reading the pattern in which they land, must be performed by a qualified spiritual leader. Before the day I had the cowries thrown for me, I did not realize the potential that such identification might have to transform experience.

I had arranged to meet with Mae Tiana, the leader of a small congregation to which I had been introduced several weeks before, at her house, which also served as her *terreiro*, the Candomblé equivalent of a church or temple. The house was in a working class neighborhood made up of other colorful concrete houses and cramped storefronts, and full of the noise and activity of hundreds of people, stray dogs, cars, and buses. In this chaotic setting it was hard to believe that Mae Tiana's tiny, nondescript house was also a place of worship.

The largest room of Mae Tiana's house served as the *barracão*, the space where ritual events are staged. It was a bright, open room sparsely furnished with several long benches for spectators and a few large, regal-looking chairs where the *mae de santo* and other senior initiates sat during *festa*s (public rituals). When I arrived for my divination, however, Mae Tiana did not take me to the barracão. Instead, she ushered me into her dark, cramped living room, where I perched awkwardly on the edge of a lumpy couch. Mae Tiana, a very small, somewhat round woman in her mid-sixties with her grey hair in a knot on top of her head, and wearing a loose-fitting house dress and a pair of mules, was not exactly an imposing figure. With very little ceremony she took out her bag of cowry shells and, muttering something under her breath, she shook them onto a small woven mat on the low table between us. In spite of the informal setting and lack of ritual trappings, as Mae Tiana began to study the shells dispassionately, I realized I was excited and a little bit nervous about the revelation she was about to make. After studying the shells for several more moments, she gathered them back up, threw a few of them again, nodded to herself, and announced the owner of my head: it was Iansã, a female warrior goddess (and her own patron deity). My second-in-command, she went on to reveal, was another warrior, the male deity Ogum. I belonged to not one, but two warrior deities!

As Mae Tiana listed the qualities typically possessed by children of these two orixás, I was surprised by the little surge of pride I experienced. Filhos of these warrior deities are known for their fierce strength, confidence, adventurousness, and passion.[2] What, if anything, I wondered, did it say about me that I was identified with not one but two such gods? Did I possess some inner power or vitality of which I was not even aware? Perhaps I should try harder to cultivate these attributes. I straightened a little in my seat just thinking about it.

When I had had a chance to reflect on it further, I realized that the experience of having my orixás identified was like being offered a supernatural guide to my self—it was like having someone look inside me and pronounce with a kind of cosmic certainty, "These are the characteristics that you possess." But how was I to understand Mae Tiana's role in making this identification? Was this simply what the pattern of the cowries indicated, or had Mae Tiana's perceptions of me influenced her reading? I had always aspired to be strong and confident—there seemed an uncanny fit between my aspirations and Mae Tiana's divination. It was as if she had performed some kind of personality analysis on me that included not only my existing personality, but aspects of my desired self as well.

The more I thought about it, the more I came to see the powerful implications that this experience had for what anthropologists call "subjectivity"—the basic modes of perception, thought, and emotion that inform our fundamental, and not necessarily conscious, sense of who we are (Holland and Leander 2004; Ortner 2005). I had responded to Mae Tiana's divination by embracing the traits it revealed, by identifying with and incorporating them into my sense of self. In other words, the divination process had caused me to not only measure and reflect on my own sense of self, but also adjust it in relation to the attributions presented. There was thus an inkling of something transformative in this experience. What is more, I began to realize that this hint of transformative potential extended beyond a shift in the *ideas* I held about my own personality characteristics. As I sat in Mae Tiana's living room thinking about how I might possess the strength, confidence, and adventurousness of my patron deities, I changed my posture. A shift in my sense of self had brought about a momentary shift in my default way of using and experiencing my body.

This tiny gesture thus drew my attention to an important link between ideas about who one is and the experience of one's body. I had arrived in Brazil prepared to investigate whether the bodies of mediums differ from those of other Candomblé participants in ways that predispose them to experience trance and possession. I had come armed with high-tech medical equipment capable of gathering data on the internal workings of mediums' bodies by measuring their psychophysiological functioning, hoping that this would be the innovative methodology to shed new light on trance and possession. But this early participant-observation pointed toward different ways of thinking about the role of the body in Candomblé mediumship. It suggested important links between bodily experience and subjectivity, and hinted at the potential for Candomblé participation to be transformative in ways that include the reshaping of both body and self.

It is worth noting, however, that not everyone immediately experiences a sense of connection and transformation upon having their orixás divined. Several people mentioned to me that their first divination had identified them as the filhos of orixás with whom they felt no sense of connection. Because the pantheon of deities in Candomblé includes many different types of gods—warriors, hunters, nurturers, those who are gentle and fierce, wise and vain—there are a wide variety of characteristics and combinations of characteristics with which Candomblé devotees may be associated. Filhos of the hunter god Oxossi are known to be calm and controlled, intelligent and loyal; those of Omolu, the deity associated with infectious disease and healing, are shy and pessimistic, hard-working, and orderly; those of the patron goddess of motherhood and the sea, Iemanjá, are calm and sensuous, strong, protective, and arrogant. When the characteristics of the orixás named through divination fail to resonate with either the existing or desired selves of a devotee, rather than motivating him or her to cultivate particular qualities, the process can instead be somewhat alienating.

It was not unusual in these cases for the individual to have a second divination performed by the same or a different spiritual leader, in hopes of a more satisfactory result the second time around. Such misfires, understood in spiritual terms as confusion resulting from multiple orixás battling for control over the individual's head, are probably inevitable in what is surely a delicate process of matching orixás to the extant and desired selves of particular individuals. Breakdowns in this process may have to do with the ability of the spiritual leader to read particular individuals or the willingness of individuals to identify with characteristics that might diverge from their core sense of who they are. Variations in the receptiveness of individuals to these divinatory identifications may also have to do with the lived social and emotional contexts they occupy at the moment of divination. In other words, the success of this process might have to do with the subjective state of an individual at the time of his or her divination.

My divination experience, for instance, had come at a moment when I was feeling vulnerable and full of self-doubt, priming me to be particularly receptive to its transformative possibilities. Did Brazilian Candomblé participants, particularly those who would become spirit possession mediums, join the religion and begin to embrace the influence of the orixás at their own "moments of vulnerability"? Knowing that many Candomblé mediums are low-income Afro-Brazilian women, I wondered if there were ways in which these individuals were primed, perhaps by the effects of their life experiences and social positionality, to embrace the subjective implications and transformative possibilities of Candomblé beliefs and practices. As one of my medium friends later put it, there has to be a potent motivation for immersing oneself in this "*mundo sobrenatural*" (supernatural world).

It was striking to me that even in my mild state of vulnerability, and even without a conviction that the identification of my orixás was channeled through the mae de santo straight from the gods themselves, my sense of self was affected by the divination experience. But how much more powerful would this experience be for someone both more deeply in need and more deeply steeped in the Candomblé cosmology? And what about those who not only know these supernatural beings and the universe in which they exist intellectually, but who know them experientially through their embodiment of the deities in the context of spirit possession?

In spirit possession, the medium's consciousness is suspended while her body takes on the characteristics of the orixás or other spirits who possess her. If the identification of my orixás had been enough to affect my bodily experience even momentarily, then the potential for spirit possession to transform the bodies of mediums was immense. This form of religious participation might therefore be a means of reshaping bodily ways of being along with self-understandings.

And so I came away from my divination experience with a sense of how potent the convergence of religious beliefs and meanings with bodily experiences and practices could be. What is more, I began to appreciate the powerful impact such convergence could have on subjective experience. With the tools I had brought to the field with me, I was uniquely positioned to trace the effects of these processes on the minds and bodies of mediums. Using ethnographic methods, I could offer a close examination of the lived experiences of mediumship, while the tools of psychophysiology would allow me to use measurement of autonomic nervous system regulation over cardiovascular activity as a window inside mediums' bodies.

What might the processes through which meaning and bodily experience converge look like in peoples' lives and in their physiologies? And what might the effects of such convergence be for individuals who became involved in Candomblé mediumship at "moments of vulnerability"? Could the transformation of subjectivity and selfhood through religious belief and practice act therapeutically for vulnerable individuals? These were the questions at the center of the research I conducted during a year of fieldwork among Candomblé spirit possession mediums in Brazil. The aim of this book is to answer them.

The Argument

Spirit possession involves the displacement of a human's conscious self by that of a powerful, immaterial being—a spirit, god, ancestor, or demon—who temporarily animates the human's body while he/she is in a state of trance. Spirit possession mediums enter into long-term relationships with these powerful others, becoming regular vehicles for their materialization in the human world. Mediums thus regularly experience what to many of us would seem like dramatic shifts in our relationship to self and body—their everyday self-awareness becomes suspended, while their bodies continue to operate without a sense of volition. The medium typically has no memory of the events that take place, yet she knows that her body has performed under the direction of some other consciousness, in ways that are not obviously linked to her own sense of identity and intention. To many people, these seemingly radical transformations of subjectivity make spirit possession appear quintessentially exotic—a novelty or example of the ways in which "others" are fundamentally different from "us."

While intimate, sensory experiences of God have become common in some forms of contemporary Evangelical Christianity (Luhrmann 2012), many of us simply do not have a frame of reference for these kinds of subjective transformations. Even hearing God speak in vivid ways would represent an extraordinary experience for many of us, yet mediums appear temporarily to *become* one of their gods. This is why such experiences are so frequently understood in terms of analogy to what are commonly understood as pathological alterations in consciousness associated with dissociative disorders[3]—the most extreme version, known as dissociative identity disorder (DID), involves the experience of multiple, discrete identities housed within a single person. On the surface, possession trance looks a lot like DID. Both involve violations of the Euro-American cultural expectation that people's memories, identity, and awareness should form a single coherent self. Faced with such exotic phenomena, questions inevitably arise about the "authenticity" of trance states, whether possession is "real" or "merely" performance, and whether it is a form of pathology. Above all, questions arise about what might motivate individuals to seek out or endure such extraordinary experiences.

Through the close examination of the experiences of Candomblé spirit possession mediums offered in this book, however, I will demonstrate that far from being exotic and "other," this form of spirit possession mediumship represents a privileged site for understanding important aspects of our shared human experience.

Spirit possession is particularly valuable for drawing our attention to the ways in which individuals are shaped by and embody elements of their lived contexts. In particular, spirit possession is an ideal context in which to investigate *the effects of meaning on the body*—in which to undertake a close examination of the processes and mechanisms through which ideas, beliefs, and discourses can actually shape and transform the states and dispositions of people's bodies.

The effects of meaning on the body have recently become the subjects of increasing attention in both the social and clinical sciences, as it becomes more and more clear that peoples' interpretations and attributions about their experiences can have powerful effects on their health and well-being. Thus, while an analysis of spirit possession may seem far removed from research on the ways in which things like discrimination, stigma, social support, loneliness, and positive regard affect mental and physical health, I will show how spirit possession can actually help us to better understand these phenomena.

In broad terms, then, study of spirit possession has the potential to shed light on basic but crucially important questions about the convergence of individuals and sociocultural systems, and of minds and bodies. For example, the seemingly radical transformation of subjectivity that takes place in spirit possession can be understood as a particularly visible example of the more general process through which systems of meaning and embodied experiences come together to shape peoples' sense of self, and affect their well-being. These are not exotic processes, but mundane ones that each of us experience throughout our lifetimes in more or less visible ways, as we enact and internalize the messages and meanings communicated by the people, institutions, and material structures that surround us.

Much of the time the interactions between systems of meaning and embodied experience result in a gradual process of learning, affecting subjectivity in ways that are subtle and incremental. The very "otherness" of spirit possession throws these processes into relief. In other words, we are able to see the embodied effects of religious belief vividly when mediums become possessed because possession seems to many of us like such an extreme and foreign expression of belief. What is more, the exaggerated visibility of these processes in spirit possession may reinforce this sense of foreignness. Because many people from Euro-American backgrounds are not accustomed to seeing such obvious effects of meaning on the body, we may think that "others" are somehow more susceptible. Yet more familiar examples of the embodied effects of meaning are all around us. The so-called placebo effect is an obvious example in which the symbolic act of consuming a substance that is understood to have therapeutic effects can actually produce such effects. If we take the time to really think about what this means—that consuming a substance that *by definition*[4] can have no effect because it is inert (i.e., a sugar pill) makes people feel better simply because they believe it will—then we begin to more fully appreciate the power of ideas, of expectations, of *meaning* to effect bodily change.

Other examples of the effects of meaning on the body include the mental and physical benefits of yoga practice (Beets and Mitchell 2010; Lin et al. 2011), the capacity of cognitive behavioral therapy (CBT) to improve outcomes among cancer patients (Penedo et al. 2007), the amelioration of alcohol addiction through the 12 steps

(Cain 1991), and the adverse effects of psychosocial stress on health. Recent anthropological research has contributed to our understanding of such stress–health dynamics, demonstrating that psychosocial stress is largely a function of meaning. That is, the interpretations and attributions—or meanings—that people make about their social situations influence their experience of stress.

Such research includes evidence that complex dynamics associated with relative social status are strongly associated with negative health outcomes ranging from suppressed immune function to high blood pressure (McDade 2002; Sweet et al. 2007; Dressler et al. 1998; Dressler and Bindon 2000; Gravlee 2005). When different markers of status like skin color and socioeconomic status (SES) conflict with one another, health is affected negatively. This clearly demonstrates that shared ideas about what status markers mean and how they should relate to one another have effects on bodily well-being that are independent of the effects of material disadvantage. The social meanings of status markers like skin color or material possessions affect individual well-being in part through their effects on self-understandings; seeing oneself as lower status compared to those around one, or compared to one's own expectations, is stressful.

These kinds of meaning effects are relevant to understanding the experiences of vulnerability that characterized the lives of many prospective Candomblé mediums. As I came to know the mediums in the two small terreiros where I conducted the bulk of my research, it became clear that as in many other places where spirit possession is practiced, individuals attracted to the mediumship role in Candomblé are often socially disadvantaged, or in some way "marked" and marginal. In a society characterized by rigid class divisions, racial inequality, and a history of patriarchy and gender divisions, the mediums I came to know were mostly poor or working class Afro-Brazilians, females, or homosexual males.[5] Many participants had thus faced immense challenges associated with their membership in particular social group(s). Others were marked not by group membership but by their failure to fulfill social expectations in some way. Some, for instance, had failed to take on an expected social role. Others, having taken on such a role, had failed to perform it successfully. Mediums thus had histories of psychosocial stress shaped both by political, economic, and institution structures of power, and by the dominant sets of meanings in their sociocultural contexts.

Unsurprisingly, the social suffering these individuals experienced was often accompanied by forms of emotional and physical suffering—another common example of the effects of meaning on the body. The stories of the mediums I encountered were filled with descriptions of chronic stress, distress, and bodily affliction. Before their initiations, mediums struggled to make ends meet, lost loved ones, had nervous breakdowns, and suffered from mysterious heart palpitations, rashes, and fevers. These experiences made them vulnerable, and it was at especially acute "moments of vulnerability" that they came to be involved in Candomblé.

Yet the dominant theme of their stories was not one of suffering or conflict; it was one of healing and transformation. As they recalled their initial engagement with Candomblé and the role of medium, their narratives traced an arc from a state of suffering to one of well-being. What is more, the movement between these states was coincident with their transformation from individuals with an unacknowledged spiritual calling, to initiated religious experts. Here again the effects of meaning on the body seem to be implicated.

One of my goals in this book is to make sense of the passage from suffering to well-being that is at the core of many mediums' experiences. How do initiation into mediumship and ongoing immersion in Candomblé help individuals deal with the forms of distress they faced prior to initiation? How, in particular, does religious participation affect the bodily states of mediums, so that they experience recovery not only from the emotional afflictions suffered prior to their engagement with Candomblé, but the physical ones as well? What are the mechanisms through which this kind of religious participation can heal?

For many participants, the convergence of meaning and embodied experience in Candomblé spirit possession mediumship facilitates a process of healing through self-transformation. What I mean by this is that becoming a medium is associated for many with a fundamental change in the sense of self—both in terms of who these individuals understand and experience themselves to be and how they project themselves into the social world. The transformation of selfhood in turn contributes to healing—not only from social and emotional forms of distress, but from bodily afflictions as well. While Candomblé spirit possession mediumship is inextricably linked to its unique social and ontological context and cannot be reduced to processes of self-transformation and healing, understanding it in these terms not only helps to shed light on mediumship, but serves to further illuminate these processes themselves.

My argument is based on the following set of interrelated premises. First, the process of self-transformation in Candomblé mediumship is an embodied one. The transformation that mediums experience is not merely intellectual, but experiential—they act and *feel* differently. Second, selfhood is itself fundamentally embodied. Self-transformation is not merely intellectual because *self* is not just an idea, it is a way of being in the world that is located at the intersection of mind and body. Third, because self is embodied, transformation of the whole self must involve not only discursive but also embodied forms of learning. When acquisition of new ideas and beliefs about self is complemented by forms of training that involve new ways of using and experiencing the body, self-transformation is particularly profound. Fourth, embodied learning is a biocultural process and as such involves bodily mechanisms, including psychophysiological ones. Embodiment is reflected in and produced, at least in part, by biological processes designed to be responsive to social and cultural input. A particularly critical and unique contribution of this study, therefore, is the use of data from psychophysiological measurement to explore the biological dimensions of embodied learning among Candomblé mediums. Fifth, transformation of the whole self has the potential to heal because it affects both embodied processes, including psychophysiological ones that may contribute to symptoms of bodily affliction, as well as discursive and meaning-related processes that, through their effects on interpretations and perceptions, may transform bodily experiences from symptoms of illness, to markers of spiritual capacity. Sixth, and finally, cultural systems like spirit possession, which synchronize embodied and discursive forms of learning, are particularly effective at facilitating transformations that heal.

Thus, while healing self-transformation is arguably an extraordinary outcome, the general shaping of selfhood and well-being through the interaction of meaning and embodied experience is not extraordinary. Instead it is a function of the nature of selves.

Self

But what do we really mean when we use the term "self"? Since it is central to my argument, it seems important to examine the notion of self and its relationship to spirit possession in some depth before proceeding. Self is a concept used by philosophers, psychologists, and anthropologists in somewhat different ways. Anthropological scholarship on self has been dominated by approaches that understand it primarily in terms of language and representation. From this perspective, self is a semiotic process through which we represent ourselves cognitively to ourselves, and discursively to others, through language (Ewing 1990; Gergen 1991; Ochs and Capps 1996). This broad approach to self, which we might call the "cognitive-discursive" model, draws our attention to several aspects of selfhood that are crucial to understanding its relationship to spirit possession. First, self can be thought of both as a kind of internal dialog through which we mentally sort out and represent our own experiences, motivations, memories, and desires and as an external dialog through which we represent these aspects of ourselves in our social worlds. The internal and external dialogs are, of course, also in dialog with one another: the way that people in my life respond when I represent myself as a good mom or a hardworking scholar inevitably affects my own internal representations of myself as a mother and scholar.

Thus, self is the locus of interaction between individual and culture—it is where the qualities of individuals, some of them shared and some idiosyncratic, come together with the qualities of their lived environments. As such, self is dependent on processes internal to the individual, especially the human capacity for self-awareness (Hallowell 1955). It is because of these individual-level self-processes that we are able to reflect on and evaluate our experiences, accumulate self-knowledge, and form concepts to make sense of this knowledge. For instance, it is self-awareness that allows me to recognize when I have a thought, and to recognize that the thought is my own. Perhaps I think that I should go to the gym today. I do not simply experience the thought as a motivation or impulse. Instead, I can represent the thought to myself symbolically, through language, and experience my own awareness of it. I know the thought is mine partly because it links to aspects of an established self-concept that I already hold—maybe I understand myself as someone who stays "in shape." Moreover, I am motivated to behave in ways that are consistent with this idea of myself. Hence, self is an important mediator of the link between ideas/beliefs and behaviors.

Sociocultural factors, including political economies and power relations, fundamentally shape our motivations and desires, canalize our experiences, and direct our attention to the aspects of experience that are most salient, while also driving expectations about what kinds of selves these elements should comprise (Hollan 1992; Kusserow 2004; Miller 1994).[6] Some cultures tell people that their social roles and relationships to others are defining features of their selfhood (Shweder and Bourne 1981). My culture tells me that taking care of my health through exercise is a central element of successful personhood and that as an autonomous individual it is my personal choice and responsibility stay in shape. As a member of this culture, I have internalized these values in the form of desires, motivations, and goals that are integral to my self-concept. Whether or not I go to the gym is another story, but if I do not go, I may have an emotional response or feel a sense of discomfort associated with failing to act in a way that is consistent with my self-concept. The inability to act in ways that are consistent with self-concept on a regular basis may create the perception of dissonance and lead to an ongoing experience of negative emotion or stress (Seligman 2010).

Self can thus be thought of as *inward* in the sense that it involves the internalization and filtering of cultural and social influences through intrapsychic processes like self-awareness, concept formation, perception, and affect. These processes are in turn shaped by their interaction with cultural and social influences and structures of power. The ways in which the intrapsychic aspects of self are shaped by such structural influences is often referred to under the heading of "subjectivity" (Biehl et al. 2007; Holland and Leander 2004; Ortner 2005).

At the same time, self is also *outward*. It is the medium through which we project ourselves into the social sphere, the way we represent ourselves to others, and the social object with which people and institutions interact. The outward dimensions of self encompass both what we think of as identity and personhood—those aspects of self that are most closely tied to social roles and expectations. The way my boss represents himself when talking to me is not the same way he represents himself when talking to his daughter, and this is in large part due to the fact that he does not expect or want me to interact with him in the same ways that his daughter does. Because it unfolds in particular contexts, shifting incrementally, and at times more dramatically in response to changing demands and experiences, self can also be thought of as a process, or "processual." Self not only shifts contextually, but over time, as we adjust our goals, consolidate our memories, and adopt new characteristics. My self of today is not the same as my self of 20 years ago, although the changes may have been incremental, and I may feel some degree of continuity. On the other hand, selves can also change more abruptly or radically—in a short time I could go from being highly self-centered to being deeply focused on my responsibilities and commitments to others.

Self-narrative, or the stories we tell ourselves and others about ourselves, can be understood as a crucial mechanism through which different aspects of self—the inward and outward, old and new—are integrated (Ochs and Capps 1996; Ricoeur 1992; Ewing 1990; McAdams 1989; Seligman 2005b). My story of self may be a means through which I make sense, conceptually and socially, of my change from self-centered to other-focused—for instance, I may narrate this change in relation to an event or experience (I became a mother, got sick, found god, or had an epiphany)—and cultural meanings serve as an important resource for this process (Stromberg 1985; Obeyesekere 1981). Understanding the ways in which self links individuals to their sociocultural contexts through discursive and representational processes is crucial to understanding self-transformation in spirit possession. In particular, it can help us to understand how religious beliefs serve as cultural resources mobilized in the process of reshaping cognitive self-representations and self-narratives among Candomblé mediums.

However, focus on the discursive, representational, and processual aspects of self by many anthropologists has meant that its embodied dimensions have been relatively neglected (Quinn 2006). Yet self is not only a product of mental consideration, or detached reflection, but also of sensations and feelings (Elias 1939, 1956). In fact, some have argued that despite cultural variability in the kinds of self-representations and concepts people hold, all selves are fundamentally grounded in the experience of occupying an individual body, separate from other bodies (Mauss 1934; Scheper-Hughes and Lock 1987). Phenomenological theories of self in particular maintain that it is constituted not only by representation, but also by our experiences of "being in the world"—experiences that are mediated by our bodies (Csordas 1993). For example, whenever I am standing up, I can feel my feet on the floor, my arms hanging from my shoulders, I can feel that my head is higher than my feet, and I can feel gravity's gentle tug. I *feel* or *experience* all of these sensations, even when I am not consciously reflecting on them. The experiences in which self is grounded are thus structured not only by our sociocultural environments but also by the nature of the physical bodies we occupy and the ways in which our bodies operate in and interact with our environments—things like our sensations and sensory perceptions, bodily movements and postures.

What is more, the direct involvement of our bodies in the world is experienced prior to and fundamentally shapes the processes of reflection and self-objectification upon which the representational dimensions of self are based (Csordas 1993, 1994; Seligman 2010; Taves 2009). This is why the metaphors we use to represent different aspects of self and experience are so often based on bodily structures, sensations, and processes (Lakoff 1993; Kirmayer 2004). The moral connotations of being an "upstanding citizen," for instance,

are linked to the experience of upright posture, just as the character-
ization of the struggle to achieve a goal as "an uphill battle" is drawn
from the experience of the physical effort involved in moving our
bodies uphill (Lakoff and Johnson 1999).

The fundamental role of embodied experience in selfhood helps
explain why serious, and especially chronic, illnesses are often so disruptive to people's sense of self. The pain and disability that often
accompany illness can dominate attention, preempt other thoughts,
and reshape perceptions. The need, for instance, to concentrate on
the performance of formerly taken-for-granted, elementary physical
tasks can deeply affect the experience of self. Such bodily experiences also undermine the ability to behave in ways that are consistent with one's self-concept—it is difficult, for instance, to interact
positively with friends and family, or be productive at work, when
experiencing severe pain. The sense of dissonance this produces may
force individuals to abandon old self-representations and script new
self-narratives (Becker 1997). Embodied and representational dimensions of self are thus deeply interdependent.

Here I draw on both "cognitive-discursive" and phenomenological
theories in using the concept of self to refer to embodied experiences
of being in the world, as well as the representational processes that
grow from, but also help shape, our awareness of those experiences.
I demonstrate how, for Candomblé mediums, embodied experiences
of operating within a particular cultural and social sphere combine
with reflections on, and representations of, those experiences, to constitute selfhood. When I argue that for some participants, spirit possession facilitates a process of healing self-transformation what I aim
to draw attention to, then, is how the practices and beliefs, meanings
and bodily experiences associated with this role come together to
re-shape *both* the embodied and representational aspects of selves in
ways that reinforce one another and positively affect well-being.

Self, Healing, and Self-Healing in
Spirit Possession

Past models of the relationship between spirit possession and healing have often failed to account for the role of self. These models
have typically either treated spirit possession as a kind of "culturally constituted defense mechanism" that allows individuals to cope
with pathological tendencies in sanctioned ways (Spiro 1965), or as
an actual form of psychopathology, albeit a culturally elaborated

one (Goodman 1988; Ward 1989, 1994). These models understand possession as equivalent or analogous to dissociative disorders and other forms of psychopathology for which altered states of consciousness and transformations of subjectivity represent symptoms (Bourguignon 1989; Cardeña 1992). While these explanations have been appropriately criticized for their reductive and medicalizing approach, there is something of value in their concern with accounting for both the embodied nature of possession (with a focus specifically on trance and altered states of consciousness), as well as the psychological and social status of individual participants. Yet these approaches do not effectively model the relationships among these elements, in part because they fail to recognize that *self* is a key mediator of these sociocultural, psychological, and bodily processes. In other words, they fail to recognize that interactions between the representational and experiential processes that make up selfhood are key to understanding both mental illness and spirit possession, and the differences between them.

Thus, these models reify a surface resemblance among mental illness, psychotherapy, and spirit possession because they misunderstand the nature of the relationship among them. What connects these phenomena is the ways in which meaning and embodied experience come together to shape subjectivity and moral personhood in each case. In each, the interactions between a set of experiences and the variously pathologizing, psychologizing, or religious attributions made about these experiences shape subjectivity and define the opportunities for enacting particular forms of personhood. In other words, similar experiences of emotional and somatic distress and entry into altered states of consciousness do not represent symptoms of a universal disorder that, depending on the context, has merely been culturally elaborated or mobilized a culturally specific treatment. Instead, the different meanings these experiences evoke and the different contexts of selfhood in which they take place fundamentally alter their effects on both the inward and outward, experiential and representational dimensions of selfhood. They form the basis of different kinds of self-concepts and self-narratives, and they lead to different forms of self-awareness, perception, and affect.

An individual who suffers from emotional and somatic distress and enters into altered states of consciousness in mainstream US culture, where these experiences violate normative expectations for selfhood, will often be understood to have the symptoms of a disorder—a disorder that has its source inside the individual. In such a context these experiences are likely to lead to subjective experiences of distress and dysfunction, and the kind of moral personhood associated with the sick role. In other words, in the dominant US culture, these symptoms are likely to make one mentally ill.

Alternatively, where they are understood from an ontological perspective that includes the idea that human bodies may be controlled by powerful nonhuman others, these same experiences may be viewed as signs of a spiritual calling visited upon the individual by the gods. This attribution may lead to a reduction in the subjective experience of distress, and instead of the sick role, the kind of moral personhood associated with being a medium (Seligman and Kirmayer 2008). In each case, the effects of cultural and social attributions on well-being are mediated by their relationship to the self.

The more that self is implicated in either the causes or consequences of suffering, the greater the impact of that suffering. Forms of suffering that are attributed to causes accessible to the individual's control, or which directly violate highly valued aspects of identity, are particularly self-implicating. By undermining an individual's self-understandings or usual embodied experiences of being in the world, such forms of suffering have the potential to create a sense of internal conflict, disjuncture, and fragmentation. For example, suffering that causes an individual to become dependent on others in a cultural context in which independence and productivity are highly valued, may create a sense of self-fragmentation because it leads to experiences that directly conflict with goals and desires central to self-understanding—in this case, a culturally instilled desire for independence and productivity (Hay 2010). On the other hand, suffering for which responsibility is located outside the individual's control is often less self-implicating. Certain forms of medicalization, in which suffering is blamed on organic disease processes, are less likely to create a sense of internal conflict because the self is seen as a victim of natural forces, and therefore not implicated in the causes of suffering. Attributing illness and misfortune to spiritual causes external to the individual similarly serves to buffer the self by linking suffering to *super*natural forces not expected to be under his/her control.

In addition, discontinuities in the experience of self may themselves be a source of suffering. This is the case especially when such discontinuities are unexpected, unsanctioned, and resist attribution. Thus, in the context of the dominant Euro-American culture, in which there are high expectations for a unitary, coherent self, there is a lower tolerance for such experiences and a relative dearth of meaningful, nonpathologizing explanations available for them. The few nonpathologizing models for such discontinuities that do exist in the United States tend to understand them in relation to a substance (i.e., alcohol) or stimulus (i.e., video games) that allows these experiences to be explained away, as fleeting responses to external triggers (Stromberg 2009; Snodgrass 2011).

For example, individuals who get very drunk may behave in ways that are out of character and that they cannot later remember, thus demonstrating discontinuities in aspects of self, like self-awareness, memory, and identity. However, because such antics can be blamed on the consumption of alcohol, they are not understood to violate expectations for self-coherence. In such cases, the self is not seen as fundamentally unstable or fragmented, it is merely thought to have been temporarily destabilized by the action of a powerful substance. In this case, alcoholic spirits are responsible for the individual's behavior rather than supernatural ones. But while these nonpathologizing models make such experiences intelligible, they are not connected to a set of positive meanings within the dominant US culture—we do not tend to think of the individual who "becomes a different person" when drunk as representing our deeply held values or fulfilling an essential social role. In other words, such experiences, even when they are not seen as evidence of mental illness, are still relatively marginalized.

Furthermore, when such discontinuities occur in the absence of obvious material triggers, and when they are more enduring, fragmentation or disruption in the integration of different aspects of self are unlikely to be normalized in most mainstream US contexts, and are therefore more likely to cause distress (Seligman and Kirmayer 2008). Importantly, discontinuities or disjunctures in selfhood are both expected and meaningful in the context of Candomblé as part of the experience of control by the orixás. In fact, divisions between aspects of self-awareness like intention and memory are invited by mediums in the form of trance and possession.

Hence, one mechanism of the movement from suffering to well-being for many of the mediums with whom I worked is immersion into a system of meaning that provides novel attributions for their experiences (Nuckolls 1991; Taves 2009). I saw, for instance, that filhos come to understand their history of suffering and its effects on self in terms of the influence of their orixás. Participation in Candomblé enables filhos to explain failures, losses, stress, and pain in terms that locate causes outside of the self, in the universe of spirits and beings whose personalities, motivations, and desires shape the human world. Such an understanding contributes to altering their perceptions of, and narratives about, themselves in ways that are therapeutic.

At the same time, the practice of mediumship also exposes individuals to novel experiences that contribute to production of new forms of socio-moral subjectivity. Possession, for example, involves the experience of being controlled by a powerful other, a being who has different attitudes, emotions, and capacities, and a different kind of relationship to other people. Most individuals who become mediums have experienced social constraints that limit their choices, the roles they are allowed and expected to play, and the behaviors in which they can engage. When possessed, however, mediums take on the behaviors of a spirit who is typically not constrained in the same ways.

Thus, as many anthropologists have noted (cf. Evans-Pritchard [1956] and others), the experience of being controlled by a spirit or deity can be ironically liberating, given that it releases individuals from quotidian expectations, allowing them to behave very differently. A woman who works as a maid for a rich family and spends her days taking orders, being polite, and serving others has the opportunity when possessed to channel the power and dominance of her orixá, or to take on the hard-drinking, rude-talking persona of her *caboclo* (indigenous South American spirit). Possession thus opens up alternative ways of being in the world, allowing mediums to enact novel characteristics and occupy a radically different structural position from that to which they are accustomed.

The experience of occupying a new structural position extends beyond possession states as well, as by their own accounts mediums also experience shifts in subjectivity associated with the role they take on within the religious community as ritual experts and mediators between the human and spiritual worlds. Individuals who have had little access to social and political power within the wider Brazilian context are thus able to access a new form of power by virtue of their structural position within the religion. These observations are consistent with theories of spirit possession that understand it as a form of social communication that allows marginalized individuals new ways of talking about, reflecting on, and performing selfhood and identity, thus giving them the opportunity to reposition themselves socially (Lambek 1981; Boddy 1993; Ong 1987).

I build on such arguments by demonstrating how these social and communicative functions of spirit possession serve to transform both internal and external dimensions of the cognitive-discursive self, and in doing so contribute to a form of "self-healing." The term self-healing refers to healing that is specifically effected through the reshaping of subjectivity and personhood. Such healing entails both mending of the self itself, as well as amelioration of the afflictions from which many prospective mediums suffer, via the transformation of self-concepts, self-narratives, and internal self-processes like attention and perception. Self-healing occurs at the intersection of individual and sociocultural context in the sense that shared religious meanings and socially defined expectations are the resources from which these new forms of subjectivity and personhood emerge.

Critical to a complete understanding of how self-transformation ameliorates the suffering of prospective mediums, however, is also an exploration of the ways in which mediumship operates at the intersection of mind and body, and thus has the capacity to reshape *embodied* dimensions of self as well. Over the course of my time in Brazil it became clear to me that the experiences through which mediums' subjectivities were most deeply affected were mediated by their bodies. This is in part because the body figures so centrally in Candomblé practice. Not only is it the main instrument of ritual devotion—used for the movements of ritual prostration, dancing, and spiritual celebration, the consumption of ritual foods, and the accumulation and transfer of *axé*, or spiritual power—but experiencing and even inviting *changes* to one's bodily state is an essential element of this practice.

Such changes include the bodily dimensions of initiation, like shaving the head and observing dietary restrictions, which alter the body in ways that are understood to prepare it spiritually to be a medium for the deities. Learning and practicing ritual behaviors and trance induction techniques also changes the bodies of mediums in ways that make these practices increasingly natural to them. Over time, the bodies of mediums slip into the dances and movements of ritual performance, and even into the altered states of consciousness associated with trance, in ways that are increasingly automatic. Altered states of consciousness themselves represent an important kind of bodily change invited by mediumship, as the relationships of filhos to their bodies shifts dynamically each time they relinquish and regain control of their material forms from the spirits.

These observations suggest that regular engagement in the bodily practices of Candomblé alters the ways that mediums use, experience, and understand their bodies. These alterations ultimately result in an even grander form of bodily change—one in which mediums' bodies go from being the material sources or sites of debilitating somatic suffering before initiation, to the experiential ground of an empowering spiritual gift afterward. In other words, mediums' bodies are not only healed, but transformed through their religious participation.

This crucial change is captured in the spiritual life history narratives I collected, in which bodily illness was the most common immediate precipitant of initiation, and its alleviation figured as the narrative resolution. The body is thus involved at both ends of the trajectory that these mediums follow in relation to their role—it represents both a cause of suffering and disrupted subjectivity that motivates their involvement, and the locus of their spiritual formation and healing.

Influential theories of spirit possession that view it as a form of social communication have not ignored the body, but have treated it as an additional channel through which participants come to articulate a more expansive form of selfhood. That is, new ways of using the body, new forms of action and behavior, are viewed from this perspective as part of a communicative performance through which mediums transform their social selves and interpersonal relationships (Lambek 1981; Schieffelin 1985; Stoller 1992; Wafer 1991). In such approaches both possession and self are seen as roles, and the body as an essential instrument of role performance. But I found that among Candomblé mediums, embodied practices do more than just contribute to new ways of performing self, they contribute to fundamental changes in the *experience* of self. To put it more concretely, I observed that for many of the mediums in my study, the embodied practices of spirit possession represent an opportunity to relearn bodily ways of being, shed old patterns of behavior, and even to reshape physiological responses that reflect a past form of selfhood.

These observations suggest that we might think of the role performance of Candomblé mediums as a form of "deep acting." In theater, deep acting is distinguished from its alternative, "surface acting," by the degree to which actors actually experience the emotions they perform. In surface acting, emotions are behaved but not really felt—tears are shed, but there is no corresponding feeling of sadness. In deep acting, on the other hand, actors perform emotions by actually evoking them—the actor finds a way to *feel* sad, in order to shed tears. The emotional performance thus extends beyond surface expression to include the actor's body in a deeper form of self-engagement.

For mediums, then, bodily engagement creates a kind of deep acting in which role performance serves to *evoke* fundamentally different bodily states, and new bodily states contribute to the performance of a different kind of self. The medium's role enactment, in other words, conjures a shift in his/her embodied state—and vice versa. However, animating the role of medium really goes beyond enactment altogether, in the sense that transitory shifts in embodied state, like those involved in trance, are linked to more enduring changes in the medium's embodied ways of being. In other words, mediumship is not merely a performance in which the actor actually feels what he or she enacts, rather it is a part of a genuine transformation of self. In fact, transformations of both the embodied and representational aspects of self are integrated through this form of religious participation, largely because spirit possession promotes such deep engagement of both mind and body. A central premise of this book is therefore that the process of self-transformation in Candomblé spirit possession mediumship is a process with the potential to *heal* both mind and body.

Embodiment

In many ways Candomblé spirit possession exemplifies how selfhood is embodied.

On the one hand, new experiences, performances, and understandings of self that are associated with becoming a medium contribute to shifts in bodily states: as the self comes to be understood as one who gets possessed rather than one who suffers, old patterns of bodily response are unlearned and new ones learned. Conversely, as mediums accumulate new bodily experiences, their sense of self is changed: the medium learns to induce trance states and incorporate the deities, and in doing so, she comes to understand and experience herself as spiritually empowered. Thus, changes to individual subjectivity are produced through a process of embodied learning.

A second central premise of this book is, therefore, that in order to understand self and self-transformation in Candomblé it is necessary for us to better understand the process of embodied learning that takes place in this religious context. It is not enough to say that patterns of bodily response and behavior are reshaped through a process of embodied learning in Candomblé, we also need to ask *how* such bodily learning takes place, through what mechanisms within the body do the cultural meanings and practices of Candomblé become absorbed? There is a need, that is, to explore the specific bodily processes implicated in what we call "embodiment."

Bodily processes involved in religious participation include the obvious sensory engagement with the sights, sounds, smells, and tastes of ritual practice—the sounds of drumming and music, the sights of ritual objects and costumes, the taste of ritual foods, and so forth. They also include the kinesthetic, proprioceptive (relating to perception of relative position and effort of one's body parts), and interoceptive (relating to perception of internal bodily stimuli like pain and hunger) processes associated with the movements, sensations, and behaviors of religious enactments—the feeling of dancing, of consuming ritual food, of sleeping on the floor during initiation—and the emotional responses activated by all of these forms of religious engagement. But embodied religious learning also involves less obvious *psychophysiological* processes. There is mounting evidence that patterns of cardiovascular, endocrinological, and neurochemical activation are entrained by learning and experience, and that learning and experience are conditioned by these psychophysiological processes (Boyce and Ellis 2005; Cacioppo et al. 2000; Schwartz et al. 1999; Suomi 1991). Yet the psychophysiological dimensions of embodiment have not been explored by anthropologists.

In fact, while a great deal of contemporary anthropological scholarship invokes notions of embodiment and embodied learning (Blackwood 2011; Freeman 2011; Ivry 2009; Mascia-Lees 2011a; Van Wolputte 2004), not only is there often very little specificity about what this means, but the physical body is notably absent from most of this literature. The term "embodiment" is most often used in the anthropology literature to refer to the ways in which bodies are understood in social terms, and how their treatment, presentation, and care reflect the values and norms of particular cultures. This includes a concern with the ways in which political-economic conditions and power relations are "inscribed" on individual bodies. Recent examples include analysis of the meanings surrounding, and treatment of, pregnant bodies—what kinds of practices pregnant women are expected to engage in, and how their bodies are regulated through medical intervention—in terms of what these tell us about the "embodiment" of particular cultural values (Ivry 2009). Exploration of the ways in which religiosity contributes to the "embodiment" of particular forms of agency and personhood among Islamic women is another example of work that employs embodiment in this rather discursive sense (Mahmood 2001). While this use of the term is relevant to the ways in which the bodies of prospective mediums reflect their pre- and post-initiation contexts in symbolic terms, treatment of the inner workings of the body in such approaches is often relatively superficial.

A related use of the term embodiment has been in reference to certain kinds of bodily learning and knowledge that are the products of interaction with our social and cultural contexts, particularly the structural features with which we come into regular contact (Connerton 1995). This usage resembles and is often explicitly linked to Bourdieu's (1984; 1990) concept of the habitus. Embodied knowledge, in this view, is knowledge that does not pass through conscious awareness, but is learned instead through interactions, behaviors, and routines (Jackson 1983; Strathern 1996). Routinely sitting at a table and using a knife and fork to eat meals, for example, produces a particular kind of embodied knowledge that is quite distinct from the kind of embodied knowledge learned by sitting on a floor mat and eating with chopsticks. Such knowledge affects everything from facility with chopsticks, to the kind of posture one associates with and automatically assumes while eating, to the kinds of contexts that stimulate one's appetite—and it does so in ways that are largely unconscious.

This approach to embodiment draws our attention to the crucially important ways in which practice—what we *do*, our culturally prescribed actions—contributes to forms of implicit learning through which our everyday experiences become powerfully internalized. Such theories are extremely relevant to thinking about the suffering many of the prospective mediums I worked with endured prior to initiation—suffering that was closely tied to structural conditions. From this perspective, we might understand such suffering as a form of *embodied knowledge* accumulated through the day-to-day behaviors, routines, and interactions of prospective mediums—especially since many of these everyday experiences involve physical struggles and psychosocial stress associated with the marginal social, political, and economic position these individuals occupy within Brazilian society. Conceptualizing embodiment in this way can also help us think about the processes of unlearning old bodily habits and internalizing new forms of bodily knowledge that take place through religious practices of initiation and ongoing devotion. Mediums rehearse ritual behaviors over and over again until these behaviors become second nature—until they become unconscious, embodied knowledge.

However, these theories of embodiment leave us to wonder about the *mechanisms* through which bodies are conditioned by experience and practice. What does it really mean to say that a body possesses "knowledge" or has "learned" something? Though they locate this learning or knowledge in the body, what many of these theories seem to be describing is really a form of non-narrative, implicit memory formation (Mulligan and Besken 2013; Roediger 1990). These forms of memory are often consolidated without conscious reflection and recalled in the same way—nonverbally, in the form of behaviors, practices, and intuitions (including things like "taste" that Bourdieu (1984) discusses). In other words, such memories actively inform our ways of "being in the world" in spite of the fact that they often resist conscious articulation.[7]

However, multiple systems within our bodies are affected by experience and can "learn" patterns of response that are not tied directly to memory. Such patterns of response represent a form of embodied knowledge accumulated within the physical operation of the body. Biological systems are sensitive to and may be entrained by repeated exposure to types of environments (everything from cold to social deprivation), inputs (from types of food to forms of grooming), and behaviors (from athletic training to trance induction). Such factors shape patterns of response in diverse physiological systems including our metabolic, endocrine, immune, neurotransmitter, and cardiovascular systems (Kendler et al. 2000; McDade 2003; Weyer et al. 2000; Wiley 2004).

For example, a growing body of research suggests that metabolic systems "learn" about the nutritional environment in which individuals live, and that this information results in a kind of physiological programming that persists across generations (Kuzawa et al. 2012). This is an example of the ways in which material—in this case nutritional—deprivation becomes embodied via pathways that have nothing to do with memory. Moreover, these forms of learning not only constitute a form of embodiment in and of themselves, but also affect what Csordas (1993) has referred to as our "somatic modes of attention."

The concept of "somatic modes of attention" suggests the centrality of attention and perception in the way we experience both the world around us and our bodies themselves. In a sense, attention and perception act like filters for our experience of our cultural and physical environments. This is because the processes that govern what we attend to and how we perceive the objects of our attention occur prior to and form the basis of conscious awareness of our experiences and surroundings (Csordas 1990). The body mediates these processes; it is the instrument through which attention and perception occur, and as such, its characteristics matter. If we put a particular kind of filter on the lens of a video camera, certain aspects of what is recorded will be enhanced, and other aspects reduced.

Similarly, the qualities of our bodies, which are shaped by the cultural and social influences they have already encountered, enhance or reduce our attention to aspects of experience—and do so without the need for conscious reflection. Bodily symptoms of illness or physical disability, for example, are likely to shape attention and perception in ways that exaggerate or obscure certain aspects of experience. Importantly, such bodily characteristics may also enhance attention to *themselves*—that is, those who perceive their bodies to be ill or disabled may find their attention directed more frequently at their own bodies or directed at their bodies in particular ways. Thus to say we attend "somatically" means that we attend both to and through our bodies.

The *entrainment* of physiological systems, by which I mean the shaping of patterns of physiological response through experience,[8] is deeply implicated in establishing the qualities of our bodies that in turn influence perception and attention. But these influences are multidirectional in the sense that the entrainment of physiological systems is also a product of the ways in which people attend to, perceive, and ultimately experience their environments. To give an example, a Muslim-American who has repeatedly been singled out and searched or detained at the airport is likely to become physiologically entrained to mount a stress response every time he goes to the airport. Thus, he will attend to his experiences there with a kind of hypervigilance that is a product of his stress physiology, and his hypervigilance combined with the physiological symptoms of stress (i.e., rapid heart rate, sweating, gastrointestinal disruption) will be perceived by him as evidence that the airport experience is threatening and unpleasant. But the establishment of an automatic stress response in that context is also a *product* of his perception that the airport is a threatening place.

Understanding embodiment in this way underscores how the qualities of our bodies and the characteristics of our cultures are inherently intertwined through the interaction of physiological entrainment, attention, and perception. These critical insights can help us to think about the ways in which the bodily experiences of mediums are shaped by and in turn serve to shape perceptions of and attention to their own experiences. Similar to our hypothetical Muslim-American at the airport, the bodily pain, discomfort, and illness these individuals suffered before becoming mediums were rooted in patterns of physiological response that were learned through their experiences—experiences of stressful and traumatic events, of poverty and material deprivation, and so on. These patterns in turn shaped and were shaped by the way they attended to and perceived their preinitiation experiences.

The trance and possession experiences that mediums are then exposed to through initiation and ongoing practice result in similar patterns of reciprocal influence among physiological systems, attention, and perception. I observed specifically that as mediums induce trance they focus their attention with increasing intensity on ritual cues, including sounds like the pounding drums and ringing bells that call the orixás down, and which gradually divert attention away from a state of self-conscious awareness.[9] Distinctive patterns of bodily response make visible the onset of possession, including shuddering, eyes rolling back in heads, and the entire body lurching to one side as if thrown off balance. Mediums also report experiencing goosebumps and a feeling of dizziness. These bodily experiences, in the context of Candomblé practice, are perceived as positive signs of possession and are cultivated through further attention, which serves to reinforce and amplify them. As a result, bodily symptoms like dizziness and goose bumps, whenever they are experienced, come to be attended to and perceived in ways that are consistent with these spiritual meanings.

In sum, I am arguing that Candomblé practice results in a form of embodied learning. These changes reshape the way that mediums attend to and perceive their experiences, especially their bodily experiences, ultimately reshaping the meaning of these experiences. Changes in attention, perception, and meaning in turn reinforce changes in patterns of bodily response. We might, then, expect there to be evidence of some form of physiological entrainment among mediums—some physiological markers of the embodied learning mediums undergo, measurable with the right kinds of tools. The methods for psychophysiology measurement that I brought with me to the field were intended to look for just such evidence, and the data I collected with these tools support the idea of physiological entrainment. Briefly, these data reveal a distinctive pattern of cardiovascular activation among filhos. This pattern indexes an overall style of psychophysiological self-regulation that has been shown in other research to be associated with the bodily capacity to dynamically respond to challenges and stimuli in the social and physical environment (Berntson et al. 2008a, 2008b).

These data are important because they begin to illustrate the role of physiological entrainment in religious embodiment, something that has not been shown in the anthropology literature before. The dynamic nature of the particular pattern of psychophysiological response revealed is especially significant because it suggests that filhos may have a learned capacity for powerful bodily responses to social and cultural cues and meanings—the kinds of cues and meanings so richly represented in Candomblé ritual practice. In other words, this quality of mediums' bodies may predispose them to a "somatic mode of attention" that is particularly well-suited to mediumship.

Central to the idea that attention, perception, and meaning not only depend upon but shape bodily dispositions is a notion of

multidirectional influences—a notion that circular or looping relationships connect these aspects of mental and physical experience
to one another. Borrowing from Ian Hacking (1999), I use the term
"biolooping" to capture the circularity of these processes and to refer
to the ways in which bodies are shaped, and physiologies entrained,
by learning and experience. At the same time, I use the term to draw
attention to the way that entrainment loops back to shape future
experience and the manner in which new cultural knowledge becomes
embodied. The concept of "biolooping" is thus central to the theory of embodiment I develop in this book. I use the term to introduce the role of
biology into a model of how meaning affects the body[10]—and this is
where our theoretical discussions of embodiment, selfhood, and self-
healing come together. Biolooping is the process through which the
embodied dimensions of self are shaped and reshaped through their
interactions with sociocultural meanings, discourses, and practices.
As you will recall, the embodied dimensions of self are in constant
dialog with its discursive or representational dimensions. The concept
of biolooping can thus help us to better understand the larger looping process through which meaning and experience transform bodily
states, and in so doing, contribute to and reinforce transformations in
self-understandings and self-related meanings, which in turn contribute to and reinforce transformations in bodily states and so on.

The practices of trance and dissociation associated with spirit
possession are particularly implicated in these sorts of "looping"
processes, since by definition these practices involve both the manipulation of meaning and experience and of physiological and subjective
states. Ultimately, I argue that cultural forms like Candomblé capitalize on biolooping processes to contribute to changes in multiple
levels of subjective experience at once, and as such, these forms are
particularly capable of fostering therapeutic self-transformations.

Fieldwork and Methods

Taking what could be described as a "bio-psycho-cultural" approach
to the study of selfhood, embodiment, and healing in spirit possession
required a degree of methodological innovation. Broadly implicated
in the transformation and healing of mediums' selves are complex interactions among sociocultural, intrapsychic, and embodied
(including psychophysiological) processes, which simply could not
be apprehended through a single channel of data collection, even one

as rich as ethnography. While ethnographic methods like participant observation, interviews, and informal conversations were the center-pieces of my research, I also incorporated methods less traditional in cultural anthropology research. These methods included the use not only of standardized psychological inventories designed to measure aspects of intrapsychic experience and emotional well-being, but also use of psychophysiological measures designed to record patterns of physiological arousal and activation (see appendix for more details on methods and research instruments[11]).

During the course of my year of fieldwork in Salvador, I frequented numerous Candomblé religious centers, or terreiros, and spent time in the homes of mediums and other Candomblé participants. I became a regular attendee at two terreiros in particular, one of which was operated by Mae Tiana, the mae de santo who performed my divination and several other rituals on my behalf (washing the rit-ual beads that symbolically connected me to my patron orixás, for instance), and who in that sense became my primary spiritual guide in the realm of Candomblé. I got to know the religious participants at the two terreiros where I spent most of my time, and spent hours informally interacting with the lay people, initiated participants, and spiritual leaders there.

There were approximately 25 initiated mediums, or *filhos de santo* (sons and daughters of saint), shared between the two centers, only 20 of whom participated regularly in the rituals and public events of the religious community during my time there. In addition to the filhos de santo, the joint community boasted approximately 15 other nonmedium initiates. The number of lay people affiliated with the two terreiros is harder to gauge, since the devotion of the uninitiated is often spotty. While I was there, around 30–50 different lay people seemed to regularly attend public rituals at the two houses.

Most of the participants at the two terreiros were working class or poor. Of the combined group of lay people and initiates whom I interviewed, 80 percent were unskilled laborers, and the other 20 percent were unemployed. Participants ranged in age from chil-dren to elderly, although those who participated in my study were all between the ages of 18 and 65. The lay people at the two terreiros were a fairly even mix of men and women, and there was a slightly high number of male than female nonmedium initiates. However, fil-hos de santo are disproportionately female,[12] and for this reason, I recruited more women than men (nine and two respectively) to par-ticipate in the formal aspects of my research.

I was a participant observer in upward of 40 public Candomblé' rituals at these two terreiros and many others. As an uninitiated participant in the religion there were certain practices that I was unable to observe directly, including practices associated with initiation. However, being closely affiliated with Mae Tiana's terreiro and having had my orixás divined and my sacred beads ritually washed, I was able to observe and participate in many private or semiprivate ritual preparations—including everything from sacred foods and animal sacrifices (at a distance), to herbal baths used for washing spiritually afflicted humans and ritually cleansing sacred beads.

I conducted 41 formal interviews with Candomblé participants at all levels within the religious hierarchy and 6 extended life history interviews with mediums. I also collected data using several standardized psychological inventories (The State/Trait Anxiety Inventory and Dissociative Experiences Scale) as well as a Brazilian screening instrument for depression and anxiety called the *Questionario de Morbidade Psiquiátrica dos Adultos* (QMPA). For the purpose of comparison, I collected psychological data from 30 individuals outside the Candomblé religion, 20 of whom were matched for SES and 10 of whom were high SES. Psychological measures were also used with the 41 Candomblé participants I interviewed. Finally, I collected psychophysiological data on interindividual differences in autonomic nervous system activation from a total of 21 Candomblé participants (10 nonmedium initiates) using a method called impedance cardiography. By monitoring the heart rate responses of mediums at rest as well as during the course of the semi-structured interview, I collected data that could be used to detect differences between people and between groups of people (i.e., mediums and nonmedium initiates) in a physiological parameter for which interindividual variability has been tied to important differences in physical and mental health outcomes.

The two groups of initiates (mediums and nonmediums) were chosen for comparison in terms of psychophysiological measures because they were relatively comparable in their degree of commitment and responsibility within the religion, and were differentiated in religious terms primarily by whether or not they had been chosen by the orixás as mediums. In other words, they were distinguished mainly by their capacity to enter trance states and become possessed. Since this is the central embodied practice of mediumship, differences in the characteristics of mediums' bodies compared to nonmedium initiates were likely to be related to this distinguishing aspect of their role.

The intent of the mixed methods approach was to provide access to multiple ways of knowing about the experiences of mediums. As Thomas Weisner and colleagues (Yoshikawa et al. 2008; Weisner 2012) have argued in the context of research on child development, mixed methods approaches are especially critical to the study of "dynamic, transactional processes." Embodiment and religious healing represent such processes, yet mixed methods approaches have rarely been used in anthropology to study these phenomena. Moreover, the particular mixture of *biological* and *ethnographic* methods that I have used is, to my knowledge, completely unique. Yet the diverse data these methods generate are not only desirable, but necessary to illuminate the complex and mutually constituting interactions of mind, body, and self. The application of different kinds of methods to address the same research questions and the collection of varied data at multiple levels of analysis provide us with a multifaceted, layered understanding of the motivations, experiences, and outcomes associated with mediumship that can inform these larger issues. To put it more concretely, data on mediums' cardiovascular responses tell us something different about, yet related to, their own descriptions of bodily experience and can thereby inform us about how bodily processes, perception, meaning, and representation interact.

An additional premise of this book is, therefore, that there are crucial advantages to taking a biocultural or bio-psycho-cultural approach to questions of anthropological interest, particularly questions related to embodiment and healing. In particular, I argue that conducting biocultural research that is deeply ethnographically grounded is key. It is my hope that the research presented here can serve as a model for studies of this sort. My use of psychological and psychophysiological methods in the context of ethnographic research was at once fruitful and challenging. Inevitably, there were some things that worked well and some that did not, ways in which this approach was constraining and other ways in which it was immensely beneficial. In the hope of helping other scholars who might be interested in designing this kind of research project, I discuss my methodology, along with its successes and failures, at length in the next chapter.

Candomblé

The two small terreiros where I conducted the bulk of my research were located in a working class Salvador neighborhood and the *favela* or shantytown that spilled down the hill beneath it. These terreiros were among countless others tucked away in similar neighborhoods across Salvador. As capital of the northeastern state of Bahia, where slavery and sugar production were both particularly concentrated, Salvador has long been the most African city in Brazil, both demographically and culturally. This history helps to explain the concentration of Candomblé terreiros in Salvador, which has been referred to as "Black Rome" in reference to its role as the epicenter of the religion (Selka 2007). Current estimates put the number of terreiros at over a thousand, though this estimate could be low.[13] Each terreiro can have anywhere from tens to hundreds of members, putting the total number of Candomblé participants in Salvador today easily in the hundreds of thousands.

Beliefs and practices within contemporary Candomblé can be traced to a variety of African traditions brought to Brazil by slaves (Harding 2000). Candomblé communities often identify their tradition according to the African *nação*, or nation, from which they believe it is derived; for example, terreiros that identify primarily with Yoruba tradition identify themselves as belonging to the "*Nagô* nação," those who identify with the Ewe tradition belong to the "*Jejê* nação," and so forth. In contemporary Brazil many believe that authentic Candomblé is drawn from the Yoruba tradition, therefore Nagô terreiros are understood to practice a more "pure" form of the religion.[14] However, because Candomblé is a noncanonical religion, meaning that there is no central text or doctrine codifying religious beliefs and practices, there is a great deal of variety across different communities—even among those terreiros that identify with the same nação.

Moreover, beliefs and practices with their roots in different African traditions have not only blended together over time, but have also evolved in uniquely Brazilian ways as they have been practiced on Brazilian soil over hundreds of years. For example, worship of a set of native South American spirits, called caboclos, was developed in Brazil. Similarly, because of pressure on slaves to convert to Catholicism, hybrid worship of orixás and Catholic saints in which particular orixás are equated with particular saints (i.e., Iansã is equated with Santa Barbara), represents another uniquely Brazilian development. Terreiros identifying with different "nations" are more or less likely to incorporate these hybrid practices, and while some houses still equate orixás with Catholic Saints, others have explicitly rejected these "syncretic" Catholic elements in an effort to practice a more purely "African" form of Candomblé (Selka 2007).

In spite of this variability, there are elements of Candomblé worship that are common to most terreiros. First and foremost, all Candomblé devotion revolves around the pantheon of orixás. Practitioners thus share a cosmology that involves the existence of superhuman beings who occupy a higher spiritual plane. Nevertheless, this plane is still intimately connected to the human world, and this connection is a key feature of the religion. While devotees also share a belief in a supreme being, Olórun, who resembles an all-powerful Judeo-Christian god, he is so far removed from the world of human affairs that he is not directly worshipped. Devotees focus instead on the orixás, who are much more actively involved in human affairs. This illustrates the larger ethos of Candomblé, which, in spite of a cosmology that includes higher spiritual realms and supernatural beings, is really focused on celebration and improvement of the earthly lives of its adherents (Voeks 1997).

Thus, although the Candomblé orixás were originally derived from the gods of Yoruba and other religious traditions brought to Brazil by slaves, some observers have pointed out that the particular set of deities that has been maintained over time is one with particular resonance within the Brazilian context. Warrior gods like Xangô and Ogum have thrived, for example, because they are symbols of power that have held understandable appeal as potent resources for intervention in the lives of an oppressed Afro-Brazilian population (Voeks 1997).

Though there is some variation across nações, and even across specific terreiros within nações, most practitioners of Candomblé recognize a core set of about a dozen orixás that typically includes: Xangô, Ogum, Iansã, Logum-edé, Oxóssi, Oxalá, Omolu, Oxum, Nanã, Oxumaré, Iemanjá, and Ossâin. Exú, the trickster spirit who serves as a messenger between humans and the orixás, is also recognized across Candomblé traditions. What varies, however, is whether each of these orixás is understood to be singular or multiple. In some traditions the orixás and *exús* are understood to manifest in multiple ways—there might, for instance, be 15 or more versions of Oxum, each of which is a variation around the central character of the goddess. In other traditions, like those followed by the terreiros where I did my research, there is a single manifestation of each deity.

The orixás are each linked to a particular element of nature that they control and from which they draw spiritual power, or axé—they are sometimes even referred to as "nature gods." Different deities are associated with fresh water, the sea, the forest, earth, thunder and lightning, and so forth (Bastide 2001). Each deity is also understood to have a distinctive personality and the characteristics of the natural domain with which an orixá is associated are intimately linked to his/

her temperament—Xangô, the god of thunder, is fiery-tempered and fierce, while Oxum, the goddess of fresh water, is stable and nurturing. Each deity is also understood to have particular preferences and taboos around things like colors, foods, and days of the week. Oxalá, for example, wears only white and abhors black and red. His sacred day is Friday; he requires sacrifice of chickens, doves, and female goats; and his taboos include crab and salt (Voeks 1997).

The personality characteristics, relationships, and exploits of the orixás are the subjects of an extensive mythology known in more or less detail by most devotees. These tales include sex, intrigue, trickery, family conflict, love, and nurturance. For example, Candomblé mythology holds that Omolu is the son of Nanã and that he contracted small pox shortly after birth. Nanã could not cure him of the illness, so she left him in a basket on the beach, where he was found by the goddess of the sea, Iemanjá. Iemanjá raised him but also later facilitated his reconciliation with Nanã. Another myth holds that Iansã became wife to Xangô after he "stole" her from Ogum (Prandi 2001). The gods thus represent both archetypes of, and influences over, human characteristics and relationships, and these kinds of stories may be invoked as explanation for the behaviors, affinities, and fates of the deities' human sons and daughters (Matory 2005).

Central practices of Candomblé, like divination, blood sacrifice, song, dance, and possession, are all oriented toward cultivating relationships to, and communicating with, the divine, in ways that can positively affect human lives. Divination, for instance, is a direct form of communication in which messages from the orixás are read by qualified spiritual practitioners, and it is often used to seek counsel from the deities to help solve human problems like illness or misfortune. Animal sacrifices and offerings are a means of feeding and pleasing the gods, and song, dance, and possession are ways of celebrating the human–divine relationship and a means of calling the deities forth into the material realm.

Each of these practices, therefore, is understood as a way to increase human access to axé, or the spiritual life force that animates all living things, and of which the deities are the ultimate source. The accumulation of axé through proper spiritual practice is understood to be a source of spiritual power, health, and prosperity for Candomblé practitioners. But, like matter, axé can neither be created nor destroyed. Instead it is transmitted—among objects, people, and orixás. Blood is a particularly potent source of axé, and thus animal sacrifice figures centrally in Candomblé practice as a powerful way to shore up the well-being of the terreiro and those connected to it.

The relationships among participants within a given terreiro are organized around levels of axé to form a kind of loose hierarchy. It is useful, however, to think of the sociospiritual structure of each house in terms of concentric circles, rather than a ladder or some other common metaphor of hierarchy, because the structure revolves around proximity to the áxe that exists at the center of each terreiro. Axé is, as one observer put it, at once a "container" and a "content" (Wafer 1991). It is a container in the sense that it is the larger circle within which the Candomblé community as a whole resides. Anyone who is affiliated with the terreiro falls within its axé to some greater or lesser extent. It is a content in the sense that it is the spiritual essence of Candomblé, contained within the ritual objects, people, spaces, foods, and practices of the religion.

Those with the most áxe are those who reside within the innermost circle of the Candomblé hierarchy. These individuals are the maes or pais de santo, and maes/pais *pequeños* (little mothers or fathers), who are senior initiates of the house and function as seconds in command. Those within the innermost circle have the most intimate relationship with the deities, and they are the ones who oversee and disseminate proper ritual practice within the terreiro. Filhos de santo occupy the next circle in relation to axé, and their places relative to one another within a mini-hierarchy of mediums is determined by their spiritual age or time since initiation. *Ogãs* and *ekédis*, the respective names for the male and female nonmedium initiates who serve as ritual assistants and dignitaries of the terreiro, but who do not enter trance states or become possessed, are one step further removed from axé; and uninitiated, or lay participants, occupy the furthest ring outward from the spiritual power center of the terreiro.

Activities within the terreiro include rituals and events open to initiated members, lay people, and the public, as well as a variety of events limited only to initiates. The central public event at most terreiros is the festa or *toque*. Each festa is dedicated to a different orixá, and the order and timing of these celebrations is determined by a yearly ritual calendar. These elaborate rituals are akin to birthday parties for the deities, and involve festive decorations and clothing, ritualized song and dance devoted to the orixá being celebrated, performance of possession trance by initiates (and occasionally audience members), and consumption of ritual foods.

Other ritual activities open to the public are *consultas* or spiritual consultations with a mae, pai, or filho de santo. Lay people typically use consultas to seek spiritual advice about problems and illnesses, or general guidance in some area of their lives. The consultation process often includes divination, and in some terreiros the spiritual consultant may also enter trance and dispense advice directly via his/her caboclo spirit. Remedies proffered may include spiritual cleansings or instructions for performance of specific acts of devotion (i.e., making an offering to a particular deity).

Initiated members of the community also engage in devotional practices, participating in formal rituals know as *obrigações*, which frequently involve animal sacrifice. These rituals, due to the large amount of axé they involve, cannot be attended by the uninitiated. As a result, I was only able to observe select aspects of particular obrigações, and often at a distance, in order to limit the amount of axé to which I was exposed.[15]

Accumulation and depletion of axé are understood to be fundamentally embodied processes. Hence, material, bodily practices like sacrifices, consumption of sacred food and feasting, rituals of cleansing, ritualized movements and physical acts of devotion (e.g., prostration), dancing, and trance and possession, all serve to increase levels of axé. As initiated possession mediums, filhos have learned, through the process of initiation and subsequent practice, to enter trance at appropriate moments during ritual performances in response to induction cues (certain types of drumming, singing, and dance). Embodiment of the spirits and deities creates a particular identification between filhos and their possessing others, through which they come to understand and experience the characteristics of these others as their own. Moreover, their ability to become possessed increases their levels of axé, and as ritual experts filhos' knowledge and skills allow them to engage in other axé boosting ritual practices and obrigações as well.

These obrigações are not understood as optional, however (hence the term, which can be translated as "obligation"). Filhos are obligated to perform particular ritual duties and serve a special role within the larger community. The ability and responsibility to channel the spirits and deities is central to this role. Ritually induced possession trance is the central practice of a practice-heavy religious tradition, but filhos are the only ones with the spiritual and technical proficiency to engage in this practice.[16] Possession thus has important implications for the relationship of filhos not only to the spirits and deities but also to the rest of the human religious community. The ability to invite possession allows filhos de santo to use their bodies in the service of religious belief both on behalf of themselves and of those around them. In other words, it is the role of filhos to put the rest of the community into closer contact with the spirits and deities, and by extension, the axé. In this sense, by becoming mediums and committing to a long-term relationship with the spirits and deities, filhos also make a kind of commitment to, and enter into a special relationship with, the other people in their religious community. The centrality of both community and practice in Candomblé is directly linked to its noncanonical nature. Because there is no doctrine in Candomblé, individuals are "indoctrinated" not through exposure to a shared text, but rather through exposure to shared practices—actions and behaviors that are passed from individual to individual through direct experience and modeling. Such shared practices include methods of initiation, animal sacrifice, ritual cleansing, preparation of ritual foods and offerings, and trance induction techniques. It is through the learning of such practices that the more discursive aspects of Candomblé belief and knowledge also tend to be transmitted. In fact, belief per se is rarely made explicit within Candomblé. Instead, like axé, knowledge about the spiritual world is accumulated and internalized by participants through their embodied participation (Johnson 2002). For instance, it is through the practices of initiation that novice filhos learn the characteristics of their orixás, and come to understand and experience these characteristics as part of themselves. Belief and practice are thus extremely tightly linked in Candomblé and the processes of embodied learning in which they converge are critical to religious formation as well as to the accumulation and maintenance of spiritual power through ongoing devotion.

Furthermore, the central role of social transmission in the communication of embodied knowledge and power marks Candomblé as a fundamentally relational tradition. This relationality is both underscored and reinforced by use of a language of kinship within each terreiro. Discourses of family dominate internal understandings of the Candomblé community's hierarchy, with labels of mother and father, little mother and father, and brother and sister attached to the central players. It is even said that one is "born" into the terreiro upon initiation. The family metaphor not only emphasizes the social transmission of knowledge and power within the terreiro, but also serves to link the dual emphases of body and relationality together. By invoking kinship and the process of birth or rebirth, this language underscores the power of the bodily and spiritual transformations that take place through initiation, and draws attention to the depth of the relationships that tie initiated bodies together within the terreiro.

The important links between embodied practice and social ties were highly visible in the two terreiros at the center of my research. The houses were related to one another both in spiritual and social terms. Pai João, the pai de santo of the second terreiro, was *feito* (literally "made," or initiated) by Mae Tiana many years before. Thus, Mae Tiana was understood to be João's spiritual "mother." In response to the demands of his primary orixá João had eventually opened his own terreiro at the other end of the neighborhood, after fulfilling all of the requisite ritual obligations. Most of the participants in both terreiros came from the surrounding neighborhood, and many of the same individuals frequented both houses—though initiated members belonged formally to either one or the other depending upon which spiritual leader had "made" them. The two terreiros often held joint festas for the orixás at one or the other of the houses, during the cycle of ritual celebrations. The relationships among the initiated members of the houses were thus further cemented by shared practices—not only in the sense that they learned and embodied the same set of practices, but also in terms of their tendency to practice together.

Thus, many of the initiated members of the two terreiros had intimate relationships to one another and frequently emphasized in conversation how much they were like family; as one filho put it, "It's like we're really a family—if one has and the other doesn't, one covers the other." Like a family, they look out for and even provide resources to one another when in need. Yet the hierarchy of relationships was also important among the members of the two houses, including between Mae Tiana and Pai João. In spite of the fact that João was more successful than Mae Tiana (in the sense that his terreiro attracted more people, he performed more consultas, and had more financial resources), Mae Tiana was still deferred to by Pai João, was given the most privileged position at joint festas, and was paid respects first by all of the initiates during rituals. This is a perfect example of how the Candomblé hierarchy shifts and redefines power in such a way that indicators of status from the world outside (i.e., affluence and social influence) are trumped by the power of spiritual knowledge, experience, and seniority within the religion. Religious power is thus no less real than the kinds of social and economic power that determine status outside the religious sphere (Keller 2002).

In sum, the structure of Candomblé, with its internally defined power relations, access to close social ties, spiritual meaning system, and ethos of embodied learning creates a set of conditions under which the selves of filhos de santo can be remade and redefined through a variety of channels at once. However, some further exploration of the wider Brazilian social and political-economic milieu, and the place of Candomblé within it, will help us to better understand how the selves of prospective mediums are shaped and reshaped by the lived social, emotional, and physical contexts they occupy before and after their religious formation.

The Brazilian Context

African derived religions in Brazil, or *"religiões Afro-Brasileiras"* as they are known, uniformly involve belief in unseen spirits who influence and intervene in the material world of human beings. Far from gradually dying out in the context of a Brazilian state eager to "modernize," these religions have instead grown and diversified. Though officially one of the largest Roman Catholic countries in the world, Brazil also has between five and ten (depending on how they are divided up) different forms of mainly African-derived, mystical religious tradition. These include Candomblé and regional variants, like Macumba and Xangô, as well as Umbanda, a religion that mixes elements of African-derived traditions with Spiritism.[17]

The historical, political-economic, and racial factors that have contributed to the growth and prosperity of Candomblé and other African-derived religious traditions in Brazil are directly relevant to understanding who participates in these religions and why. Candomblé in particular has developed a specific set of social and political meanings in the context of a historical lack of overt political organizing around race in Bahia, and the past failure of the Brazilian state to develop a social welfare system. These factors, which have also shaped the development of Brazilian moral personhood, have determined the significance of participating in these religions for particular individuals and social groups.

Historically, issues of race and racism have been viewed by Brazilians (academics and the general public alike) as secondary to the problem of class (Skidmore 1999). Indeed class has always been a problem of epic proportions in Brazil; it has long been among the top five countries in the world with the largest disparities between rich and poor (Baer 2002; Cooper and Frasca 2003), although this disparity has recently begun to shrink somewhat (Rapoza 2012).[18] Moreover, until quite recently, there has never been a safety net in Brazil, due in part to what DaMatta has called "the radical and authoritarian separation between two social positions that are objectively or conceptually differentiated in terms of the rules of classification of Brazilian culture" (cited in Levine 1999). In other words, according to the rules of classification in Brazil, the rich are rich and the poor are poor and there has never been a sense of moral obligation to alter this state of affairs. Yet while class is a central element of structural inequality in Brazil, it is no coincidence that Afro-Brazilians have always been disproportionately represented in the lowest income groups of the country. Clearly racial discrimination is, and has been, a major issue in Brazil (Hanchard 1999; Lovell 1994; Selka 2007). Many scholars have attributed the lack of emphasis on racism to the so-called myth of racial democracy, the essence of which is the idea that the opportunity for social advancement is equally available to individuals of all racial categories (Skidmore 2000). While more recent scholarship suggests that Brazilians are aware of racism and its effects within their society, there continues to be a more fluid understanding of racial categories in Brazil than in the United States (Sansone 2003; Selka 2007). In spite of this fluidity, however, blackness is still associated with the bottom of the social hierarchy, and whiteness with the top (Hanchard 1999).

As a result, Afro-Brazilians in Salvador are largely "marginal to the formal economy"; that is, unemployed or concentrated in the service or informal sectors, working as vendors, maids, janitors, and doormen for wealthy whites (Greenfield and Prust 1990:124). With jobs mainly in the service sector, the Afro-Brazilians I worked with were constantly faced with the disparity between their own lifestyle and that of the elites for whom they worked. Whereas the elites live in quiet, secure, climate-controlled high-rise apartment buildings, the poor live primarily in rundown, chaotic neighborhoods and favelas, typically dense areas of makeshift houses perched precariously on hillsides, often with no sanitation system and only pirated electricity. Thus, in addition to struggling for jobs, resources, and material comfort, the poor are often exposed to unsanitary conditions, noise pollution, overcrowding, and increasingly, gun violence (Muggah 2014; Nehamas and Oliveira 2012).

In addition to racial discrimination, Afro-Brazilian women are also victims of gender discrimination. A history of patriarchy combined with a widespread acceptance of the notion that Afro-Brazilian women are wild, sensuous, and in need of control (Gregg 2003) have placed these women under suspicion and made social advancement particularly difficult for them. These women, who have historically suffered more from the gender gap in earnings than the racial one, are concentrated in the very lowest paying sectors of the economy. Thus, the Candomblé mediums with whom I worked, who were overwhelming female, occupied among the lowest status positions in Brazilian society, in that they were members of not one, but two groups facing social and economic discrimination (Lovell 2000).

These social realities and power relations are key elements of the sociocultural context in which Brazilian self and personhood are shaped. Normative moral personhood in Brazil has long been defined by economics, and poor selves are understood to be less morally valuable. Selves are shaped by such normative ideologies of personhood, which canalize experience, shape motivations and desires, and direct attention to the most salient aspects of experience. In this context, many of the Afro-Brazilian men and women who ultimately get involved in spirit possession occupy devalued forms of moral personhood located at the bottom of the social hierarchy. Yet even those at the bottom of the hierarchy are socialized into embracing the dominant models of successful personhood that include social mobility and a comfortable material lifestyle, and implicitly accept the notion that they should be motivated to achieve these goals in spite of the oppressive circumstances they face (Dressler et al. 1998; Dressler et al. 2005). Similar dynamics can be found in the United States and many other countries with high levels of social inequality (Rose 1998).

Because normative expectations or models of lifestyle, success, and life-course transition are internalized as goals and desires integral to self-understanding, the failure to fulfill these goals and desires often becomes self-implicating—reflecting negatively on the individual's sense of self and moral worth. The stories of many of the mediums with whom I worked reflected this dynamic—they included normative expectations and desires, like the desire to own a home, to find a good job—alongside failed aspirations and hardship, like the humiliation of not being able to pay the rent, the despair of joblessness, the grief of repeated social losses. The emotional conflict such dynamics create stands alongside other forms of embodied suffering associated with psychosocial stress and material deprivation—from the symptoms of mental and physical illness in many mediums' narratives, to more diffuse forms of existential distress.

Dressler et al. (1998) have shown, for example, that stress resulting from the incongruity between the culturally shared model of a desirable lifestyle in Brazil, and individuals' actual realities, accounts for previously unexplained effects of socioeconomic status on a number of stress related symptoms, ranging from blood pressure to depression (see also Dressler et al. 2005). In addition, the living conditions of the underclass are known to contribute to negative health consequences through the vehicles of poor diet, exposure to

Table 1.1 Mean number of symptoms on the *Questionario de Morbidade Psiquiátrica dos Adultos* (QMPA), a Brazilian screening instrument for anxiety and depression

	Mean QMPA Scores	Mean QMPA Somatic
Filhos	11.9	4
Ogãs/Ekédis	12.8	3.7
Frequentadors	11.4	3.2
SES matched controls	10.4	2.8
High SES controls	4.6	.8

infectious disease, prevalence of harmful behaviors such as smoking, and psychosocial stress (Dressler et al. 1998; Marmot 2005). These pathways represent mechanisms of embodiment by which the shared system of meaning in Brazil translates, via structural inequalities and the internalization of social expectations, into physical outcomes.

Not coincidentally, all of the low SES participants in my study showed elevated rates of depression compared to their high SES counterparts, while mediums had somewhat higher numbers of somatic symptoms (table 1.1). These findings highlight the ways in which structural factors may contribute to emotional and somatic suffering and a sense of dissonant or disrupted selfhood.

However, Afro-Brazilians should not be viewed as passive victims of these structural factors or passive absorbers of normative social expectations. In fact, Candomblé has played a central role in the ways in which Afro-Brazilians have worked against these constraints. While there has been a historical lack of overt political organization around race in Brazil, due in part to the fact that for a variety of reasons Brazilians have not tended to think of race as an explicitly political issue (Selka 2005), this should not be taken to mean that there has been a lack of racial consciousness. Instead, race-based organization in Brazil has taken a unique form that has often been characterized as "cultural" rather than overtly political. What this means is that Afro-Brazilians have focused their efforts less on political resistance and confrontation, and more on the creation and maintenance of Afro-Brazilian cultural forms and social institutions, of which Candomblé has been one of the most successful. The religion has long provided Bahian blacks with a variety of resources not available to them in the dominant culture (Butler 1998a, 1998b; Harding 2000). One result has been that Candomblé is seen as "a potent emblem of racial consciousness" in Brazil, and especially in Bahia (Selka 2007:1).[19]

However, these were not issues with which participants at my primary research sites seemed to be particularly concerned. While a few ogãs mentioned the link between Candomblé practice and racial identity, most participants in the two terreiros did not talk about their participation in political terms, or as a way of performing Afro-Brazilianness. Instead, they spoke of being attracted to the religion for aesthetic, spiritual, social, and pragmatic reasons. In particular, participants at various levels within the spiritual hierarchy mentioned becoming involved with Candomblé because of its beauty, its spiritual meaning and superiority over other religions (i.e., Evangelical Christianity), the involvement of family and friends, and especially, out of *need*—the need to petition the gods to address life problems, illnesses, and existential suffering.

It is important to note however, that the place of Candomblé within Brazilian society as a central symbol of racial identity is a result of the same set of forces that have also contributed to making the religion a key social institution through which the needs of Afro-Brazilian participants have often historically been met. In other words, through the work of specific political-economic and power dynamics, Candomblé has come to serve the needs of the Afro-Brazilian community in a *variety* of different ways—politically, socially, symbolically, and materially.[20]

In practical terms, as a social institution Candomblé has provided access to social networks and patron–client relationships within the community that make available both material resources and a system of social support (cf. Brown [1986] and Greenfield and Prust [1990] on Umbanda). At the same time, by virtue of its connection to the notion of African heritage, involvement has come to symbolize Afro-Brazilian identity and racial consciousness. Moreover, the effects of the alternative hierarchy within Candomblé, which allows individuals to gain levels of power and prestige that they would be unlikely to achieve outside the religion, illustrate that these political and social, practical and symbolic aspects of participation are overlapping.

For most participants, motivations for and benefits of Candomblé participation are understood in simultaneously worldly and spiritual terms. From a scholarly perspective, therefore, we must also try to understand the various meanings and outcomes of Candomblé participation in a way that acknowledges the experiential unity among its political-economic, social, and religious dimensions for devotees. Participants may seek out Candomblé for help with a material problem, like job loss, but they understand both the cause of the problem and its treatment as spiritual. The spiritual and material are thus deeply intertwined in the Candomblé worldview. What is more, by virtue of the intimate connection between the material and spiritual, this religious practice actually refigures the social and political-economic dynamics of Brazilian society in ways that are not merely figurative (Keller 2002).

There are, for example, specific spiritual counterparts to, or inversions of, the way that the social and moral dimensions of personhood have historically been constituted in Brazil. Whereas in the context of slavery and a rigid class hierarchy the worth of persons has historically been measured in monetary terms, in Candomblé it is measured in terms of axé. This symbolic inversion of moral value is enacted most overtly in a mock "auction" practiced in some terreiros, in which a filho de santo is sold back to her family upon the completion of her initiation (Johnson 2002).

Similarly, whereas social and economic relationships in Brazil have historically rested on a patron–client system, which makes success about who you know, who is looking out for you, and with which member of the elite class you have aligned yourself, through Candomblé individuals enter into patron–client-like relationships not only with their mae/pai de santo but with the spirits and deities as well. Mediums in particular commit to stable reciprocal relationships with their orixás, in which the orixás act as the powerful figures who offer protection and aid in exchange for the devotion and spiritual work of their mediums. The Candomblé worldview likewise gives a different twist to the well-known phrase used by Brazilian elites to put people in their places, "*Você sabe com quem está falando?*" (Do you know who you're talking to? Levine 1999). In the world of Candomblé one can never be sure to whom one is talking, and the possibility that the human with whom one is interacting is occupied by a powerful, immaterial other is a very real one.

Hence, the spiritual worldview of Candomblé forms the basis for alternative models of personhood, including different criteria for measuring success and different expectations for the life-course. These shared refigurings of moral personhood are the basis upon which individuals may reconstruct their own self-understanding and rescript their self-narratives. Similar refigurings may also be a subtext of Spiritism[21] and many of other the religiões Afro-Brasileiros in which powerful immaterial forces are also understood to affect human affairs. The density of these religions means that the intervention of spiritual forces in the politics of everyday life is something that is widely accepted in Brazil, making this kind of spirituality part of a shared ethos, as well as a potential source of resilience for many individuals in need.[22]

The Brazilian setting is thus extremely dynamic and complex: it is a place where class is rigid, where race is supposedly fluid yet blackness is devalued, where cultural institutions serve as safety-nets, and where there is a pervasive sense of the spiritual in everyday life. It is in this context that mediums' selves are shaped and reshaped through the meanings and embodied experiences they encounter, in ways that are at once political and social, practical and symbolic, phenomenological and discursive.

Organization of the Book

One of the central arguments of this book is that systems of meaning and embodied experience shape and are shaped by one another. My goal is to convincingly demonstrate the ways in which domains of experience like discourse and embodiment, belief and practice, public and private, mind and body, which have traditionally been thought of as separate, are actually intimately linked and mutually reinforcing. Nevertheless, for narrative and heuristic purposes the book is organized into chapters that treat some of these domains separately, before ultimately attempting a grand synthesis.

I begin in chapter 2 with a description of and reflection on the methodology used for this study, focusing in particular on the motivations and consequences, costs and benefits of incorporating psychological and psychophysiological methods into ethnography. In chapter 3, I dig into the main argument of the book, by exploring the process through which initiated mediums come to produce a new self-narrative based on shared meanings, or cultural models, learned through participation in Candomblé. Using several case studies, this chapter explores the intimate relationships among the individual and social, public and private domains by detailing the process through which shared meanings simultaneously become the basis of a transformation in the internal, cognitive and external, discursive representations of mediums' selves.

Chapter 4 turns to a consideration of the embodied dimensions of self-transformation, exploring in depth the process through which religious practices shape embodied experience, and demonstrating how such embodied learning is instantiated in psychophysiological function. I return to the notion of biolooping, presenting evidence in support of a circular relationship between bodily processes and sociocultural meanings. Chapter 5 brings together ideas from the previous two chapters through a close examination of the ways in which particular mediums have experienced a process of healing self-transformation scaffolded by Candomblé belief and practice. I detail the ways in which developing a relationship with the orixás through initiation and ongoing devotion heals the suffering, fragmented selves of these mediums via mutually reinforcing effects on both the representational and embodied dimensions of self. In chapter 6, I return to the central theoretical premises that selves are embodied, that embodiment is a biocultural process, and therefore that systems of meaning and embodied experiences can converge to shape peoples' selfhood and affect their well-being. I conclude by exploring the implications of these ideas for understanding how self-related embodied learning can affect well-being in a variety of different contexts.

Chapter 2

Reflections on the Challenges and Rewards of Integrative Research

Traveling without a Roadmap

I embarked for my fieldwork in Brazil with the usual trappings of the novice ethnographer: tape recorders, notebooks, appropriate "fieldwork clothes," a laptop computer, and a pile of academic books that I was unlikely to read but felt compelled to carry along with me. I also brought with me something far less typical for a cultural anthropologist heading into the field: a hard-sided suitcase specially fitted with foam inserts in which was cradled a piece of high-tech laboratory equipment, called an "impedance cardiograph." Filled with the anticipation of trying something really new, and deeply motivated by a set of research objectives that spanned the cultural, psychological, and biological domains, I set out with the intention to integrate measures of psychological and biological function into a traditional ethnographic process anchored by participant observation and ethnographic interviewing.[1] Consequently, in addition to the tools of the ethnographer, I was equipped with a set of psychological questionnaires and a portable system for psychophysiological measurement. Thus began the intellectual and methodological adventure I have come to think of as "bio-psycho-cultural ethnography."

Impedance cardiography, as the use of an impedance cardiograph like the one I brought to Brazil is called, is a popular method for collecting psychophysiological data in psychology labs because, combined with a regular electrocardiograph, it has a unique capacity to generate data on the regulation of cardiovascular activity by both the parasympathetic and sympathetic branches of the autonomic nervous system (ANS). The use of impedance cardiography in a fieldwork setting had, for a number of good reasons, never been tried before. The kinds of language used to describe the method hint at some of the reasons why: words like "lab" and "autonomic nervous system" do not, on the surface, seem particularly compatible with ethnographic research. These words evoke both important practical and epistemological obstacles that have kept most anthropologists from even considering the use of such a method in the field. Trepidations about my technical proficiency with the psychophysiology equipment aside, I was cautiously, perhaps naively, optimistic that I could overcome whatever obstacles I encountered and use this decidedly nonanthropological method to shed new light on a very old area of anthropological inquiry: spirit possession.

While there is nothing particularly novel about using "biocultural" methods in anthropological research (see, e.g., an abundance of excellent work including McDade [2002]; Gravlee et al. [2005]; Dressler et al. [2005]), my approach differed from other biocultural studies in a number of significant ways. One major difference was the use of traditional ethnography—by which I mean long-term participant observation and various forms of ethnographic interviewing—as a way to investigate the more cultural aspects of my research questions. To date, most biocultural studies have used cultural consensus modeling and related tools as a way to study culture. This approach allows researchers to *correlate* biological findings with those from quantifiable cultural measures. While this method has been used to great advantage in many biocultural studies, it was not well suited to my research objectives. For my purposes, participant observation along with various forms of open-ended interviewing made more sense as a way to research questions related to the experiences, beliefs, and social contexts associated with a particular form of religious participation. Using data from these methods, I aimed to *contextualize* my biological findings through thick description and a rich sense of phenomenology.

A second major difference in my research relates to the role of biological measures. Most biocultural studies have used biological markers like blood pressure, stress hormones, and markers of cell-mediated immune function to examine the relationship between aspects of culture and health outcomes. In such studies health outcomes are the dependent variables and cultural factors the independent variables. In my research, on the other hand, physiological characteristics were hypothesized to be embodied qualities that brought individuals, and were brought by them, to the role of medium. In other words, I was not interested in investigating biology as an outcome, but rather as one of several interacting factors contributing to mediumship. Hence, in my study design biology was intended to be an independent variable, and mediumship the dependent variable, or outcome of interest.

Not only did this design invert the role of biology in most biocultural studies, it also turned the traditional approach to studying the biology of trance and possession states on its head. Past scholarship had always been oriented toward trying to measure neurophysiological activity in the midst of such states, but has had little success since such measurement has been made unfeasible by the sanctity of the ritual contexts with which such states tend to be associated. Instead of trying to measure the neurophysiology of trance states themselves, I designed my research to investigate a set of questions about how trance and possession are influenced by the psychological states and autonomic regulatory capacities of the individuals who engage in them. Methodologically, conceptualizing the relationships among biology and spirit possession in this way allowed me to do two important things. First, it allowed me to apply physiological measures in nonreligious settings since they were modeled as relatively enduring dispositions of the individual that would *interact* with specific contextual and behavioral cues, rather than as states *induced* by such cues. And second, it allowed me to compare different groups of religious participants in terms of a set of social, psychological, and psychophysiological factors, rather than trying to compare one set of people as they occupied different states.

This relates closely to the third important way in which my research differed from other biocultural studies, which was in terms of the type of biological measure used. As I alluded to earlier, no other anthropology study has empirically investigated the relationship between culture and autonomic nervous system function. This may be partly a matter of convention, but it is primarily related to the fact that in studies that use measures of biology to index health outcomes, there are many methodologically simpler and more straightforward biomarkers that could be used, including blood pressure (Dressler et al. 1998; Dressler et al. 2005; Gravlee et al. 2005; Sweet et al. 2007) and a variety of immune markers that can be easily measured in a drop of blood (McDade 2002).

By contrast, for an investigation of how physiological characteristics might contribute to the outcome of mediumship, measuring ANS function was an ideal candidate, since such measures have a long history of use as predictors of various kinds of social, psychological, and health outcomes (Cacioppo et al. 1995a; 1995b; Coe et al. 1992; Liang et al. 1997; Biederman et al. 1995). For years, psychophysiologists have used impedance cardiography (which measures cardiac function by sending low frequency electrical signals through the thorax via electrodes—see appendix for more details) together with electrocardiography to gather data on the relative influence of the parasympathetic and sympathetic branches of the autonomic nervous system. The relative degree of control exerted over cardiac activity by each branch has been found to have important implications for the kinds of outcomes people experience—SNS is typically associated with negative outcomes like stress sensitivity and cardiovascular disease, and PNS with positive outcomes like self-regulatory capacity and adaptability (Alkon et al. 2003; Berntson et al. 1996; Cacioppo et al. 1998; Porges 1992; Uchino and Cacioppo 1995).

High sympathetic cardiac control could thus help explain why mediums experience bodily suffering in response to psychosocial stress prior to their initiations, and could be a reason that particular individuals are drawn to the potentially stress-buffering benefits of mediumship. High parasympathetic control, on the other hand, could mean that mediums have a heightened capacity to self-regulate arousal. Such a capacity could increase the ability to narrowly focus attention on induction cues and meanings related to trance and possession, and make particular individuals especially suited for these transformations of subjectivity. Use of impedance to investigate the autonomic origins of cardiac activation among mediums could therefore function as a window onto how the dynamic and shifting biological capacities of particular individuals, or what we might think of as their embodied trajectories, interact with a set of religious beliefs and practices to shape individual outcomes.

Without a model for how to incorporate impedance cardiography into biocultural research to guide me, however, I was in many ways traveling without a roadmap through the journey of designing and conducting a study using this method. Even with a model to guide the process, designing a study is in many ways a process of imagining—imagining how the research process will unfold, how methods will work when applied, what kinds of results will come from the data gathered. This imagining is typically guided by theory; methods are selected and applied in ways that are targeted to illuminate the theoretically based questions and objectives driving the research. In the process of imagining, however, it is sometimes more difficult to address the gap between the theoretical utility of a method and its practical applicability. In other words, our ideas about how methods are supposed to work, or how we want them to work, do not always match how they work in reality.[2]

This is particularly true when we venture into unfamiliar methodological territory, or when we attempt to borrow from the methods of other disciplines—both of which I did in this research. Not only was I unable to imagine the myriad small and large obstacles and challenges associated with the methods I chose, individually and especially in combination with one another, I was also unable to fully anticipate how the materialization of these methods in the field had implications for many more abstract and relational dynamics that really mattered.

Methods in Practice

In concrete terms, doing "bio-psycho-cultural ethnography" meant figuring out how to use several very different kinds of methods more or less simultaneously. For the purpose of gathering data about the internal workings of mediums' bodies, I had the quantitative, "scientific" method of impedance cardiography. To gather data about the psychological states of mediums, I had psychological questionnaires. And to collect data about the lived contexts, behaviors, and experiences of mediums, I had ethnography. In practice, combining these methods turned out to be more complicated than it had seemed in principle, since their very juxtaposition raised a number of unanticipated, sometimes challenging, and often thought-provoking epistemological and practical issues.

I first began to get a sense for these issues early on in my research, when it came to thinking about the physical location in which my research activities would take place. In particular, I needed to figure out where it was practical to conduct the psychophysiology portion of the research, and how the location of this method would work in relation to my ethnographic endeavors. At first, I had hoped to be able to take all of my methods with me to where my participants lived and gathered, rather than requiring people to come to me. I soon realized, however, that the idea of setting up this supposedly "portable" equipment anywhere, anytime was unrealistic at best for a variety of reasons. For one thing, while the equipment was sufficiently portable to transport into the field—it was not a huge piece of equipment that had to be permanently installed in a lab—in reality, it was too unwieldy and delicate to throw in a bag and take anywhere.

Worse still, the quality of the recordings generated by the equipment was deeply affected by something called electrical "noise"—that is, random electrical signals that disrupt information-carrying signals within an electrical circuit. Consequently, the machinery absolutely had to be plugged into a grounded outlet to ensure that the data signal would be clearly detectable and not swamped by noise. As I soon discovered, the outlets in most Bahian working class neighborhoods are not grounded, and since electricity in favelas is most often pirated, not only are grounded outlets not available, but the power itself is unreliable. I could not, therefore, count on the very basic but extremely necessary ability to successfully power up the impedance cardiograph in these settings.

In addition, attaching the impedance electrodes required interactions, such as lifting up participants' shirts in order to position the electrode tape in very specific places on the neck and torso, which were both intimate and challenging and required my full concentration. Thus, they were best conducted in a private setting with few distractions (the procedure for attaching participants to the impedance cardiograph is described in detail in the appendix). Time spent in the homes of participants, where family members and neighbors constantly wandered in and out of already cramped spaces—sometimes settling in to chat, other times just hovering curiously—contributed to my sense that such settings were not well suited to this purpose.

Combined, these constraints on portability convinced me that I needed to create a dedicated space in which I could perform the psychophysiology measures under more "controlled" conditions. I decided to use an extra room in my apartment for the purpose, setting it up with the impedance equipment and my computer, chairs, a desk, and a few decorations. Once the electrician I hired was done, it even had a grounded outlet. In retrospect, I realized that what I had created was a kind of "lab" space in which to conduct these measures. The benefit of this lab-like setting in principle was that, as in more traditional psychophysiology research, I could better control the conditions under which recordings were made so that differences in arousal could be reliably attributed to interindividual differences in psychophysiological traits, rather than differences in the conditions under which the measurements were made.

But these "controlled conditions" were ultimately traded-off against other important practical and phenomenological concerns. For example, by asking people to come to me to participate in this portion of the research, I effectively made the stakes much higher for participation. Participants would have to be strongly motivated and committed in order to literally go out of their way to participate. Just getting themselves to my "lab" was an obstacle since the neighborhood in which most participants lived was some distance away from where my apartment was located, and their low economic status meant that most were reliant on public transportation to get there.

Cognizant of these issues, I offered to pay taxi fare for participants to get to and from my house, which everyone who participated gladly accepted.

Yet there were issues here as well. I could not really give people the taxi fare in advance, since the money was meant to help facilitate participation and participants paid in advance could, in principle, fail to ever show up to participate. Instead, I was forced to reimburse people for their costs, but this meant that they had to have the money to pay for their transportation up front, which would be an issue for participants who were unemployed and struggling financially. I began to suggest that people have the taxi driver wait while they came up to get the money. This worked well, as those who had the money to pay up front could do so and be reimbursed, while those who did not could still take a taxi if they desired. Some people, I am sure, came by bus and pocketed the reimbursement, for which I was glad, since my other efforts to compensate participants had failed. As I will discuss in a moment, people who participated tended to be socially or spiritually motivated to do so. The exchange of money was inconsistent with these motivations.

Because it required that I have relationships within the religious community that were robust enough for people to want to go out of their way to work with me, and for them to feel some sense of responsibility to keep their commitment once they had agreed to participate, the issue of motivating participation was even more difficult than the logistics of getting people to my "lab." Getting people to agree to participate in the psychophysiology research required that I first be a good ethnographer. Hours and hours of participant observation were needed to build the kinds of relationships that convinced people not only that I was trustworthy, but also that it was worth their time and energy to participate in the formal aspects of my study.

In Bahia in particular, where Candomblé has become something of a tourist attraction, I had to convince Candomblistas that my presence was not just for entertainment value. In the context of a religion in which people are particularly protective of spiritual relationships and knowledge, participant observation was the only way to establish my legitimacy.[3] I had to show my face over and over again, be there for rituals and festas and talk to people at every opportunity, and establish a relationship with a spiritual leader and with the orixás.[4] All of this served to demonstrate my genuine interest, a basic understanding and commitment to understand further, and a degree of spiritual legitimacy. Hence, not only was participant observation a crucial method in its own right, through which I was able to access key information about the internal logic of Candomblé and the experiences of participants, it was also a key method for recruiting Candomblistas into the psychophysiological portion of the research and ensuring their willingness to go out of their way to participate.

Perhaps because of my own, at the time inchoate, sense that bringing people into the lab could undermine my relationship with them, I never invited anyone to participate in the psychophysiology until I was certain they would not say no—and no one ever did. On the other hand, lots of people agreed but failed to show up at the appointed time, and many, whether intentionally or not, simply made it impossible to actually schedule an appointment with them in the first place. For these and probably a number of other reasons, I did not end up with as many participants in this portion of the research as I had originally hoped for. Yet for these very same reasons, each time I successfully brought a participant into the "lab" it felt like a major triumph.

In addition to the practical issues raised by conducting the psychophysiology portion of the research in my makeshift "lab" were more phenomenological issues related to the ways in which such settings shape experience. Impedance cardiography is, by its very nature, a method likely to feel alien and perhaps even a little uncomfortable to most participants (this is true in the United States as well, but probably especially true for my particular set of Brazilian participants). Applying this method in an unfamiliar, laboratory-like setting located outside participant comfort zones could only serve to increase the foreignness of the experience. On the other hand, ethnography centers around collection of data within the flow of people's daily lives in ways that are as unobtrusive and integrated into ordinary experience as possible. Hence, the settings within which these methods took place, and the kinds of experiences they created, were in fundamental tension with one another.

Cognizant of the ways in which these two forms of participation might impinge upon and influence one another in the experiences of my participants, I made an effort to conduct the psychophysiology portion of the research in a way that was as "ethnographic" as possible within the chosen setting. However, in order to minimize the kinds of interindividual differences in experience that might interfere with the ability to compare results across participants, I still had to create a kind of standard protocol for use of the psychophysiology procedures and measurements. Most psychophysiology researchers use protocols that are experimental, presenting stimuli to participants and measuring their physiological responses. Such protocols typically include experimental tasks—things like mental arithmetic—that function as stressors. While such tasks may work well in highly educated, Euro-American samples, they are culturally inappropriate, or lacking in "ecological validity," for use within study populations like mine (Seligman and Brown 2010). The challenge was thus to create a more ecologically valid protocol, that would better reflect the daily lives and experiences of participants and would, in this way, remain consistent with the demands of my ethnographic research.

The protocol I designed used a kind of case study approach, combining interviews and psychological questionnaires with the use of impedance cardiography. The ideal protocol went like this: first, informed consent was administered and the protocol and procedures were explained in detail to participants. Participants were then connected to the psychophysiology equipment, a procedure that involved attaching electrode tape around the neck and chest and then attaching wire leads between the electrode tape and the impedance machine (see appendix for a detailed description of the procedure). Participants were given some time to relax and get used to wearing the electrodes and wires, and afterward a baseline recording was made before the start of the interview. Administration of a semistructured interview and set of three psychological questionnaires followed while the impedance recordings were ongoing, and a second baseline recording was taken upon completion of the questionnaires (see appendix for description of the research instruments). After participants were disconnected from the impedance cardiograph, they were invited to debrief and chat over juice and cookies.

By interviewing participants while the psychophysiology measurements were being recorded, I hoped to kill two birds with one stone. Not only could the interview itself serve as an "ecologically valid" stimulus, physiological responses to which could be compared across participants (Ewart and Kolodner 1991), but by immersing them in an interview, I hoped also to make the experience less "sciencey" and more "ethnographic." Since under the best of circumstances the use of interviews within ethnography may pause, slow down, or distract from participation in daily life, I hoped that moving these interviews a bit farther outside the ordinary experiential and spatial settings of participants would not substantially compromise them. Moreover, since interviews tend to invoke participant life worlds, their use within the "laboratory" setting could serve to engage people in the familiar, even within an unfamiliar context. I hoped that integrating psychological questionnaires into the ethnographic interview would serve to make them seem less strange as well.

Combining interviews with impedance recordings was thus intended to soften the edges of the more alienating method/interaction and reduce the tension between ethnography and psychophysiology. But this combination may also have succeeded in sharpening the edges of the ethnographic interview, making it less intimate and comfortable for participants. What does it do to the interview process, for example, when the interviewee is wired to a machine? How is the ability to invoke the life worlds of interlocutors affected by the material presence of unfamiliar objects and practices, which invoke instead a world of "scientific research"? And what about the effects of combining interviewing and impedance on me, the researcher? Trying to use both methods at once could not help but affect the intimacy and comfort I experienced in conducting interviews, since I found myself distracted from each method by the other. In fact, doing both proved to be challenging enough that I sometimes had to ask my Brazilian research assistant, Rilda, to help conduct the interviews while I monitored the psychophysiology recordings or vice versa.

Thus, as I made efforts to address the ways in which the more "scientific" and "ethnographic" forms of participation might impinge upon and influence one another in the experiences of my participants, I also became increasingly aware of the implications of these two different forms of research for my own positionality as researcher vis-a-vis the people with whom I worked. The position of the ethnographer relative to her interlocutors is very different from the position of the scientific researcher collecting psychophysiology data from a group of study participants. For the purpose of quantitative data collection, every research participant should be treated the same way to ensure comparability across individuals. Hence, for the psychophysiology portion of the research, I needed to try to use exactly the same methods in exactly the same way for every participant. Moreover, for such research it is not necessary or even desirable to have a relationship with any of the participants, since the goal is to remain "objective" and treat all participants the same. In addition, in order to provide adequate statistical power for quantitative analyses, bigger sample sizes are better in such research, in spite of the decreased intimacy possible with such samples. Thus, for the psychophysiology research, it seemed that I needed to try to be a "scientific fieldworker," privileging methodological uniformity, objectivity, and social distance.

For the purpose of my ethnographic research, on the other hand, social intimacy and methodological fluidity were desirable. A fluid approach allows ethnographers to discover unexpected differences across individuals, and to follow them wherever they might lead rather than sticking to a rigid protocol. Ethnographic research also allows for a process of constant reevaluation as new information is learned, while quantitative research is constrained by the need to maintain standardization. Ethnographic research takes place in any relevant setting, however chaotic or messy, while psychophysiology research requires a more controlled context. Moreover, ethnographers may return repeatedly to interlocutors to gather new information, while psychophysiology research tends to take place over the course of one or two sessions.

Thus, ethnography both depends on and leads to the establishment of social intimacy with interlocutors. Such relationships allow a degree of trust to be created, enhancing access to more confidential forms of information. Yet this social intimacy is not commonly shared among participants and researchers in psychophysiology studies, despite the fact that they require interactions with a degree of *physical* intimacy to them. Though minimally invasive, impedance cardiography still requires that electrodes be attached to a participant's bare chest. This requires lifting or removing shirts, sometimes adjusting the position of a bra, and delicately touching bare skin as the electrode tape is applied. In psychophysiology studies, these seemingly intimate interactions are made less intimate, and therefore less socially awkward, because they are performed in a sterile, neutral environment with a kind of clinical detachment facilitated by the anonymity of participant and researcher. Social intimacy impedes the adoption of such a clinical stance, increasing the potential for social awkwardness in these physical interactions. Being both "scientific fieldworker" and ethnographer thus required me to navigate two different kinds of positionality, tacking back and forth in the same encounter between the neutral, clinical tone suited to the psychophysiology aspects of my research, and the more socially intimate persona suited to the ethnographic aspects.

Moreover, unexpected local realities often piled onto these challenges, making the attempt to find the right kind of positionality all the more difficult. An example that has to do with the local reality of *sweat* in Salvador will serve to illustrate what I mean. Given the climate in Bahia, it is impossible to go anywhere or do anything in Salvador without getting seriously hot and sticky. Participants often asked me for a towel to clean up with before the interview, or wanted to delay starting until they had stopped sweating. One ogã, a confident young man named Edmundo, even asked me if he could take a shower. While this seemed very strange and slightly inappropriate to me at the time, this was the way I learned firsthand what others have observed before me: that Brazilians tend to be fastidious about personal hygiene. As Nations and Monte (1996: 1017) observe "taking innumerable baths per day, using deodorant and dousing oneself with cologne (from sweet smelling herbal water to imported French perfume, depending on class), wearing clean, pressed clothes and spotless shoes in public are valued across socioeconomic groups in Northeast Brazil." It was thus distasteful and even degrading for people to come to my "lab" space all sweaty and have me apply electrodes to them without first giving them time to attend to their personal hygiene. Asking participants to allow me to attach the electrodes while they were still sweaty was therefore not only something of a social misstep that affected my relationship with them, but also belied my efforts at creating the neutral comfort of "clinical distance" by making people uncomfortable in a way I had never anticipated. To correct the problem, I built a cooling-off and "freshening-up" period into the protocol so that participants would no longer be forced to ask me for these things. But the experience of coming to this practical insight exemplifies the kinds of added challenges that came with combining ethnography and psychophysiology in a field setting in particular.

Local realities were also at the heart of the problems I encountered in dealing with something called "movement artifact" when taking the impedance measurements. During my training I had learned that the quality of impedance recordings can be seriously affected by the way in which movements can change the impedance signal. If a participant moves, say lifting his/her arms, fidgeting in the seat, or scratching his/her face, this alters the waveform being recorded from the impedance signal. A movement here or there causes only short-lived interference with the signal, but a lot of movement can interfere in important ways with the quality of the data. In fact, a standard part of the protocol I had been taught to use was to instruct the participant before beginning the recording to try to sit as quietly as possible and relax while the recording was being made.

I knew, therefore, before I began collecting data in Brazil, that the movements of my participants should be kept to a minimum. What I did not know, however, was how foreign "sitting still" would be to the majority of my participants. As many times as I reminded them, my participants simply could not stop themselves from moving. Bahians tend to be expressive, active people. They move. They dance. They reenact. They talk with their hands—a lot. They do not sit still. It is funny now to think about how I asked one participant who was gesticulating vigorously with his hands to try sitting on them in order to keep more still. He dutifully complied. But with his hands stilled, his legs began to move, jiggling up and down as he talked. I finally gave up after reminding some participants up to ten times during an hour-long interview to sit as still as possible. It became clear that my admonishments were futile, and I took to simply marking the periods in the impedance recording when a participant was wiggling a lot. The movement artifact would be dealt with during data analysis through a painstaking process of hand cleaning the data. And ultimately, the baseline periods at the beginning and end of the interview were the results I used for comparison, and these, luckily, were the periods during which most participants actually did sit fairly still. So in the end, on the surface at least, this problem did not really seem to affect my results.

Yet use of a method in which, built into the technology, is an expectation for a lack of movement, within a group of participants for whom lack of movement is decidedly *not* built into the habitus, is clearly loaded in some ways. What are the implications, for instance, of having to ask people repeatedly to stop moving—for the flow of the interview, the relationship of researcher to participants, and perhaps even for the data recorded itself? It is one thing to ask this of people while in the persona of "scientific fieldworker," but how might it have changed the dynamic as I switched between modes and sought to become ethnographer again?

The major challenge to combining ethnography and psychophysiology was thus maintaining a balance between the strategies and prerogatives of each—building rapport with participants while still recruiting a large enough sample, establishing social intimacy while maintaining "clinical distance," incorporating new information into the research design without altering quantitative instruments, controlling the setting and circumstances of the research without alienating participants, trying to enter people's life worlds while at the same time asking them to enter my "lab," and so on.

I have often thought that if I had used a psychophysiology method that was less invasive, more portable—even ambulatory (meaning the participant could move around normally while wearing it), it would have been easier to bridge the gap between ethnographer and "scientific researcher." Such a method would have allowed me to conduct the research in any setting, opportunistically taking measurements within the flow of people's daily experiences. And if I had the research to do over, I would probably look harder for such a method. The tradeoff of choosing a different psychophysiology method would have been losing the ability to collect data on both branches of the autonomic nervous system, since impedance cardiography is the only method to allow this. But this tradeoff might have been preferable to some of the other tradeoffs made necessary by the constraints of impedance.[5] Yet, other methods and their technologies would have come with their own sets of challenges. Moreover, the process of gathering psychophysiology data in situ, if I had been able to do it, would undoubtedly have presented unexpected practical and phenomenological complexities in the same way that using the psychophysiology methods in my makeshift lab did.

One of the lessons learned through my research thus relates to the ways in which the materiality of incorporating nonanthropological methods into anthropological research is a profoundly theoretical matter. The issues thrown into relief by this research process ultimately tap into broader theoretical concerns about power and authority within research relationships. Both in the ethnographic and scientific process, we must cultivate certain kinds of relationships with the people who are the subjects of our research, in order to accomplish our goals. The instrumental qualities of both kinds of relationship, and the efforts we must make to position ourselves in ways that maximize this instrumentality, is made especially visible by the tensions that arise in their juxtaposition.

Findings: Limitations and Opportunities

The tensions between more classically "scientific" and ethnographic modalities are also relevant to thinking about the analysis, interpretation, and limitations of my findings. Borrowing the intellectual tools and practical methods of another scholarly field and integrating them into one's own paradigms is complicated by the fact that different fields have very different ways of knowing (Weisner 2012). These epistemological differences are the basis of important disparities in the conventions surrounding things like standards of evidence and genres of writing, reporting, and representing findings. For example, while cultural anthropologists value ethnographic ways of knowing through participant observation, repeated interaction, interlocutor perspectives, qualitative interviews and theory-based interpretation, psychophysiology is part of a scientific community deeply invested in the results of complex statistical modeling. While cultural anthropologists value thick description, psychophysiology research is disseminated in the kind of dry, formulaic writing oriented toward objectivity and replicability. Thus, integrating across these fields means combining very different ways of knowing and representing what is known.

Faced with these disparities, my strategy was to conform as much as possible to the conventions of each field for analysis of the data corresponding with its respective method, and to bring the findings from each to bear on those of the others in the process of interpretation. Thus, on the one hand, I used traditional anthropological methods for coding and analyzing my ethnographic data (which took the form of field notes generated through participant observation and data from formal and informal interviews). On the other hand, I used statistical analyses to make sense of the psychological and psychophysiology data. For the most part these were the kinds of analyses best suited to the different types of data. Searching through the voluminous psychophysiology record for regularities or themes in the way that one would code ethnographic data would have been a waste of time, for it is unlikely that I could have discerned true regularities from chance patterns or coincidence.

Yet it bears pointing out that the idea of distinguishing what is "real" from what is merely chance already assumes a certain standard of evidence that is built into the conventions of statistical analysis. Rules based on probability theory about when a pattern is regular enough to be considered meaningful are central to the statistical conventions that many of us take for granted. Notions of what is meaningful in such analyses are crystallized particularly in the conventions surrounding p-values (i.e., $p < .05$), which are so often used to define statistical "significance." I began my psychophysiology analyses by using a conventional analysis of variance (ANOVA) to compare group means. I found a substantial difference between the means of the two groups—they were a half a standard deviation apart—but the results of this statistical test were not significant by conventional standards, meaning that the difference between groups was not robust enough to be definitively distinguished from chance. These findings would, therefore, not be considered meaningful by such standards. Yet especially given the small size of my samples, the differences were certainly suggestive.

Knowing that small sample size causes a lack of statistical "power," and was therefore likely the cause of my less than significant findings, I did some research on statistical analyses for small samples. I found that nonparametric statistics are considered to be a better fit for such samples, since these tests do not assume a normal distribution or equal variances the way that parametric tests do (Corder and Foreman 2009; Pett 1997). Since small samples often do not fit these parameters, these tests do not work well in such studies. This is interesting from an epistemological perspective as well, as it suggests that the most common kinds of statistical analyses have many assumptions built into them about the characteristics of a typical sample (i.e., normal distribution). These kinds of tests are thus best suited for certain kinds of research, especially research with large, representative samples. This is not the kind of research in which most anthropologists engage.

I subsequently reanalyzed my findings using a nonparametric test that compares group medians instead of means, and found that mediums have a substantially higher median score on the cardiovascular measure used than nonmedium initiates. This finding is marginally significant by conventional standards ($p = .07$). And while this result would likely be considered more meaningful by most scholars, it is still not the kind of statistical finding that is likely to impress those who place high value on such standards of evidence. My small sample size, which was in large part a result of the unique challenges of combining psychophysiology and ethnography, thus affected my ability to meet the conventional standards of evidence within psychophysiology. An additional tradeoff of combining these two kinds of methods might therefore, ironically, have been a lack of statistical power—something I would not have had to worry about if I had used ethnographic methods alone.

This is because the ethnographic approach to figuring out what is meaningful is very different. Certainly as anthropologists we are interested in detecting patterns and regularities in our data. Things that come up repeatedly in our interactions and interviews grab our attention, but so do the exceptions—the things that seem not to fit a pattern. Yet trying to quantify my ethnographic data and subject them to statistical analyses instead of using more interpretive methods would not have been particularly useful, since it would have eliminated all of the contextual detail that we tend to use instead of numbers to tell us when things are meaningful. As anthropologists we are interested in thinking about how the things we have observed and recorded make sense in relation to one another and to larger theoretical ideas. In fact, part of how we know when something constitutes a pattern or regularity worth noting is by thinking about how it relates to what we know about the bigger picture. I was interested, for instance, not only in the patterns and regularities I discerned across mediums' spiritual life history narratives, but also in the internal logic of each particular narrative, and its relationship to the broader social and religious context.

What is more, I was interested in the way the different *types* of data I collected combined to form a gestalt. Piecing together ethnographic data on differences in the motivations of mediums for religious participation with the distinct and recurring theme of transformation within and across their narratives, for instance, formed a meaningful picture of the embodied effects of this form of religious participation. The psychophysiology data were intended to complement those other forms of data, to add to the big picture by providing information about whether and how such embodied effects leave traces at the biological level. The pattern of difference I found between mediums and nonmediums in ANS function seemed to indicate just such a trace. In other words, the psychophysiology evidence fit into the larger picture formed by my other findings in a way that felt far from coincidental, in spite of its failure to meet strict standards of statistical significance.

Certainly from an anthropological perspective these findings are compelling—not because anthropologists do not understand the issues at stake in defining statistical significance, but because we understand that these issues are not the only ones that matter. The question of how to handle the conflict between these different standards of evidence, then, seems best answered in terms of the intended audience. For some audiences the fact that the psychophysiology results are only marginally significant will matter a lot. Yet for many others, the very fact that there was a difference at all between such small comparison groups will seem compelling, particularly in the context of the larger story my data have to tell.

The lack of significant results from most of the psychological inventories I used may also be a result of small sample size and limited statistical power. But I suspect that there is an additional explanation that also has to do with differences in epistemology. Lack of results from these methods may also relate to issues of cultural and contextual validity of the instruments. Such standardized inventories are designed to measure risk for what are understood to be universal forms of psychopathology. The assumption built into such tools, therefore, is that people from all populations are susceptible to these forms of pathology, and that while the language of the inventories may need translation, the concepts that form their basis, do not.

Scholars from transcultural psychiatry have shown, however, that this is not the case and that many of the psychological constructs measured by such questionnaires lack cultural validity (Canino et al. 1997), much as the experimental protocols of psycholophysiology studies often lack ecological validity. While I was aware of such issues, my desire to be able to compare results from mediums to other populations convinced me to try using these standardized tools anyway. However, such conceptual problems may explain why only the Brazilian instrument (the QMPA) seemed to produce more meaningful results. The nonfindings from the other inventories are therefore meaningful in a way, since they suggest that there may be cultural specificity to the ways in which things like anxiety and depression are experienced in the Brazilian context. The QMPA, for instance, includes a number of somatic symptoms that are not the same as the "vegetative" symptoms that form part of the DSM diagnostic criteria for depression (Santana 1982). Similarly, the dissociative experiences scale (DES) may lack cultural validity among Candomblé participants since it asks only questions about pathological and distressing dissociative experiences, and not religiously meaningful ones. Hence, while in some ways the use of these culturally questionable inventories represents a missed opportunity, I do not see it as a major limitation of the study.[6]

For me, the most nagging limitation of this study has to do with the inability to know with any certainty the direction of causality between mediumship and patterns of physiological function. This is a limitation of the cross-sectional study design, but interestingly, it is not a limitation that can be neatly tied to, or explained in terms of tensions between the conventions of psychophysiological and ethnographic research, since psychophysiologists often employ cross-sectional designs as well. The limitation of such designs is that they do not allow psychophysiology data to be tracked over time and across development the way a longitudinal design can. In my research, this means that we cannot differentiate between the embodied qualities brought to the role by mediums, and the effects of embodied religious learning on these bodily processes.

Lamentably, a longitudinal design simply was not feasible for this study—as a graduate student I had neither the time nor the resources necessary to conduct this research over the course of multiple years. In addition, the small sample size and challenges of recruitment prevented me from being able to simulate this kind of longitudinal design through comparison of mediums at different stages (i.e., preinitiation and postinitiation).

Interestingly, however, the inability to know whether psychophysiological results are a cause or effect of religious participation is shared by much of the current research on religiosity within the psychophysiology literature. Most studies to date have compared individuals with low and high scores on "religiosity" or "spirituality" measures in terms of their ANS function, and have found correlations between high religiosity and patterns of ANS function that resemble those that I found (Berntson et al. 2008a; Cacioppo et al. 2005; Miller et al. 2003). As in my research, the very fact that there is a relationship at all between these two things is compelling. But, because these studies are also cross-sectional, they are not able to answer the important question of causality in this relationship. Does religiosity result *from* these autonomic differences, or does it result *in* these differences?

The default assumption seems to be the latter, that religiosity results *in* autonomic differences,[7] but without longitudinal data these studies are in much the same boat as mine—they must speculate about causality based on other available data and theory. And in this regard, my research is at a clear advantage. Rich ethnographic data on how mediums experience their relationship to the spiritual world both before and after their initiations can tell us a lot more about what aspects of religious belief and practice might affect or be affected by autonomic function, than constructs like "religiosity" and "spirituality" on which psychophysiologists must rely. My data, because they involve a form of religiosity that includes deeply embodied practices and entry into altered states, can help, for instance, to elucidate some of the cognitive and behavioral components of the health/religiosity link. These data suggest that connections between ANS control, attention and information processing, cognitive attribution processes, and even self-transformation (giving over control to an other, lack of personal responsibility, etc.) may all be connected to the positive effects of religious participation on health.

Hence, although neither type of study can tell us definitively about the direction of causality in the relationships observed, the use of ethnographic methods provides the material for a more compelling story about how autonomic function, health, and religious participation might influence one another. The merits of this approach are unlikely to convince psychophysiologists to stop doing laboratory studies and start doing ethnography. But maybe, just maybe, some anthropologists and scholars of religion will be convinced that taking such an integrative approach is worth the trouble.

Conclusion

To summarize: doing integrative research can be complicated and difficult. At some point it really sunk in for me that this is why it is not done more often. It is difficult to be an expert in disparate theories and methods, to straddle forms of positionality, and to meet divergent standards of evidence. However, I have come to see the knowledge gained through navigating the tensions and challenges encountered in *doing* both ethnography and psychophysiology, and in *being* both ethnographer and scientific fieldworker, as an added advantage of having used this integrative methodology. If we are cowed by the challenges and unwilling to accept the limitations of doing such research, then we will never transgress our intellectual borders. Yet such transgressions are often immeasurably rewarding as they help us to become more aware of, and to resist tacitly accepting, the pervasive epistemological assumptions within our own fields. The rest of this book speaks to the many other important ways in which doing such integrative research can advance our knowledge.

Chapter 3

Sometimes Affliction Is the Door: Healing and Transformation in Narratives of Mediumship

To become a filho de santo, or possession medium within Candomblé, individuals must undergo an intensive initiation process typically lasting from 21 days to 3 months. This alone makes taking on the role of medium a major commitment. But mediumship also involves a great deal of ongoing responsibility, endless ritual duties and considerable expense, regular entry into an altered state of consciousness, submission of one's body to powerful spirits and deities, and many other practices and experiences that could be viewed as difficult, dangerous, or burdensome. This is not, therefore, a role that anyone takes on casually. In fact, by the accounts of Candomblé participants at all levels within the spiritual hierarchy, no one seeks out or even desires mediumship.

It seems far from clear, therefore, how and why anyone does end up in this role. Are there certain kinds of personal experiences and individual characteristics that push certain people to become mediums? Are there aspects of the role that pull some people toward it? What kinds of factors, in other words, move some people to become mediums in spite of the conventional wisdom that says it is not something to which anyone aspires? And for those who do become mediums, what is the effect of taking on this role?

In the semistructured interviews I conducted with each participant in my study, I asked these very questions: why did you become involved in Candomblé (*porque você se envolveu no Candomblé*)? Did your life change after becoming involved (*a sua vida mudou desde que se tornou envolvido*)? How did it change (*como é que a sua vida mudou*)?

As it turns out, those who became mediums were more than six times as likely as those involved in the religion in some other capacity to explain their participation as a response to an illness (table 3.1).

The illnesses they described ranged from tuberculosis-like symptoms and skin rashes, to vomiting, diarrhea, and weight loss. Filhos de santo were also twice as likely to mention having had a mental health problem serious enough to motivate visiting a mental health professional prior to becoming involved in the religion—with symptoms resembling anxiety, depression, and even psychosis. In addition to illnesses, filhos also described being afflicted with a variety of social problems that also helped to motivate their initiations. Their illnesses and afflictions had often reached a point of crisis by the time these individuals became involved in Candomblé, making their initiations relatively urgent matters.

By comparison, other religious participants rarely mentioned illness or affliction as a motivation for participation. Instead, these participants overwhelmingly attributed their religious involvement to affiliations with other participating family members. Yet while 82 percent of mediums also had family members who were involved in the religion, they rarely linked their participation to family (table 3.1). In addition, most of the filhos I worked with talked about seriously approaching the religion for the first time right before their initiations, but lay people tended to be lifetime participants. Even ogãs and ekédis, who are themselves initiates, were typically involved in the religion for an extended period before becoming initiated. In other words, none of the other kinds of Candomblé devotees understood their participation to be urgently motivated by some form of affliction the way that filhos did.

Other participants were also much less likely to associate their participation with a major change in their quality of life, while in talking about how religious involvement had affected them, mediums overwhelmingly said that their lives, and particularly their health, had improved. Mediums' narratives thus traced an arc from suffering and affliction to health and well-being. These findings strongly suggest that affliction and the possibility of its resolution, are among

Table 3.1 Results of semi-structured interview questions for three comparison groups within Candomblé

	Motivated by illness (%)	Have family in Candomblé (%)	Sought mental health care (%)
Filhos	63	82	54.5
Ogãs/Ekédis	10	80	20
Frequentadors	5	75	25

the most important pushes and pulls associated with becoming a medium. As one medium told me by way of explaining why she had become a filho de santo, "In order to be brought to Candomblé, there had to be a door." Affliction or illness frequently acts as the "door" or entry point into Candomblé mediumship.

Yet to say that people become mediums in order to be healed in a conventional sense would be a vast oversimplification of a much more complex phenomenon. Illness or affliction may represent a proximate motivation or immediate catalyst for entry into mediumship, the way that it might motivate a visit to the emergency room. But filhos' narratives illustrate that the process of becoming a medium is ultimately a process of transformation rather than simply one in which individuals return to their pre-illness states of being. In other words, becoming a medium seems to fundamentally change individuals rather than simply treating and resolving their symptoms, the way that we would expect a trip to the ER to do.

The metaphor of the door introduced by my medium friend invokes this transformative process, drawing attention to the fact that the relationship between illness and healing in Candomblé mediumship is more complex than just a case of cause and effect. The idea of a door conjures an opening or entry—in this case, an entry into a new spiritual world that might not be accessible or even desirable to individuals who have not had the experience of illness. While a door suggests an element of agency and choice—one must choose to open the door and walk through it—affliction represents a door that individuals are compelled through. As the same medium friend put it, "I realize now, that things I saw and heard were signals that I would have a connection to this supernatural world. Not because I wanted to—nobody ever wants to—but somehow destiny was bringing me to this thing." Thus, for many prospective mediums affliction is what moves them from a state in which they cannot or will not access this spiritual world to one in which in some sense they cannot resist it. Affliction is thus symbolic of a lack of volition or agency. The agency in this case is in the hands of the gods, who are responsible for inflicting such illness and suffering upon human beings.

Illness and affliction can therefore be thought of as a kind of threshold for mediumship, in multiple senses. Illness crises are powerful enough experiences to push people into mediumship. They represent a threshold, then, in the sense of the level or point at which something (in this case mediumship) begins to happen. At a certain threshold of illness, people are willing to go to the emergency room—or, in the case of prospective mediums who have exhausted other solutions, they are willing to become mediums. But a threshold can also be defined as the starting point for an event or experience (Oxford English Dictionary). It is in this important sense that illness represents more than just a cause or catalyst. It represents a starting point for a new stage in a prospective medium's life—the thing that pushes her toward a new state of being.

These meanings are captured in the concept of liminality—the root of which, *limin*, not coincidentally means threshold. Liminality refers to a kind of social or psychological in betweenness (Turner 1969). To be liminal is to occupy the ambiguous territory between roles, stages, or states, where ordinary rules and expectations do not apply.[1] Illness makes people liminal because the physical limitations it imposes prevent them from fulfilling ordinary roles and expectations. Religion, and in particular ritual practice, makes people liminal by bracketing time and space, setting it apart from the ordinary. Occupying this bracketed time and space temporarily places the ritual participant outside the reach of day-to-day rules and roles.

Liminal states can also be characterized as states of becoming. Because everyday roles, behaviors, and expectations—everyday selfhoods, in other words—are suspended by liminality, this puts individuals in a uniquely receptive position to learn to inhabit new roles and behaviors, to become committed to new beliefs, to transform. Liminality can thus be an opportunity for individuals to become someone new. Rituals of initiation capitalize on these characteristics of liminality to intentionally move people into new social and religious roles (Van Gennep 1960; Turner 1969). For Candomblé mediums, illness and affliction represent the initial entry into a liminal state that ends when they have completed their initiations. That is, mediums *become* liminal through affliction, and *remain* liminal through ritual initiation, until they emerge in a new role with new behaviors and expectations attached to it. Illness thus defines the beginning of a process of self-transformation for prospective mediums—a passage from a pre-illness state of being, to a new, postinitiation form of selfhood.

But how does this kind of change end up making mediums *feel* better? Somehow the process of transformation that takes place causes a change that is profound enough to move individuals from a state of suffering to one of well-being—to heal them of their afflictions (Dow 1986). This transformation seems to be largely a function of a shift in the orientations of prospective mediums toward the spiritual, a change in their relationship to the religion, the religious community, and themselves. How can such a change in orientation actually alleviate suffering? Much of the rest of this book is devoted to exploring this process of transformation and to investigating how healing takes place *through* the transformative process.

While I will ultimately argue that a self-transformation profound enough to create the experience of healing must include *integrated* changes in both the representational and embodied dimensions of self discussed in chapter 1—that is, in the way that mediums think and talk about themselves as well as their experientially grounded ways of being in the world—I focus my analysis in this chapter on the thinking and talking piece of selfhood and experience. Through close examination of mediums' narratives of becoming, or what I have referred to elsewhere as their "spiritual life histories" (Seligman 2005b), I explore how transformation in this representational domain is effected, how it contributes to healing, and how such changes relate to the larger process of transforming the self as a whole.

Religious Self-Transformation

When I asked what had brought her to Candomblé, Ana, a 34-year-old Afro-Brazilian woman who had been a medium for 11 years, immediately described an illness she had suffered prior to initiation. The skin all over her body had erupted in sores, she said, that her doctors were never able to diagnose or treat. But in the same context, she also mentioned that she had never been able to find or keep a job before becoming initiated. In fact, problems with work and money were a central theme of her larger narrative, coming up repeatedly. Moreover, Ana identified being without money as the most stressful thing in her life, and told a story about trying to rent a house and not having enough money to make a deposit as an example of a particularly traumatic event about which she still harbored feelings of stress and shame.

The problems that led Ana to initiation thus appear to be a complex mix of social constraint, emotional distress, and bodily suffering. Her skin disease was the immediate catalyst, but her unemployment and financial struggles were mixed into her narrative as equally salient sources of distress. As we shall see, such themes are standard in the narratives that filhos in my study told. In such tales, both the problems that precipitate initiation and the transformations effected through participation seem to play out in multiple domains of experience at once—the social, psychological, and embodied. In other words, these accounts suggest not only complex causes, but also complex *effects* of mediumship.

In fact, in the lived experiences of prospective mediums, both the causes and effects of involvement seemed to transcend the specific list of problems and resolutions enumerated in their stories, to include a more encompassing sense of affliction and healing—a change to the larger experience of selfhood or subjectivity. Ana told of experiencing the resolution of each of the problems that had plagued her before initiation—since becoming a filho, she told me, her problems with work have resolved, she is no longer sick, and she is happier. But the net effect is really that Ana has become a different kind of person—a happier person, a healthier person, a person who no longer struggles in the same way with employment and economic hardship. How does religious involvement precipitate such encompassing experiences of self-transformation?[2]

One model for thinking about religious self-transformation comes from the literature on conversion. Understood as the movement from religious nonbelief or lack of participation to avid belief and active participation, conversion has appeared to many to be motivated by or to motivate a global change in individual characteristics and worldview.[3] How else, observers have wondered, could the same individual so radically change his or her patterns of behavior and ideas about how the world works? In fact, in his early seminal work on the subject William James (1885) characterized conversion as a "regeneration" of self through which the individual overcomes a sense of brokenness and conflict. James thus understood conversion as a process through which the self is fundamentally transformed.

James approached this process of transformation primarily in psychological terms, exploring the role both of individual will and the subconscious in effecting personal "regeneration." Much of the scholarly literature since James has also emphasized the individual and psychological dimensions of conversion, characterizing it as a sudden, emotional, and singular transformation of an often passive subject (Richardson 1985). Conversion is most often seen, in other words, as something that happens *to* people: an individual has a revelatory experience and is changed by it. The change is seen as private, internal, and psychological—having to do with the individual's worldview and sense of self, rather than his or her social identity. Moreover, the convert is typically not understood as a social agent who actively seeks out such transformation and the "new forms of relatedness" it entails (Austin-Broos 2003; and see Stromberg [1993] for an excellent counterexample).

The literature on spirit possession, on the other hand, has long been focused on the social dynamics of religious self-transformation. The "social-communicative" analyses I described in chapter 1, for example, have convincingly demonstrated that by allowing individuals to inhabit or be inhabited by spirits, these religious traditions provide a means through which participants can transcend the constraints of their social situation and expand their social horizons (Boddy 1994; Lambek 1981, 1989; Kapferer 1979). In other words, they get to behave in ways they could not otherwise because their behaviors are attributed to the spirits. This approach understands participants as agents who actively seek to transform their social identities, and participation in spirit possession is seen at least in part as a means to accomplish these social goals. Consequently, many students of spirit possession have argued that it is particularly attractive to those who occupy marginal positions within their society, for such individuals stand to benefit most from such forms of social repositioning (Lewis 1971). These analyses are thus focused on exploring how spirit possession facilitates a transformation of the social dimensions of self.

But unlike the scholarship on conversion, the spirit possession literature has had little to say about how these religious experiences affect the individual psychological aspects of self. The kinds of psychological and emotional dynamics that James identified at work in religious conversions—the sense of brokenness and emotional conflict that motivate a regeneration of self—have been less frequently explored in the context of spirit possession (notable exceptions include Obeyesekere [1981] and Boddy [1989]). Yet people's desires, fears, and perceptions are always deeply implicated in the ways in which they engage with the social world, and vice versa. The stresses and defeats that Ana experienced as a member of the underclass affected not just her possibilities for social role enactment but her *internal* sense of self. Thus, Ana and people like her who radically change their religious commitments and seek new forms of social identity do so because they have some mental and emotional skin in the game. Becoming a medium may allow individuals to address their mental and emotional needs at the same time, and through the same processes, by which they redefine their social selves.

It is no coincidence, moreover, that so many mediums talk about symptoms of mental and physical illness as their "door" to mediumship. Because symptoms of illness have both communicative and experiential dimensions, they are, by definition, both social and individual phenomena. Somatic symptoms often function socially as a sanctioned means for individuals to draw attention to the difficult social situations in which they find themselves (Kirmayer and Young 1998; Nichter 1981). In a social context in which a woman cannot freely express distress at her husband's infidelity, her mother-in-law's controlling behaviors, or her social isolation she might instead suffer from weakness, dizziness, headaches, dissociation, menstrual problems and other symptoms that indirectly draw attention to her social predicament and demand some form of social response (Nichter 1981; Guarnaccia et al. 1996).

At the same time, abundant evidence demonstrates that stressful social experiences are linked to measurable effects on health via a variety of physiological pathways. For example, racial discrimination associated with skin color has been shown to affect blood pressure (Gravlee et al. 2005; Sweet et al. 2007), and psychosocial stress associated with low relative social status can both increase blood pressure and suppress immune function (Dressler et al. 2005; McDade 2002). Even the likelihood of contracting a common cold is affected by the experience of psychosocial stress (Cohen et al. 1991). Hence, social and psychological distress may precipitate bodily or "psychobodily" ailments, while these ailments may also begin the work of repositioning the social self. I introduce the term "psychobodily" here in place of "psychosomatic," in order to capture the links between mind and body that allow such symptoms to be both psychologically and physically produced, experienced, and expressed, without the implication that they are somehow not real. I will discuss the very real processes through which social experiences become embodied in depth in the next chapter, but the point I want to make here is that social dynamics always have psychological and embodied—or psychobodily—dimensions, just as psychobodily symptoms and experiences have both social causes and effects. The self is where these dimensions of experience converge, and its qualities are defined by the complex interactions among them.

These complex interactions are represented in Ana's story and the self-narratives of other mediums. As the stories we tell ourselves, and others, about ourselves the intersection of the social and psychobodily is clearly visible in such self-narratives. These are stories used to shape and represent who we think we are as people in socially and culturally meaningful terms. As such, these narratives have both an expressive and instrumental dimension—in other words, we use them to express and make meaningful our experiences, but we do so in ways that may also serve to strategically affect our social contexts (Hunt 2000; Ewing 1990; Seligman 2005b). Hence, narratives of religious becoming are the means through which prospective mediums come to understand and represent their experiences of affliction and of resolution and healing, in religiously meaningful terms—both in their own minds and in their social worlds (cf. Stromberg 1993). It is for precisely this reason that these self-narratives play a crucial role as both an expression of, and vehicle for, the process of healing self-transformation.

Beings and Being in Candomblé

But, as I quickly discovered, in order to understand the narratives of mediums and how they contribute to a process of self-healing, it is first necessary to understand the ontological foundations of self and personhood in Candomblé. Philosophers use the word "ontology" to refer to theories of the nature of existence—including conceptions of what entities exist in the universe and how they are related to one another. For instance, some people might understand the universe to include only human entities, each one independent from the others and innately valuable, while other cultural and religious traditions understand the universe to include humans and other spirits, supernatural or ancestral or both, all of whom are connected in an intricate web of interdependence (Vivieros De Castro 2004). These ontological orientations fundamentally shape ideologies of selfhood, providing the basic outlines for the kinds of selves people are expected to have—whether highly individuated or relational, unique and will-driven or dependent on hidden and shared energies for their fortunes.

Making sense of mediums' narratives thus requires us to understand how they are shaped by such ontological orientations—how their spiritual worldview and the specific beliefs and meanings they hold shape the way these individuals understand themselves and represent their experiences. Deciphering mediums' stories requires, for example, making sense of one medium's casual statement that her aversion to a particular food is not a simple matter of personal preference but something supernaturally predetermined. It challenges us to understand how another medium's construction of her interpersonal problems as a spiritual issue, not a social one, both depends on and contributes to a particular understanding of human selves in relation to the rest of the universe.

Within the Candomblé cosmology the universe is populated by a number of different, but related, types of spirits—some of them closer to the human world of matter, and some of them further away. These supernatural beings are a part of everyday reality, influencing the material world. Mediums' accounts of how they came to be mediums are fundamentally shaped by these ontological commitments, and the shaping of narrative in terms of this "metaphysics of being" (Hallowell 1955; Vivieros De Castro 2004) is deeply implicated in the process of self-transformation. In other words, Candomblé provides the basic outlines for a new form of selfhood that is defined in large part in relation to these spiritual entities.

The supernatural beings in the Candomblé universe can be roughly organized in terms of their proximity or distance from the human world of matter. The most distant figure is the supreme being, Olorun, who is so distant from the world of matter that he is typically not even worshipped directly by devotees. The pantheon of orixás represents the next highest order of spiritual entity in Candomblé. Occupying lower strata are the caboclos, exús and *exúas*, and *erê* spirits.[4] Caboclos, who are indigenous South American spirits, are one level down from the orixás, closer to the realm of matter. Below caboclos are ewês, or child versions of the orixás, who often possess a medium after the orixá has left and before the medium regains (human) consciousness. Before coming out of trance mediums are thus often possessed by spirits who have a closer connection to the material world—almost as if to prepare their bodies for the transition to such earthliness.

At the lowest level, closest to the realm of matter, are the trickster characters known as exús and exúas (the female version), who are the slaves of the orixás, and who serve as mediators between humans and gods. While there is often understood to be a single exú who is more on par with the orixás, there are also multiple exús and exúas who exist at this lower stratum (Wafer 1991). Exús/exúas are the most accessible of all Candomblé spirits to human beings. Because they are closer to matter, unlike the orixás, all of the lesser spirits partake in material consumption, and interact more directly with human beings. Thus caboclos—known as the somewhat rough characters stereotypically associated with the indigenous population in Brazil—drink heavily, smoke cigars, and party all night. Exús also partake in drink and smoke and ewês, because they are child spirits, like to eat sweets and drink juice and soda. Furthermore, all of the lesser spirits may speak directly to humans, and therefore it is often these spirits, particularly the caboclos, who offer advice to humans seeking their counsel about practical problems and health matters. The exús are the spirits most often petitioned for help with everyday problems, and on any given Monday (exús' day of the week) one can see the city dotted with offerings made by individuals in need of some immediate help.

Yet, in spite of their higher spiritual status, orixás are intimately connected to the world of matter in a variety of ways—not least of which is their influence over human lives and fates. Every human being has a primary orixá, known as the "owner of the head," and a secondary orixá or *juntó*, who together govern individuals' behaviors, personalities, and fates. The personality of the orixá is thought to be part of the true nature of the individual whose head it owns, so that individuals frequently share personality characteristics and preferences with their orixás. For example, Oxum, the goddess of sweet water, is known to be vain, sensuous, and maternal in nature (Verger 1981).[5] Individuals whose heads are owned by Oxum are expected to possess some of these same characteristics. Ogum, on the other hand, is a warrior god whose filhos tend to be bold and courageous, but also competitive and quick to anger. Pedro, a medium with whom I worked closely, had a long history of beach brawls that were knowingly attributed to Ogum by Pedro himself as well as others in the terreiro.

Mediums often recognized aspects of the deities in themselves, but were also very aware of the ways in which they were different from their patron orixás. Adriana, a *filha* whose head was owned by Iemanjá, goddess of the sea, acknowledged that like the goddess, she is vain and enjoys bathing and primping. But, she told me, unlike the goddess who is known to be fairly calm, "I am still temperamental." As another filho put it, "I can't be exactly the same because he (the deity) is an orixá and I am only matter."

The orixás themselves are like larger than life versions of humans—they have personalities, desires, and preferences, they behave badly, have relationships, share exploits, and experience adversities. In fact, the myths about the orixás are often more outrageous than a *telenovela* (Brazilian soap-opera), since all of the orixás are related to one another as well as being married to, cheating on, and double-crossing each other on a regular basis. The gods thus represent both archetypes of, and influences over, human characteristics, and in this sense are tied closely to the world of human beings (Bastide 2001; Walker 1990).

Moreover, as I described in chapter 1, each god has a special connection to other worldly phenomena, including certain colors, days of the week, animals, and natural elements (i.e., Xangô is the god of thunder and lightning, Iemenjá is the goddess of the sea, etc.). Humans have the potential, then, to make links to the deities through the material—for example, by wearing red and eating goat, an adherent links herself to Xangô. In addition, since humans are expected to mirror the characteristics of their superhuman counterparts, it would not surprise anyone if a filho of Xangô particularly *enjoyed* wearing red and eating goat. Many Candomblé ritual practices operate under the same principle of making links to the spiritual world through the material. Material offerings and behaviors serve to please and feed the deities, while at the same time bringing some *axé*, or spiritual force, to human beings. Such practices are thus a means of materializing the spiritual power of the supernatural for the benefit of humans, in order to improve the earthly lives of adherents. Evidence of the degree to which this ontological orientation is a practical reality in the lives of Candomblé participants can be seen in the number of stores and market stalls in which can be found strings of devotional beads and materials for creating offerings to the spirits (cover photo).

The practice of ritual divination works in much the same way—as an exchange between the spiritual and material worlds. Candomblé divination uses cowry shells that are thrown and then "read" by the diviner, who is able to interpret the information presented by the pattern the shells form. Divination thus represents a form of communication through which these higher order supernatural beings, who never speak directly to humans, may make their wishes or knowledge known. Thus, the gods use a material vehicle, the cowries, as a medium to connect them to the human world. Similarly, possession uses the bodies of human individuals as mediums to connect supernatural beings to the world of matter, and in some sense it represents the ultimate link between material and spiritual.

Mediums, then, occupy a critically important position within the cosmic scheme of things. In their capacity as links between the material and spiritual worlds, filhos have the responsibility of connecting the larger religious community to the supernatural, via their own material forms. Their role also gives mediums privileged access to axé and the potential for spiritual power, health, and prosperity that come with it. At the same time, however, prospective mediums are particularly vulnerable to the material effects of not forging and maintaining proper ties to the orixás. The spiritual disturbance represented by unacknowledged mediumship in particular sends ripples through the human world, causing the kinds of illness and misfortune that plague many filhos before initiation. Thus, while spiritual leaders use divination to determine which individuals have been chosen by the orixás as mediums, uninitiated mediums can often be recognized even without divination, by the distress and suffering they experience. Affliction, then, represents a manifestation of the connection between the spiritual and material worlds and is understood as evidence of the profound influence that the orixás have over human fates.

Initiation of a prospective medium serves to resolve her spiritual disturbance, and by extension, her illness or affliction. But initiation is also a way of cultivating the spiritual–material connection. Initiation is typically performed when the deities demand it. When it does take place, initiation involves seclusion inside the terreiro, where the initiate must stay for a prolonged period and where she undergoes various rites of passage, including having her head ritually shaved, sleeping on the floor, and eating only ritual foods (see chapter 5 for a more detailed discussion of initiation). Through these material practices, initiates are imparted with, and come to embody, ritual knowledge and axé.

To summarize, the world that Candomblé devotees occupy is filled with many types of beings, some of them material, like humans, and some immaterial. While these "other than human persons" (Hallowell 1955) occupy different spiritual planes, they affect the lives of humans in numerous ways—from being available for practical help with human problems, to fundamentally contributing to who each human being is, to taking over human bodies and acting through them. In the world of Candomblé things do not just happen to people, instead the causes and consequences of events in the human realm reverberate throughout this layered universe. Things happen for reasons that are linked to the spiritual and the immaterial, but those things may manifest in very human and material ways. Job loss, for instance, is likely to be the product of a spiritual disturbance of some kind, and not just the result of economic ups and downs or the inability to get along with an unreasonable boss. Pedro and Ana, two of the mediums described earlier, both experienced repeated job loss which came to be interpreted as a symptom of their spiritual disturbance. Such misfortune, then, is viewed as evidence that the material and spiritual are "part of a single reality"—inextricably intertwined and equally real (Capone 2010:20; Hallowell 1954).

As we shall see, these ontological conditions have important implications for our understanding not only of the process through which potential mediums are identified, but also for our understanding of how selves are reshaped in Candomblé religious formation, and represented in mediums' narratives. In order to understand how the process of transformation really works, then, it is necessary to understand how these kinds of beliefs work—how they are internalized, how they come to shape self-understandings, and how they motivate behavior.

Belief, Knowledge, and Cognition

As Talal Asad (1993) and others (cf. Stromberg 1985) have noted, Western scholars of religion have tended to focus disproportionately on belief, privileging it over the practical and embodied features of religious ritual. Such scholarship assumes, in other words, that what matters most in understanding religious participation is the beliefs that people hold—the god or gods they believe to exist, how they understand the interactions between human and divine, the ideas they hold about proper behavior and sin, what is sacred what is profane—the kinds of ideas, like those I just finished describing, that structure peoples' ontological commitments. Religious practices are simply understood to follow from such beliefs, rather than playing a role themselves in shaping peoples' commitments, behaviors, and understandings. One of the central projects of this book is to trouble such assumptions, by exploring how the belief aspects of Candomblé religious devotion work in concert with the embodied aspects. An important point of departure, then, is to consider how we understand belief.

To begin with, the term "belief" is often used in opposition to "knowledge," implying that it is somehow less real or substantial than its counterpart (see Byron Good's [1994] excellent discussion of this issue).[6] In addition, both belief and knowledge are generally thought of as linguistically or discursively based aspects of mind—in other words, they are typically understood as conscious, articulable, and explicit. When you ask someone to explain their religion, the ideas they invoke are what people typically mean when they talk about belief. A Candomblé devotee might say, for instance, "There are many gods who reign over human affairs and each is connected to an element of nature." Or he/she might say, "The spiritual world and the material world are connected." From the perspective of the standard model of belief, these are merely intellectually understood ideas, propositions to which adherents are more or less committed (Harding 1987). It is hard to understand how this sort of belief could result in the kind of encompassing change to self and worldview that we have been discussing.

Yet the beliefs that one's job loss is the result of spiritual factors and one's food aversions are supernaturally predetermined seem to be connected to broader effects on the self-understandings and experiences of the mediums who hold them. Evidence from contemporary research on cognition may help us to understand how these beliefs create more far-reaching effects. Research from cognitive science suggests that such beliefs may be part of complex cognitive networks of association that operate outside of consciousness, yet fundamentally shape our motivations, desires, and reasoning (Barsalou et al. 2004; Lakoff and Johnson 1999; Westen 2001). In fact, contemporary constructivist models of mind suggest that conscious thoughts and beliefs are like the tip of a giant iceberg. From this perspective, most of what we come to learn, conceptualize, believe, and experience in our engagement with the world will remain, like the bulk of the iceberg, under the surface—outside of our awareness, never consciously reflected on or verbalized unless and until an effort is made to do so (Hollan 2004).

Experimental evidence shows, for example, that people can be primed subliminally to adopt certain values or orientations (i.e., toward success, friendship, individualism, or collectivism) (Bargh and Barndollar 1996; Gardner et al. 1999; Oyserman and Lee 2008). These values then shape the way that participants behave in subsequent experimental tasks, changing the likelihood that they help another person rather than advance their own interests, for example, in spite of the fact that they have no conscious awareness of the prime and would be hard-pressed to name the orientation it elicited. In a similar way, religious knowledge and belief may come to operate at an intuitive level for Candomblé mediums, structuring their behaviors, as well as their understandings of self and world.

One way of thinking about how such knowledge and belief become internalized in ways that go beyond a commitment to abstract propositions is in terms of "cultural models" (D'Andrade 1992; Shore 1996; Strauss 1992; Westen 2001). These mental models schematically encode knowledge in various sociocultural domains, allowing people to easily access networks of information as they construct meaning and select actions appropriate to their context (Dressler and Bindon 2000; Shore 1996). Such models are often not known explicitly or articulated easily by their holders and the more deeply held and motivating the models, the more implicit, less discrete, and harder to verbalize they tend to be.

Cognitive anthropologist Claudia Strauss (1992) makes a distinction between models that are "bounded" and those that are "unbounded." Bounded models are typically learned explicitly, and while people may endorse these beliefs, they are not always motivated to behave in accordance with them. Unbounded models, on the other hand, are typically learned through experience and tend to be taken-for-granted and difficult for individuals to articulate. Strauss's (1992) research with working class American men shows, for example, that for these men the "American Dream" is a bounded model—they believe in it, but it does not motivate their behaviors. Instead, they are motivated by an unbounded model that Strauss calls the "bread winner" model, which drives them to focus their efforts on providing for their families, rather than trying to pull themselves up by their bootstraps in a more conventionally ambitious sense.

The "bread winner" model is, for these men, the kind of belief that is so deeply held, so intuitive, that it is not easy to articulate. Yet Strauss demonstrates that the model fundamentally structures these men's sense of self. It is through their effects on self that such deeply held beliefs are capable of becoming the foundation for the social and psychobodily transformations associated with Candomblé religious formation. Moreover, understanding belief in this way makes it easier to grasp how it can contribute to a process of self-transformation that includes embodied dimensions, since implicit knowledge and intuition seem less firmly entrenched than conscious thought in the "mind," as opposed to the body.[7] In fact, beliefs of this kind may become so foundational to the sense of self that the inability to behave in accordance with them can produce a physiological stress response (Dressler 2000).

But models are not simply "a personal cognitive resource"; they are also representations shared across individuals within the same culture, and their internalization is shaped by social norms (Shore 1996:47). The working class men from Strauss's study share with one another a deep belief in the breadwinner model, and their knowledge of and adherence to this model comes in part from the way that it is learned from, enacted, and reinforced among their fathers, brothers, and peers. From this perspective, Brazilians who participate in Candomblé share with one another a number of cultural–religious models on which they base behavior and create meaning—and which for some may come to structure their sense of selfhood in important ways. The shared nature of these beliefs is essential to their potential for the kind of encompassing self-transformation I have been describing, since reshaping selfhood around such beliefs facilitates a transformation that is not only deeply personally meaningful, but also socially operative.

Cultural Models and Self-Narratives

Knowledge and belief about the relationships of orixás to humans, and the connections between the spiritual and material, form what can be thought of as a foundational model (Shore 1996) within Candomblé—a model that, when deeply internalized, has the potential to fundamentally shape the experience and understanding of selfhood. The model includes three elements particularly relevant to selfhood, and thus to the self-transformative potential of mediumship: (1) the idea that orixás can cause things to happen to people; (2) the idea that the orixás determine fundamental aspects of the person/self; and (3) the idea that the orixás may periodically take over the bodies of humans. From this foundational model emerge more complex propositions like: negative life events and misfortunes are a result of spiritual disturbance or calling; negative aspects of self can be attributed to the orixás; and elements of self, like memory, identity, and body, may sometimes become separated from one another. Following from these is the notion that suffering and misfortune are not to be blamed on something inherent to the person or self, and that human behaviors may sometimes be attributable to nonhuman forces. This model is thus the foundation of a worldview or ontological orientation that understands human selves as subject to the complex interactions of spiritual and material forces. Deep internalization of this model therefore has the potential to transform notions of moral responsibility, agency, and personality, which structure mediums' self-understandings and the way they represent themselves through self-narrative.

Candomblé participants also share a related cultural model of and for spirit possession mediumship specifically. A central feature of this model is knowledge concerning the "signs and symptoms" of a spiritual calling by the orixás. This shared model allows participants to recognize unacknowledged mediumship and to tell when someone has a legitimate spiritual calling. The content of this model was articulated in similar terms in interviews with spiritual leaders, adepts, and laypeople alike.

The cultural model includes a laundry list of signs and symptoms that one *mae de santo* glossed as forms of "suffering." These are the afflictions I alluded to earlier that so often represent the "door" into mediumship. They include chronic, undiagnosable illness; mental problems, like anxiety and depression, interpersonal problems, especially problems within the family; negative life events or general misfortune, often in the form of unemployment, financial crisis, illness, death, or injury of self, friends or family; and general malaise or existential distress. It was also agreed that an obvious sign of undeveloped mediumship is spontaneous entry into a trance state and possession by a spirit, the enactment of which also follows a particular model. But spontaneous possession alone is not enough to signify potential mediumship. Instead, such trances bring potential mediums to the attention of spiritual leaders, who may then uncover a history of other forms of suffering indicative of an unacknowledged spiritual calling. Mae Tiana, the spiritual leader with whom I worked most closely, articulated the model this way:

> I can recognize a person who needs to become a filho because they are badly made, rough…they feel something different and don't know what it is…When a person has the saint but doesn't know it, they become sick, they are uncomfortable like this, they don't get along with anyone. Yes, they have problems with relationships…sometimes they can't find employment, they will not make an effort. Like I was when I needed to be made…I suffered, suffered a lot because the orixá wanted to be made, and I didn't take care…If a person needs to be made and doesn't take care, they can even die, they can become crippled, they stay in a sick-bed, anything can happen…because the orixá wants them and the person doesn't want, so the orixás get angry and punish them. (Translation mine)

The cultural model thus treats undiagnosed or unacknowledged mediumship as a likely cause of affliction and understands initiation as an appropriate treatment. There is built into this model an expectation that becoming a medium will change individuals' fortunes, mitigate their suffering, and resolve the signs and symptoms that identified them as potential mediums in the first place. The expectation, in other words, is for some degree of transformation of the individual's earthly, quotidian self—in addition to the transformation of self expected to take place whenever the medium is possessed by the spirits.

Individuals showing signs and symptoms consistent with the cultural model are likely to be recognized as undeveloped mediums by those who have access to this cultural knowledge, including potential mediums themselves. Mediums must talk about, enact, and even experience their calling to the role and relationship to the orixás in accordance with the shared cultural model in order to make their experiences and behaviors culturally intelligible and socially legitimate as potential mediums. When I questioned mediums about what had motivated their initiations and whether their lives had changed since becoming filhos, I was thus tapping into this cultural model. For the degree to which an individual has internalized, and behaves in accordance with, the model determines whether or not she will be seen as a prospective medium.

The importance of achieving cultural intelligibility and social legitimation through proper enactment of the model was brought home to me at a public festa one night when a young, non-Brazilian woman in the audience spontaneously entered trance. Typically when uninitiated audience members enter trance spontaneously their possession is acknowledged by members of the spiritual community who minister to them carefully, often taking them to the back of the terreiro where they are either brought out of trance or supervised until their possession ends. They are then assessed by the spiritual leadership to find out whether this trance was a "one-off" possession by a frisky deity or part of a larger pattern of spiritual calling in line with the model for mediumship. Many of the mediums with whom I worked experienced spontaneous trance at the first Candomblé ritual they attended, leading to their assessment by the spiritual leader and the official "diagnosis" of their spiritual calling.

On this particular occasion, however, the young woman was actively ignored by the spiritual leadership of the terreiro until her behavior became too disruptive to ignore, at which point she was dealt with rather perfunctorily. What precipitated this disdainful treatment by the community, I realized, was her failure to perform her possession properly. Her "trance" state did not evoke the materialization of the spiritual world in the way that the trance states of other Candomblé participants do (it was too frenetic for one thing), and hence it appeared "fake" to the members of the community (see chapter 4 for a detailed description of a typical trance state). In other words, her behavior did not meet expectations and therefore failed to constitute the legitimate manifestation of possession. As a result, whether or not she had experienced other signs and symptoms of unacknowledged mediumship was destined to remain obscure because she never got the opportunity to invoke these other aspects of the model within the spiritual community. Her behavior thus failed to trigger the chain of events that might have led her to be identified as a prospective medium. This story demonstrates how important fitting the model can be to the process of being identified as a prospective medium.

On the other hand, like most models, the cultural model for mediumship represents a kind of archetype—a classic pattern around which actual experiences vary, not a rigid formula to which all individuals must conform precisely. Moreover, like all models, the cultural model for mediumship is imperfectly shared. Thus, there are many ways in which potential mediums may go unrecognized, ways in which individuals may fit the model for mediumship and yet fail to become mediums, and ways in which people who do not fit the model become mediums. While experiencing some or all of the signs and symptoms in the model signals the possibility of a spiritual calling, and the lack of these signs and symptoms makes it less likely that an individual will be identified as a prospective medium, it is important to note that sometimes things simply do not "work" in the way represented by the model—or they work differently.

One of the mediums I worked with, for instance, started out by working as a domestic in the home of her pai de santo for many years before beginning to attend some public rituals at his behest, and finally becoming possessed by an orixá at one such festa. After her possession the pai de santo performed a divination through which he discovered that the orixás wanted her to be initiated as a medium. In her account she emphasized the appeal of the aesthetic dimensions of the religion—the music, dance, and clothing—along with her relationship to the pai de santo as central to her motivation to become initiated. She did not describe experiences of affliction and misfortune prior to her initiation, and while she did say that her relationship with her husband had improved since her initiation, she did not emphasize the experience of transformation in the way that many other mediums did. Hence, in spite of the fact that she did not seem to recognize the typical signs and symptoms of mediumship in her own story, she was somehow identified by the pai de santo as a prospective medium and brought into the fold. Although her story was atypical among the mediums with whom I worked, and on the surface did not seem to conform to the model, this medium was still considered a legitimate filha by those within her spiritual community.

One of the built-in ways in which the legitimacy of all new mediums is cemented is through a public ritual called a *saida*, or "coming out," during which they are presented to the community at the end of the period of seclusion required for initiation. It is during this ritual that an initiate announces the name of the owner of his or her head and dances for the orixá for the first time, displaying both ritual knowledge and the capacity to become possessed (Bastide 2001). This ritual event is an opportunity for the initiates to be acknowledged by the community as freshly minted mediums occupying a new, spiritually potent role, the possessors of important and secret knowledge and power (Johnson 2002). In other words, it is a moment at which their social transformation is made manifest, and this moment is dependent on shared knowledge and belief. Internalization of the cultural model for mediumship allows individuals to behave in ways that are consistent with a shared belief in the existence of a spiritual calling, and belief in the power of religious initiation to transform individuals who respond to this calling. The shared model is reinforced for all religious participants through its enactment by prospective mediums and initiates in public rituals like the saida. Such cultural intelligibility and social legitimation allow the social aspect of self-transformation to take place.

Ultimately, however, mediumship contributes to the transformation of both the outward social person and the internally understood and experienced self. Because models are both shared public knowledge and internalized cognitive resources, they are fundamental to both forms of self-transformation. Like other Candomblé participants, mediums have access to the basic information contained in the cultural model of and for mediumship. But prospective mediums relate to these beliefs differently than others, using these cultural forms to express their individual needs and emotions.

This may be in part because prospective mediums have typically had the kinds of experiences that resonate with the model as signs and symptoms of a spiritual calling—that is, they have experienced various kinds of "affliction" and emotional distress. Individuals do not simply invent such experiences in order to fit the model, though as we shall see later, the model influences the way in which they interpret their experiences. But those who are motivated to fit themselves into the model tend to be those who have experienced the kind of suffering that the model entails. There is a fit, in other words, between the "door" to mediumship and the particular people who are compelled to pass through it. The social status of Afro-Brazilian women and gay men in Salvador, discussed in chapter 1, places these individuals in a position to incur high degrees of such suffering as a result of poverty and discrimination. Of the 11 filhos I interviewed, all described suffering from one or more psychosocial problems prior to initiation, especially interpersonal, employment, and money problems. Moreover, 9 of them had experienced an acute illness that could not be resolved with medical intervention (table 3.2).

For prospective mediums like these, internalizing the cultural model thus represents a means for transforming their experiences of affliction, suffering, and distress in culturally meaningful ways. This personalization of cultural meanings is what Gananath Obeyesekere (1990) terms "the work of culture." According to Obeyesekere (1981), culture works to meet individual needs in ways that are salient and meaningful both to self and others. While his analysis focuses on the manipulation of symbols like the huge, gnarled dreadlocks worn by Sri Lankan possession mediums, the "work of culture" can also take

Table 3.2   Types and examples of affliction suffered by mediums prior to initiation

Type of "affliction"	Financial/ employment	Interpersonal	Death of close relative	Acute illness
Number of Filhos	6	5	2	9
Examples	Repeated job loss; long-term unemployment	Problems with husband; street fights	Death of husband; miscarriage	Vomiting and weight loss; rapid heart beat; rash all over body

place through manipulation of narrative. In his work on Christian conversion stories, for instance, Peter Stromberg (1993) has shown that by narrating their emotional and social problems in religious terms, converts not only make sense of these problems, but transform them into a central locus of religious meaning that serves to strengthen their religious commitments.

Similarly, Candomblé mediums make their experiences and autobiographical memories both personally and culturally meaningful by using shared cultural models to rescript their self-narratives. As I discussed in chapter 1, narratives are a way of organizing and representing self-understandings both internally and externally—to oneself and to others. Because self-narratives are both public and private, in order to be successful they must convince and compel not only the individual him/herself, but also a social audience (Taves 2010). To take an example from chapter 1, I can represent myself narratively as having changed in some fundamental way—perhaps I used to be very self-centered and I now understand myself as focused on the needs of others—but if the people in my social world are not convinced, then my ability to maintain this new self-narrative will be compromised. My narrative might be particularly unlikely to convince my audience if I fail to narrate the cause of the change in terms that are meaningful within my context—if, for example, I represent the change as a product of my own willpower, but people in my social world expect narratives to link such major changes in character to an event or experience. Thus, while they are expressions of individual selfhood, self-narratives are not entirely individual. Rather they are culturally and socially scripted. They are expected to follow certain kinds of conventions, match particular genres, and highlight privileged themes and self-characteristics (Miller 1994; Bruner 1987). In other words, they are expected to conform to certain cultural models.

A common model for self-narratives within mainstream American culture is the story that justifies or contextualizes a characteristic of self in terms of a past event or experience that serves to illustrate or explain the characteristic (Bruner 1994). As an adult, for instance, I might tell a story about how I surprised everyone at a restaurant by ordering squid off of the menu at the age of five, as a way of illustrating the deep roots of my current "foodie" self. A variant of this model is the narrative that justifies or contextualizes *differences* between a current understanding of self and previous behaviors and characteristics, in terms of a "turning point"—an event or experience that caused a major reassessment of, and change in, selfhood (McAdams 1993). Becoming critically ill or being badly injured is a common turning point invoked in American self-narratives to explain a change in the goals and priorities of the current self.

Models that scaffold self-narratives are examples of those that are particularly deeply held, organizing individuals' taken for granted understandings of the relationship between self and world. Both of the American narrative models described earlier are structured by a widely shared and deeply embedded model of selves as relatively stable and coherent entities (Ewing 1990; Shweder and Bourne 1981). Thus, American self-narratives often invoke such stability, or include a major motivation for change.

Candomblé cultural models provide cultural scripts that facilitate the reworking of mediums' self-stories. For example, beliefs about the role of the orixás in causing one's experiences of suffering and in determining one's personal characteristics contribute significantly to how mediums shape new narratives, and by extension new selves. These beliefs are part of a narrative model that reframes things like job loss, relationship problems, self-destructive behaviors, and illness as manifestations of the orixa's personality within the medium's self, or the orixa's displeasure at not being properly "cared for." These models thus become particularly meaningful for prospective mediums at "moments of vulnerability," when they are in the throes of suffering and crisis, in part because fitting their experiences into these models has the potential to fundamentally transform the significance of those experiences. Narrating their suffering and misfortune in terms of a religious model that draws strong links between the spiritual and material worlds activates the important set of implicit beliefs about moral responsibility, agency, and personality that I discussed earlier. By framing the relationship between self and negative experience in this way, mediums transform the way they understand their self, from unhappy and unhealthy victim or agent of misfortune, to the ground upon which cosmic dynamics are being played out.

As I have already mentioned, however, these religious models only become transformative when they are profoundly internalized and identified with deeply, and when they are invoked in socially intelligible ways. This process does not take place all at once, but rather in a gradual, iterative manner that culminates with initiation. As prospective mediums are first recognized and come to recognize themselves as recipients of a spiritual calling, they slowly begin to match their experiences to the cultural model and a kind of proto-narrative emerges, which is then reinforced socially (Taves 2009). The mediumship narratives that follow illustrate this process, demonstrating how Candomblé cultural models create a template or broad script into which individual mediums rewrite their own stories and through which they are able to transform themselves.

Jalita

Jalita is a 54-year-old mother of seven. Her husband died of cancer 10 years before I met her, and she has never remarried. She has a junior high school education and worked as a manicurist for many years, though she was unemployed at the time I knew her. Jalita owns her own home in a neighborhood that is one step up from a *favela*, or shantytown, and shares it with her sister and five of her children. She has spent 26 years within Candomblé, and currently acts as the *mae pequeña*, or second-in-command, at a local terreiro. She is socially graceful, warm, and maternal, and appears to be very competent, relatively satisfied with her life, and to enjoy very good relationships with all of her children.

Jalita described the events leading up to her initial involvement in Candomblé in the following manner: she was married at the age of 24, and by the time she was 28, she already had three children under the age of four. It was around this time that she became what she describes as "very stressed," and began seeing a psychiatrist who prescribed medicine for her for what she describes as "*maluco*" (craziness). As she puts it,

> I went to the psychiatrist and he told me to take this medicine, and so I took it. I mean to say, if a child had cried at that time, and I had had a knife in my hand, I would have had the desire to shut him up…but there was something that controlled me…that's why I had to seek out Candomblé—I was already passing those kinds of limits.

So one day she went to a Candomblé, never having attended one before despite the fact that her husband was a participant. As soon as she got to the terreiro, she went into a trance state referred to as a *bolação* (a special type of trance that signals the need to become initiated). When she awoke from her trance, the pai de santo spoke to her, and informed her that she needed to be initiated. This made her weep, because at that time she did not really like Candomblé and was afraid of it. So she left the terreiro, despite what the pai de santo had said, and went home. By the time she got home, she had become very ill. She had a cough, fever, a headache—"everything." She became so ill that she was convinced she had tuberculosis. She had three young children to raise, and could not afford to stay sick, and so she soon went to see the doctor about her illness. According to Jalita, over the next six months, her doctor "tested for everything," but could find nothing wrong with her.

Eventually, Jalita sent her sister to a Candomblé practitioner whom they both knew, in order to have the cowries thrown. The cowrie shells agreed with what the other pai de santo had told her— that she needed to be initiated. In the meantime, her illness was worsening, so her husband finally went back to see the pai de santo in whose terreiro she had gone into trance. The pai de santo instructed that she must return to his terreiro for a spiritual cleansing. Jalita agreed to the spiritual cleansing, and after he had performed it, the pai told her she must return to the terreiro again in eight days. When she returned, there was a caboclo festa going on at the terreiro, and she immediately entered into trance and once more experienced a bolação.

While she remained in a trance state, she says that they moved her to a room somewhere in the terreiro where she awoke from her trance three months later. She describes it in this way:

> After 3-months the pai de santo finally demanded that the saints leave me, and I woke up. After I woke up, I passed my hand over my head— and in those days I had a lot of hair, very big and well cared-for—I passed my hand over my head and didn't feel my hair…I had already been initiated! I was already an *iaô* (filho novice) and I knew already the things I should know—what things I shouldn't do, and what I should…what I could and couldn't eat.

Although she awoke from her trance state already possessing such ritual knowledge, she nevertheless claims complete amnesia for the time she spent in trance. After that she stayed in the terreiro, in seclusion, for another three months, for a total of six months of initiation, despite the fact that she had three young children at the time, one of whom was only three months old when she entered the terreiro. Though it was difficult, and her sister had to care for her children during this time, she thinks of her initiation as "a great blessing" because she "has never had another thing wrong" since then.

Analysis of Jalita's narrative reveals the interplay between two of the main building blocks upon which self-narratives are constructed: the memories of life experience, and the cultural model that the individual has come to absorb. The details of Jalita's life history are organized around themes found in the cultural model for mediumship. She describes herself as suffering from both chronic, undiagnosable physical illness, as well as mental illness at the time of her initiation. She also speaks of experiencing several episodes of spontaneous trance. She describes negative life events and interpersonal problems prior to initiation, in her case centered around her family and the care of her children (i.e., "if a child had cried at that time and I had had a knife in my hand..."). According to Jalita, the psychosocial stress brought about by her recent, and rather abrupt, transition into the role of wife and mother (she went from a single young woman of 24 years, to a wife and mother of three, in less than 4 years) had reached a crisis point by the time she was initiated. Thus, represented in her narrative are key elements of the cultural model for mediumship: interpersonal problems, stress, distress, illness, and spontaneous trance.

These elements of the cultural model are not presented randomly in Jalita's narrative, however. In fact, Jalita's narrative is illustrative of a common arc followed by many mediums' stories, which often begin with some form of psychosocial suffering, then build to a crisis that either manifests as illness or is followed by illness. Help is then sought from biomedicine or psychiatry but the illness cannot be diagnosed or cured by doctors, which leads the individual to approach Candomblé for help, often resulting in episodes of spontaneous trance, and culminating in initiation. This can be thought of as the prototypical script followed by most mediumship narratives, and around which they tend to vary. In fact, the stories of eight out of eleven of the mediums I interviewed followed this basic arc fairly closely. The other four stories still shared elements of the model but did not follow the full arc. For instance, these narratives talked about psychosocial suffering of some sort (relationship or employment problems) but it was not followed by an illness crisis; or they mentioned an illness but it was not followed by failed help-seeking in a biomedical setting.

Jalita's narrative lends further insight into the links between the model for mediumship, with the misfortune and affliction it entails, and the social conditions in which many prospective mediums find themselves. Her crisis was brought on by stress associated with movement from one life stage (young adult) to another (wife and mother). This kind of life-stage-related psychosocial stress, brought about by uneasy social role transitions (or failure to make appropriate transitions) recurs in the narratives of the mediums in this study. The fact that these transitions are considered normal elements of the life course and are not experienced as stressful by most members of the society contributes to a situation in which these individuals must struggle to find a culturally appropriate way to both express and relieve this stress.

Moreover, for individuals in the Brazilian context who occupy socially marginal positions to begin with (poor women and men of Afro-Brazilian descent), there is less flexibility in the cultural expectations for the life course to begin with: there exist few life-course alternatives, and few built-in mechanisms for mobilizing support when life-course transitions do not go smoothly (Gregg 2003; Lovell 2000). It is not surprising, therefore, that problems with such transitions should lead to distress and even crisis.

However, for those individuals who occupy a social context in which there exists knowledge of Candomblé, the cultural model for mediumship can provide both a mechanism for mobilizing support, as well as a viable life-course alternative. The notion, built into the model for mediumship, that some individuals must respond to a spiritual calling or risk prolonged suffering and even death means that individuals who fit the model for such a calling have good reason not to move through ordinary role transitions smoothly. Moreover, they tap into a shared notion that spiritually afflicted individuals must let go of such ordinary life expectations, at least temporarily, in order to begin movement through the process of initiation and take on the role of religious adept instead.

Lucia

The narrative of another medium, Lucia, provides an example of the similarities and differences in the way that individuals use the same cultural model to script their individual self-stories. Lucia was 62, unmarried, and working at a museum in Salvador when I met her. She is a small, grandmotherly woman with a calm, warm demeanor.

She began the story of how she came to be initiated in the following way:

> I realize now, that things I saw and heard were signals that I would have a connection to this supernatural world—not because I wanted to, because nobody ever wants to, but somehow destiny was bringing me to this thing…For example, during my adolescence, I rebelled…they brought me to see the orixás, but my head was like the head of any other young person—I studied and I fought—I didn't have time for that side of things…So in order to be brought to Candomblé, there had to be a door, and the door was a very serious problem: I caused the death of my father.

Lucia had become very politically active in her late teens, during the time of the military dictatorship in Brazil. After several narrow escapes from the military police she became increasingly anxious about being apprehended and imprisoned, or worse, by the authorities. Eventually, her anxieties caused her to drop out of college and take a job.

Around the same time, Lucia's father suffered a stroke and lost the capacity to care for himself. Lucia and her older brother, along with their mother, shared the burden of caring for her father. She blames herself for her father's death because one night while she was supposed to be watching over him, she fell asleep. That night he suffered some sort of crisis, possibly another stroke, and had to be admitted to the hospital where he soon died. After that, Lucia says, she never went back to normal. She describes herself as barely able to function, crying all the time, and eventually she went to a psychiatrist who prescribed several medications. During this period she also had surgery to remove several large tumors from her uterus. Lucia explains that she was so nervous before the surgery that she went into what she would later come to understand as a spontaneous trance state.

At some point she began to suffer from delusions, often feeling as if she were being followed, and experiencing frequent visions of her father. At times she would throw fits, screaming and shouting, and throwing objects at her mother. She began to fear that her family would have her committed, and she recalls thinking, "If they commit me, I will kill myself." Finally, a friend suggested that maybe her problems were not mental, but spiritual, and took her to a pai de santo to have a *consulta* performed. The pai de santo did indeed pronounce her problems to be spiritual in nature. Though Lucia grew up in Rio, the pai de santo informed her that she must travel to Bahia to be initiated. Lucia followed his instructions and went to Salvador, to the terreiro he recommended, where she remains a filha de santo to this day. According to Lucia, at the beginning of her initiation the *pai pequeno*, or second-in-command of her terreiro, told the pai de santo that he must keep her on her medication while she remained in seclusion, or she would "finish his house, or finish herself." However, her pai de santo had "unlimited faith" and put aside her medicines, giving her herbal remedies of his own instead. She made it through her initiation, and became the "tranquil person" she is today.

Lucia's story is also built around themes consistent with the cultural model for mediumship; high levels of psychosocial stress and mental distress that functioned as signs and symptoms of undeveloped mediumship are central to her narrative. Yet the specific types of stress and distress experienced—including fear of the military police, the illness and death of her father, anxiety, depression, panic attacks, and even delusions—are unique to her. Her story also follows the standard arc, more or less, beginning with stressful experience, followed by an illness crisis (in this case psychological) that could not be resolved by conventional medicine, an episode of spontaneous dissociation, and finally resolution in the form of initiation into Candomblé as a medium.

Like Jalita, Lucia also struggled with social roles. Her multiple hardships led to psychological distress that prevented her from undergoing expected role transitions. She had never married and probably could not bear children (as a result of her uterine surgery), both of which were fundamental aspects of the normative life course for a Brazilian woman at the time of her initiation. In Lucia's particular social context, higher education and a career track seem to have been viable life-course alternatives, and yet she dropped out of college. These factors could only have served to exacerbate the mental distress she already suffered, just as her psychological distress contributed to her inability to undergo these social role transitions.

Furthermore, her fears about being committed indicate that Lucia experienced stress resulting from an awareness of her own deviance, and its potential consequences. However, recognition as a potential Candomblé medium served to protect Lucia from long-term social deviance and dysfunction, by redefining her affliction in spiritual terms—an idea I will discuss in more depth later. In fact, as discussed earlier, it is the experience of affliction itself that often allows individuals to be recognized as potential mediums.

However, the narrative of a male medium named Pedro demonstrates that not all mediums suffer from a dramatic physical or psychological affliction culminating in a crisis that precipitates initiation.

Instead, Pedro suffered from a series of negative life events, and a prolonged sense of dissatisfaction with his life. This pervasive dissatisfaction, or existential distress, likely relates to social marginalization he experienced as a result of being a gay man in Bahia. While these experiences left him aggressive and angry much of the time, they did not lead to an acute physical or mental crisis like those described by Jalita and Lucia.

Pedro

Pedro is a big man—tall and somewhat barrel chested, with a warm smile and an air of pent up energy. At the time I knew him he was 34 years old and unemployed. Even as a child Pedro says he was aware of Candomblé, as he had several relatives involved in the religion. However, he grew up a practicing Catholic until his late teens, when he lost interest in religion and became something of a full-time beach bum. At the age of 22, Pedro began to have serious problems. He was drinking too much and began to get into beach brawls and street fights on a regular basis. He started frequenting a *Mesa Branca* house (a variant of the syncretic Afro-Brazilian/Spiritist religion Umbanda) but the religion did not hold his interest for long. He got involved in Candomblé and almost became initiated while living in Rio, but backed out at the last minute due to his mother's objections; his mother did not want him to be initiated in Rio, fearing that his ties to the terreiro there would draw him permanently away from Salvador.

He soon drifted away from Candomblé again, and recounts that he developed a terrible infection in one of his teeth while living back in Salvador. Although it took some time to heal, the abscessed tooth was eventually cured with antibiotics. Pedro went back to drinking and fighting. He could not hold down a job, and was eventually forced to move back in with his parents. He began frequenting a terreiro in the neighborhood, where he agreed to undergo a preliminary initiation. However, when the mae de santo told him that he needed to be fully initiated, he resisted. According to Pedro, he fled from the terreiro, and fainted in the street outside. When he awoke inside the terreiro once more, he reluctantly agreed to stay and began making arrangements for his initiation. He describes his initiation experience as difficult—he says he missed his family terribly and was often afraid and uncomfortable. He did, however, finish the period of seclusion successfully and has been a filho de santo for nine years.

It is interesting to note that Pedro includes in his narrative the details of the infected tooth, despite the fact that the tooth was healed with the use of medicine prescribed by his dentist, well before his initiation. Pedro's inclusion of the tooth anecdote signals an understanding on his part that such affliction is part of the cultural model for mediumship around which typical medium narratives are scripted, and represents his attempt to fit his own story into the narrative structure. As a result, he has come to reinterpret his infected tooth as one of the symbols of his own spiritual affliction, despite the fact that it did not lead directly to his initiation. Furthermore, Pedro's story clearly shows that "affliction" is a matter of degree, and interpretation: although Pedro never suffered from an illness crisis like the ones Jalita and Lucia experienced, he has still come to reinterpret any and all distress he suffered prior to initiation as evidence of his spiritual disturbance.

In fact, this speaks to a larger point concerning the notions of suffering and affliction as they are used here. Use of these terms is not intended to pathologize the experiences of mediums, but rather to represent the range of negative life events, and the various forms of distress (social, emotional, somatic, and existential) experienced by many individuals and articulated as symbols of the spiritual disturbance that precipitated their initiations.

The fact that Pedro's narrative starts much earlier than the others, with his childhood, is also worth examining. Pedro begins his narrative by describing his early experiences with Candomblé, and a long-term pattern of approach and withdrawal from the religion gradually becomes evident. His incorporation of information regarding his long history with Candomblé seems to be designed to help legitimate his role as medium, given the fact that he lacks one of the basic elements that typically comes to define the legitimacy of other mediums, which is their past affliction. Pedro's narrative does, however, share with the other narratives the experience of chronic psychosocial stress around social role: his inability to hold a job and failure to get married and start a family, for instance, violate expectations around social role transitions. His social struggles are likely related at least in part to the fact that he is an openly gay Afro-Brazilian man, though he did not make this attribution himself.

Because the suffering experienced by mediums prior to their initiation is viewed within Candomblé as a form of spiritual affliction inflicted by the gods upon those who have failed to develop their mediumship potential, an extremely important element of the cultural model for mediumship is the notion that individuals do not choose mediumship, but are chosen for it. This aspect of the model is articulated in many mediumship narratives, including those of Jalita and especially Pedro, as the claim that the individual not only did not want to become a medium, but actively resisted being initiated even in the face of negative consequences.

By disavowing the choice, or even the desire, to become a medium ("no one ever wants this life") mediums and others who make this claim are referring explicitly to the shared notion of immense responsibility attached to mediumship. Signaling that this role is not something individuals seek out helps ensure that everyone is aware of the immense obligations to the gods and the community that the role entails. In other words, this rhetorical practice is designed to communicate that, as playful as it may sometimes appear, mediumship is hard work.

On the other hand, the devotion required of Christian priests and nuns must also be hard work, yet seeking out these roles is not only acceptable, but serves to underscore one's religious faith and devotion (Lester 2005). Clearly there is something more to this practice of disavowal among Candomblé mediums. In Candomblé, the capacity to be a bridge between the material and spiritual worlds must come directly from the supernatural world, it cannot be petitioned for or earned through devotion.[8] Choosing to become a medium would thus signal not an act of faith, but an inauthenticity and presumed lack of efficacy. In other words, being *chosen for* rather than choosing mediumship is crucial to the medium's legitimacy.

Perhaps most important of all, disavowing desire in the context of mediumship has an essential moral significance. Denying desire is also a way of denying moral culpability for any of the misfortunes and suffering that led one to the role. If mediums do not choose to be spiritually singled out in this way, the suffering they experience is also not of their own choosing, and, therefore, not their fault. The work that disavowal does is thus reminiscent of the release from moral responsibility associated with the medicalization of various conditions. Labeling alcoholism as a disease, for example, has helped to release alcoholics from the moral condemnation that has historically accompanied that condition. Assignment of responsibility to a higher power—either biology or the gods, or some of both in the case of Alcoholics Anonymous (AA)—allows individuals to escape blame for their own afflictions. What is more, disavowal underscores the shared belief that the experience of spirit possession itself is nonvolitional. It is understood that mediums are caught up and controlled by the spirits without any choice in the matter. Thus, not only is possession not under the control of the human will, it exists entirely outside the realm of human control.

In addition to this explicit notion that one must be spiritually selected for the role of medium, the initial involvement of prospective mediums in Candomblé almost always results from the subtle intervention of other human beings. In spite of the fit between their stories and the narrative model, prospective mediums cannot alone pronounce their stories to be those of the spiritually afflicted, and thereby declare themselves undeveloped mediums. Rather, becoming a medium requires a certain amount of social consensus. Typically this social process begins with the suggestion by friends, family, or acquaintances that one should seek help in Candomblé. This is part of what I have referred to elsewhere as "positive access" to Candomblé (Seligman 2005a).

By "positive access" I mean exposure to religious content in a positive context or through others who have positive associations with it, in order to tap into the cultural model for mediumship. The narratives of most Candomblé mediums include mention of the source of this "positive access" in their lives; in Jalita's case, her husband's involvement in Candomblé allowed her to access the cultural model for mediumship. For Lucia, it was the suggestion that her problems might be spiritual, and the introduction to a spiritual leader by a close friend, that were responsible for connecting her to Candomblé. For Pedro, it was a long-term familiarity with the religion, through the involvement of various family members.

The role of social recognition and positive access in connecting individuals to the cultural model for mediumship underscores the important interaction of psychobodily and social factors in the process of self-transformation. For the mediums whose stories I have related, the correspondence between their experiences and behaviors and the cultural model for mediumship allowed them to be recognized as prospective mediums by friends and family, who then helped them connect to Candomblé. At some level, this social process can be understood as part of how individuals are "chosen" for mediumship.

Positive access and social recognition set in motion a process of coconstruction whereby prospective mediums begin fitting their autobiographical memories into the cultural model for mediumship and forging their experiences of affliction into new, culturally meaningful self-narratives. As individuals increasingly come to frame their experiences in spiritual terms they receive feedback from those around them, editing and revising their stories as they go, and gradually coming to understand themselves in new terms. An analogous process that will be familiar to many readers is the coconstruction that takes place in the context of AA "personal story" telling. As in Candomblé, the shared model of AA heavily structures the personal stories that participants relate. For example, AA participants receive negative feedback when they tell stories that attempt to place blame or responsibility for their self-destructive behaviors on other people. At the same time, narratives that acknowledge the individual's own helplessness against alcoholism, and embrace the influence of a higher power, are reinforced by others. The formal telling of these stories thus creates the opportunity for the AA social group to provide feedback as individual personal stories are developed, helping to shape these narratives in a way that is potentially therapeutic largely because the meanings it invokes are so highly shared (Cain 1991).

Coconstruction can be thought of as part of a larger process of socialization through which members of mediums' social networks, especially those within the Candomblé community, help them learn to see themselves within the religious model.

It is particularly implicated in the prospective medium's encounter with his/her Candomblé spiritual leader, who identifies elements of his/her experience unequivocally as signs and symptoms of a spiritual calling. As the spiritual leader identifies certain experiences as especially significant, these elements of the prospective medium's story become further reinforced. Although this process of coconstruction was not something I was able to observe firsthand, since the mediums I worked with had already been initiated, it can be extrapolated from their accounts and those of the spiritual leaders. Mae Tiana, for instance, emphasized problems with employment and serious illness in her discussion of the ways in which an unacknowledged spiritual calling can be recognized. In her dealings with prospective mediums, she is therefore likely to place particular significance on these elements of their stories. Similarly, the accounts of mediums about their early interactions with their mae or pai de santo are suggestive. Pedro recalled, for example, how his mae de santo had always attached a lot of significance to his employment issues, and Lucia referenced her pai de santo's concern with her mental health. Through the coconstructive learning process narratives thus come to be articulated in such a way that the model becomes increasingly recognizable.

The process of coconstruction is not unique to contexts like Candomblé or AA, but applies to self-narratives more broadly, as individuals must try out their stories within whatever social contexts they occupy, and are inevitably faced with the responses of those around them (Kirmayer 2000). This is especially true developmentally, as children learn through modeling and feedback to narrate themselves in socially desirable terms (Miller 1994). Adults co-construct children's self-narratives by prompting them to include details considered particularly socially salient—a parent might ask a child, for instance, to describe how they felt when an event occurred, to name the other people who were there, or recount the actions they performed.

Not coincidentally the process of Candomblé religious formation—from recognition, to the sequence of events involved in initiation, to the coming out ceremony—can be thought of as a developmental process (see also Rebecca Lester's [2005] account of the development of Catholic nuns in Mexico). Understanding how Candomblé cultural models come to structure mediums' self-narratives in developmental terms, as a form of socialization, helps make clear that this process is at once a crucial part of how the individual's calling becomes culturally intelligible and socially legitimate, and also how the model comes to be deeply internalized. The social learning and internalization processes are reinforced in the extreme through initiation. In fact, initiation acts as a form of supercharged socialization; elements of the process, like seclusion, create an intensity and singular focus that allow initiation to accomplish in a short time levels of internalization and identification that typically take place over much longer periods. The embodied aspects of the initiation process, discussed in detail in the chapters that follow, also contribute critically to its efficacy.

Interestingly, formal performance of the mediumship stories of prospective and newly-minted mediums is not a part of Candomblé ritual the way, for instance, performance of the "personal story" is a central part of Alcoholics Anonymous, or the way performance of the conversion narrative is important in some Christian religious traditions (Stromberg 1993). Yet the development of these narratives is a profoundly social process that uses informal feedback to guide individuals formally into the Candomblé religious sphere by helping them learn to fuse their personal meanings with shared religious beliefs. The social response they receive both hones and reinforces the transformation of their self-narratives as well as their new role and the expanded social ground it entails.

To return then for a moment to our earlier discussion of beliefs, the role of models in scaffolding self-narrative demonstrates how beliefs function discursively, as linguistic representations of thoughts and ideas, but also have a deeper cognitive and affective life as intimate components of how selves are structured—or in this case, how they become restructured. In this sense, belief and knowledge contribute in important ways to the healing potential or therapeutics of mediumship, but only when the beliefs are shared within a community. For ultimately, it is the reciprocal relationship between social and individual factors that makes narrative self-transformation powerfully therapeutic, helping to heal mediums of the very afflictions that identify them as spiritually inclined in the first place.

Transformation and Healing

The process of learning to understand both self and world in religious terms creates the experience of healing for mediums in several ways. At the most basic level, the social dimension of this transformation promotes healing via the practical and material benefits it makes available to mediums. Candomblé mediumship has many such benefits, not least of which is the immediate and prolonged removal of the individual from her social situation. In the case of individuals who are suffering the negative consequences of profound psychosocial stress, removal from the sources of this stress during weeks or months of initiation functions therapeutically by forcing individuals to distance from and let go of outside expectations and thwarted goals (Johnson 2002). Not everyone is able to take a "time-out" from their lives in this way, however, and it is not uncommon for prospective mediums to delay their initiations until they can make suitable arrangements with family and work. For many, however, just committing to be initiated seems to go some distance toward ameliorating their suffering—perhaps because some benefits of mediumship begin to take effect even before formal initiation occurs.

For other individuals there is enough urgency to their suffering (including the threat of death from severe, untreated illness and the dangers of repeated, uncontrolled possession) to overcome the practical constraints associated with the initiation process. In addition, in the last several decades many terreiros have begun to offer less stringent versions of seclusion in order to accommodate the demands of contemporary life. For example, some terreiros allow individuals to go to work during the day, and return to seclusion within the terreiro whenever they are not working (Johnson 2002). When individuals do complete their initiations, they are not removed to an impersonal, institutional setting but rather to a context in which they are given an entirely new network of social support, even a surrogate family, in the form of the religious community (see chapter 1 for a detailed discussion of social support and the kin metaphor in Candomblé).

Additional material benefits of their social transformation are products of the expanded social network mediums access through Candomblé involvement, and include employment opportunities, financial help, and patron–client relationships (also discussed in chapter 1). Maes and pais de santo in particular often have many community connections and may help to secure employment or even a small loan for a financially strapped filho. These practical benefits mitigate the suffering or affliction experienced by many mediums before initiation by acting directly on the sources of their psychosocial stress. Since the spiritual and material are ontologically linked in Candomblé, these material effects are interpreted as a direct consequence of the spiritual investment mediums make with their initiations.

Somewhat ironically, however, one of the most common reasons for delaying initiation is to give the individual time to scrape up the required material resources needed to make it happen. Initiation can be quite expensive, requiring purchase of, among other things, a live goat. Most of the mediums I worked with had to call upon friends and family to marshal these resources. This suggests yet another way in which becoming a medium can be a social process. What is more, it draws our attention to the reciprocal nature of the material–spiritual link. Spiritual investment is made in part through material investment; material offerings are vehicles for the transmission of axé between gods and humans. Investment in a relationship with the deities through such material offerings is necessary in order to reap the spiritual benefits of mediumship, many of which are manifested in material ways (i.e., improved social relationships, employment opportunities, healing, etc.).

From the perspective of the community, the experiences of mediums thus reinforce belief in the connection between the material and spiritual. Watching mediums move from states of suffering to empowerment vividly demonstrates for members of the religious community that material things happen for spiritual reasons, that the gods may cause suffering in order to exercise control over and communicate with human beings, and that particular people are called by the orixás to be their earthly mediums. Mediums thus bring the entire community closer to the spiritual realm since they themselves are a materialization of the spiritual, a source of axé, and a direct point of contact with spirits and deities. Members of the Candomblé community are invested in these beliefs, and by extension are invested in the identification and religious formation of new mediums.

This is important for understanding the shift in social identity that also comes with mediumship. Because their role is central to religious belief and practice, mediumship gives individuals access to power and respect that come with being a ritual expert and spiritual intermediary, while at the same time allowing them to shed mainstream social role expectations. A medium who, like Lucia, has not gotten married and had children and has therefore failed to move through the expected social role transitions in mainstream Brazilian society may feel freed of those expectations as she settles into her role as medium. Moreover, with mediumship as her vocation, not only is she no longer limited by mainstream expectations, she is suddenly in a position of leadership within the religious community.

It should be noted, however, that the power and respect associated with mediumship are mainly confined to the Candomblé community. In other parts of their lives, outside of Candomblé, mediums may continue to have experiences of constraint and discrimination. These experiences may even be *brought on* by their participation in Candomblé, since a growing segment of Brazilian society, the Evangelical Christians, actively crusades against Candomblé and its practitioners. On the other hand, many people in Salvador respect and admire Candomblé, even if they do not actively participate, viewing it as a symbol of African heritage and authenticity (Selka 2007). Ultimately, access to power and respect, even if limited to the religious community, still has important psychological effects, changing the way that individuals view their own social status. At the same time, the practical ways in which Candomblé helps to change their status also serve to diminish exposure to psychosocial stress, even outside the religious setting.

The central practices of the mediumship role, trance and possession, also contribute to the medium's change in status. These practices allow filhos to embody different characteristics (discussed in depth in chapter 5) and to communicate with other humans in new ways, via the spirits and deities. These shifts dramatically expand the social ground on which mediums may operate, allowing them to enact a new kind of social selfhood. When possessed by a powerful orixá, a medium who has to defer to others all day long in her service industry job can enact assertiveness and even aggression. And when she is possessed by her caboclo spirit, this filha de santo can speak authoritatively to people and adopt a commanding tone in response to their requests for advice and assistance—not to mention that she also gets to swig cachaça, smoke cigars, and swagger around the terreiro! She thus has an opportunity to perform a very different kind of selfhood. Such enactments can also positively affect the quality of mediums' everyday social interactions; with a sanctioned outlet for the enactment of aggressive behaviors, for example, a medium's interpersonal relationships may dramatically improve.

The integration of individual self-narrative with the cultural model for mediumship thus functions therapeutically by allowing mediums to transform their social selves, and such social transformations often alleviate psychosocial stress and distress. But narrative self-transformation also works by altering the medium's *internal* understandings and experiences of self. The therapeutics of this internal transformation rest in part on the way it allows filhos to come to terms psychologically with their negative experiences (Witztum and Goodman 1999). Misfortune, affliction, and distress tend to undermine peoples' self-expectations, goals, and desires, creating what has been referred to as a sense of "biographical disruption"—a sense that their life-story or self-narrative has been overwritten or torn apart (Hunt 2000; Bury 1982). The failures of Jalita, Lucia, Pedro, and other mediums to move through expected role transitions may have had this kind of undermining effect on their goals and self-expectations. Such expectations are structured by the dominant cultural model of selfhood within Brazilian society, in which getting married, having children, holding down a job, and achieving material success figure prominently (see chapter 1). Failure to conform to this model may therefore be stressful and distressing, in part because it disrupts the individual's sense of self. It is this experience of disruption that makes the self-transformation associated with initiation particularly therapeutic. Rescripting narrative is a means to reconcile these inconsistent experiences, and the cultural model for mediumship provides a template for rescripting—giving built-in, socially intelligible explanations and meaning to idiosyncratic experiences of suffering, and providing an alternative model of selfhood.

Through the process of rescripting, the burden of affliction is transformed into a benefit as it comes to legitimate the individual's role as medium. No matter what type of suffering a medium experienced prior to initiation, once it is reinterpreted in the terms of the religion, it no longer reflects on her in the same way. In other words, those negative experiences are no longer self-implicating once they have been translated into religious terms—they no longer conflict with the medium's self-concept both because the meaning of the experiences is different and because the self-concept is different too. Instead of representing the failure to achieve normative selfhood, an affliction like the inability to hold down a job becomes a symbol of the medium's calling, visited upon her supernaturally. Thus, Lucia's mental health crisis and Pedro's existential distress were both rescripted as symptoms of undeveloped mediumship. The narratives of each medium reflect this shift from spiritual affliction to spiritual empowerment—a shift that is most obviously encoded in the conclusion of many narratives with phrases like "and I have never had anything wrong with me since then."

Moreover, by accepting the deities of the Candomblé religion as the source of their misfortune, individuals incorporate their affliction into a new self-understanding, while at the same time *distancing* themselves from it. Again, this process can be usefully compared to what takes place in the medicalization of certain conditions, where moral culpability for suffering can be alleviated through identification of organic causes (Dumit 2003). Such causes represent a kind of *natural* "higher power" instead of a supernatural one—but in both cases a force that is not thought to be under the control of the individual's will is held responsible for his/her suffering. To return to our previous example, an individual in treatment for alcoholism may come to incorporate his addiction to alcohol into his self-understanding ("I'm Jim and I'm an alcoholic"), at the same time that he distances himself from it by internalizing the belief that alcoholism is an organic disease of which he is a victim.

In Candomblé, the attribution to deities who are at once self (or responsible for important aspects of self) and yet are clearly distinct from self may be even more morally liberating. What is more, the meaning of affliction is doubly transformed in mediumship in a way for which there is no clear analogy in medicalization, since it moves from experience with its source in pathological and deviant qualities of the individual, to experience that not only has its source outside of the individual, but also represents a primary symbol of their spiritual legitimacy (cf. Stromberg 1993).

Lucia, who often intellectualized her own experience, explicitly acknowledged the importance of coming to terms with her own story through her involvement with Candomblé:

> After I became initiated, I became a different person. I went through a process of re-learning. I succeeded in re-interpreting that part of my life—that I never went to college, that I went through everything I did—as a learning experience, I learned to value other things that I hadn't valued before.

Lucia's comments suggest that this process of relearning and reinterpretation provides a basis for new behaviors and emotional responses—a basis for finding value in new things. Transformed self-understandings thus have the power to shape actions and reactions. To return again to a previous example, if I come to understand myself as other-focused, rather than self-centered, I am more likely to produce other-focused behaviors. This is because when I fail to produce behaviors consistent with my new self-understanding, I will feel a sense of conflict (unless I have a good narrative strategy for explaining the lapse). For mediums, coming to understand themselves as a vehicle for the gods motivates them to produce behaviors consistent with their spiritually empowered role. The mediumship narrative is thus therapeutic precisely because it is at once a vehicle for altering self-understanding, and an index of an individual's ability to behave differently: as a medium, not an afflicted person.

As emphasized earlier, only those cultural models with which individuals identify deeply have the capacity to motivate action. Because initiation is a powerful way of creating such identification it can be thought of as an important means by which individuals can disrupt negative behavior patterns. In fact, it is partly by disrupting negative patterns of behavior that initiation helps create deep identification with the cultural model for mediumship. By forcing individuals to step out of the day-to-day lives in which they have come to inhabit the role of a suffering or afflicted individual, the initiation process clears the cognitive and behavioral decks for the internalization of new, religious knowledge and ways of being. The experience of liminality discussed earlier—that sense of being removed from the rules and roles of one's normal life, of no longer being one's old self and not yet being a new self—helps open initiates to the internalization of new meanings and patterns of behavior (Van Gennep 1960; Turner 1969).

Moreover, since the reinterpretation of negative experience and the rescripting of self-narrative that serve as the basis for new patterns of behavior are rooted in a shared cultural model, these enactments of transformed selfhood are not only accepted, but supported and reinforced socially. If mediums evoke the cultural model sufficiently, then people in their social worlds will not only accept, but *expect* behavior that is consistent with the elements of healing and transformation the model entails. This is where the reciprocal relationship between the personal/psychological and public/social dimensions of mediumship is most profoundly felt, making mediumship uniquely effective at healing suffering that has its origins in social and psychobodily domains.

Conclusion: The Body

I began this chapter by posing the question: "Why does anyone become a medium?" In the past, researchers have answered this question either in medical terms, suggesting that mediumship is a response to psychological dysfunction, or in social terms, proposing that mediumship is a response to social oppression. My research suggests a far more complex answer to this question: many of those who become mediums are motivated by the opportunity for self-transformation.

While Candomblé adepts understand this transformation in spiritual terms, as a movement from spiritual affliction to spiritual attunement, it can also be understood to have *both* social and psychological causes and consequences. Through cognitive-discursive channels, including the manipulation of shared meaning and the rescripting of narrative, individuals come to understand and enact new, more adaptive forms of selfhood.

This account illustrates how religious belief can play a key role in healing self-transformation, suggesting that belief is not "merely" an attribute of conscious mental reflection or "mind" as it is typically understood. Instead, belief and knowledge are often deeply embedded in cognition and affect, and may therefore be centrally involved in structuring experience and behavior (Levi-Strauss 1963; Taves 2009). Nevertheless, hearkening back to Asad's critique of Western scholarship on religion, what is missing even from this more complex account of the social and psychological, cognitive and discursive dimensions of mediumship is a more thorough engagement with the body.

The ability of initiates to change their behavior, to adopt new patterns of action consistent with a new form of selfhood, points to the embodied nature of the transformation that takes place when individuals become initiated as mediums (Cromby 2005). Moreover, the body is central to Candomblé ritual practice, particularly for mediums, whose bodies literally become the site of spiritual incorporation. And while psychosocial factors are at the root of much of the suffering mediums experience, their suffering is not just manifested in social dysfunction or psychological distress. Somatic suffering and the healing or resolution of physical illness are central to the stories mediums tell about the causes and consequences of their religious formation.

What is the relationship between the psychosocial and physical afflictions prospective mediums suffer? How does somatic suffering affect selfhood? And how do we make sense of the resolution of somatic suffering through the process of self-transformation and the internalization of cultural meanings? Having established the importance of the interactions between social and psychological factors in Candomblé mediumship in this chapter, I explore how these factors intersect with body and practice to effect a transformation of the whole self in the chapters that follow.

Chapter 4

Looking Inside: Biological Mechanisms and Embodiment in Candomblé Trance and Possession

At 11 pm, the festa for the goddess Oxum at Pai João's terreiro was just getting under way. Fireworks had been set off in the concrete yard outside, and people who had been milling around began to wander inside. The shutters of the terriero were flung wide and some onlookers hung their upper bodies through the windows, into the barracão, or central room. The room was bright white with a thatched ceiling, and for the festa it had been decorated with streamers of white and gold. More crepe paper decorations hung in the corners, dressing the room in the colors of Oxum. Frequenters from the neighborhood trickled in, alerted by the fireworks that the festa was about to begin. Some of the ogãs (male ritual assistants) began to pound out a slow, slightly disorganized rhythm on the tall drums arranged along the back wall of the barracão. Pai João's filhos de santo, all dressed in white clothes, gathered in the center of the room. After greeting Pai João and the other senior members of the terriero with the typical prostrations and stylized hugs, the filhos de santo finally began to dance. They moved in a counterclockwise circle, or *roda*, elbows bent and feet shuffling rhythmically in a traditional Candomblé dance step. The ogãs at the drums now pounded out the songs of greeting to each orixá, and as the filhos danced and sang, members of the audience joined in, clapping their hands, swaying to the drums, and singing along.

Once the songs of greeting to each orixá had been sung, the ogãs began to drum in earnest, pounding with more intensity as they played the special rhythms designed to call the orixás down to their earthly mediums. The filhos seemed to move with more intensity as well, performing the specific dances for each of the orixás. The room was tightly packed and hot. As the dancing, singing, and drumming continued, a sense of tension seemed to permeate the room. Suddenly the first of the filhos dancing in the roda went into trance. It was Jalita, one of the mediums described in chapter 3, who had been initiated at the age of 28 after becoming physically and mentally ill. As you may recall, Jalita had begun to experience high levels of stress after getting married and having three children in just four years. Overwhelmed by the sudden transition to motherhood, a lack of resources, and low levels of social support, she suffered psychological symptoms of anxiety, depression, and possibly psychosis that were unresponsive to medication. She had also been afflicted with undiagnosable somatic symptoms including fever and cough. Now, some 26 years later, Jalita was a senior member of the terreiro serving as its official second-in-command, or *mae pequeña*, and she had not suffered from such physical or psychological distress since becoming a medium.

As she went into trance, Jalita's eyes suddenly squeezed tightly shut, indicating that she, the earthly medium, had become unconscious and a spiritual entity had descended into her body. Her head dropped forward precipitously on her neck and she began to tremble violently. In the midst of her trembling, Jalita let out a series of high-pitched cries. Then, suddenly, she swayed so dramatically to one side that she appeared as if she would fall over. She caught herself at the last second as she veered to the side, and before she could fall, hopped on one foot several times in a small circle until she stood fully upright again. Finally, she went still. As the drums pounded on and the rest of the filhos continued to dance around her, Jalita stood still, her body holding a distinctive posture with hands clasped behind her back, chin dropped to her chest, brow furrowed, and eyes squeezed tightly shut, rocking back and forth on her feet. This posture signaled that Jalita was now fully entranced—meaning that her own consciousness was entirely displaced or suppressed and her body occupied by the animating force of a deity—in this case, the goddess Oxum. As the now possessed Jalita stood rocking in the middle of the room, two ekédis, or ritual assistants, approached her. The ekédis gently stabilized Jalita and began to remove her glasses, shoes, earrings, and hairpins—for the orixás do not wear shoes, earrings, or glasses. They took a large piece of fabric and tied a sash around her middle, with a big bow in back, symbolizing the elaborate attire of the orixás. Once the ekédis had moved away, Jalita, now Oxum, began to dance once more.

Soon other filhos followed suit, their entry into trance accompanied by the same distinctive pattern of bodily movements. Their eyes squeezed tightly shut or rolled back in their heads, and the characteristic trembling began.[1] The trembling was accompanied by loud cries or guttural sounds, followed by swaying and off-balance hopping in a circle, until finally each filho came to rest in the characteristic posture of the possessed, with arms clasped behind his/her back, head down, eyes squeezed tightly shut, rocking back and forth. As filhos became possessed, they each received the same ritual preparations by the ekédis: watches, jewelry, and shoes were removed, men's pants rolled up, sashes tied around the mediums' waists.

Since human consciousness is believed to be displaced while the individual is possessed, Jalita and the other mediums said they were unaware of what their bodies were doing while possessed, describing complete amnesia for the entire period of trance. Yet, while filhos report amnesia for everything that occurs while they are possessed, many of them describe the sensations associated with the *onset* of trance in similar terms: they talk about a feeling of excitement, a tingling sensation, experiencing chills and *arrepios* (goosebumps), faintness or dizziness, and a sense of distance from their surroundings before losing consciousness.

After all of the filhos had entered trance, they were led away to a back room of Pai João's terriero, where they were dressed in ritual attire: in this case, since most of the filhos were possessed by Oxum, they were dressed in white gowns with ornate head pieces and given mirrors to hold as symbols of the beautiful and vain Oxum. Once all of the possessed filhos were dressed in their ritual garb, they returned to the roda, still in trance, to dance for the rest of the night. The movements and postures of the possessed mediums resembled the known bodily qualities of their possessing orixá—powerful, aggressive movements for Ogum the warrior, a stooped posture for Oxalá the wise senior orixá, and so on. Thus despite her age and weight, the possessed Jalita danced with great intensity for hours while possessed by her youthful Oxum, feet moving lightly across the floor, arms gliding from side to side. The ecstatic energy of this performance contrasted with the calm, deliberate energy of the unpossessed Jalita, whose only knowledge of her performance that night would come from the reports of others.

Embodiment and Bio-looping

As this description demonstrates, entry into trance evokes both the same behavioral enactments and the same bodily sensations across different Candomblé mediums. Moreover, use of psychophysiology measures to examine their bodily functioning revealed that Jalita and other mediums[2] also share a distinctive pattern of autonomic nervous system activity. I will explain the measures I used and what they mean in depth later in the chapter, but for now, the point I want to make is that taken together, these observations make evident the central role that bodies play in mediumship.

At the most basic level, the bodies of Candomblé mediums are the vehicles through which they enact their roles, and through which trance and possession are performed. Mediums are able to use their bodies as a means to express their religious belief and commitment to other members of the community, and the community as a whole uses the bodies of mediums as objects of shared meaning and sites of cultural production. What I mean by this is that collective beliefs and values concerning the spiritual and material, agency and moral responsibility, and bodies and selves are played out on and through the forms of mediums. But bodies are neither neutral nor stable objects through or upon which culture may be written (Scheper-Hughes and Lock 1987; Turner 1995). Bodies are dynamic. They absorb and integrate cultural and social information, literally incorporating experience. Thus, Jalita and the other mediums with whom I worked talked about emerging from their initiations already possessing a great deal of new bodily knowledge, including how to invite possession and how to dance for, and as, the orixás. In fact, mediums described a fundamental transformation of their bodily experience—not only during possession, but also through the broad process of religious formation—a process which for many included the experience of bodily healing.

How do we account for these experiential transformations and the accumulation of bodily knowledge associated with mediumship? And more broadly, how do we explain the ways in which practice and discourse, or peoples' socially and culturally informed behaviors and ideas, affect their bodily states? These are questions about what many scholars refer to as embodiment (Mascia-Lees 2011a). More specifically, they are questions about how embodiment works— about what processes mediate the relationship between cultural and social experiences and bodily responses, between the roles and meanings mediums enact, and their bodily states.

One possibility that has rarely been given any real consideration within cultural anthropology is that biological processes play a role. The fact that different mediums describe a similar set of physical symptoms at the onset of trance suggests, for instance, that these sensations may index a physiological process associated with their ritual performance. The practices and meanings involved in possession rituals and trance induction techniques may, in other words, result in a measurable change in the bodily states of mediums. The possibility that there is a physiological component to the experience of trance and possession is underscored by the findings from my psychophysiology measurements, which show that not only do mediums experience distinct physical symptoms at the onset of trance, but compared to nonmedium initiates (ogãs and ekédis), they also show a distinct pattern of heart rate regulation. These findings suggest a link between the bodily transformations associated with mediumship and the psychophysiological functioning of mediums.

But consistency in the way that mediums describe their sensations at the onset of trance and the near uniformity in the way that trance is performed also suggest an important role for learned meanings (Halloy and Naumescu 2012). Mediums learn to talk about the onset of trance in terms of a specific set of sensations because those particular sensations are imbued with significance. They learn both from their own experience, and from the way that other mediums describe their feelings, to associate goosebumps, dizziness, and tingling with the nearness of the gods and the onset of possession. And because those sensations are particularly meaningful, mediums learn to recognize and attend to them (Halloy 2012). At the same time, irrelevant sensations—ones that are not linked to important cultural meanings—are ignored. Mediums do not talk about feeling hot when their orixá is about to descend in part because this is not a culturally meaningful symptom—it is not part of the cultural model for trance that mediums learn when they become involved in Candomblé.

Practices like the ritual change of clothing and the adoption of physical postures and actions characteristic of the occupying spirit or god also contribute to the embodied experience of possession. It is easy to imagine how wearing a big, heavy, ornate dress, and enacting a set of stereotyped movements could make a medium's body *feel* different than usual. Moreover, these behaviors and bodily symbols communicate to the social group that a shift has taken place in the consciousness of the possessed individual, and others then reinforce the performance of her change of state by treating the medium's body differently. Hence, meaning and practice are also crucial dimensions of embodiment. The question is, how do the bodily, practice, and meaning aspects of embodiment interact?

I propose that we think about such interactions in terms of a feed-forward or "looping" process in which the mechanics of bodies are affected by learning and experience, and the characteristics of particular bodies in turn shape the ways in which they come to learn from and embody experience. In other words, the qualities of particular bodies figure as both causes and effects of experience. Deconstructing this "loop" may help to clarify what I mean. Bodies are not all the same—they differ in size, shape, strength, sensory and physical capacities, metabolism, microbial content, and so on. The characteristics of different bodies affect the way that they interact with the world. Being very tall shapes the way that an individual views his or her environment, both literally and figuratively. For a very tall person, for instance, doorways may represent obstacles or nuisances in a way that they do not for other people. These individuals will probably pay a lot more conscious attention to doorways than most of the rest of us do.

Some of the ways in which bodies differ are the product of learning. Bodies of athletes have learned through rigorous physical training to do things that the bodies of other people cannot do, and this in turn affects the nature of the activities and practices in which athletes engage. The circularity or looping that I referred to is thus in the way that the learned characteristics of bodies—how they are shaped by experience—combines with the meanings attributed to those qualities, to influence subsequent experience and shape exposure to and embodiment of new knowledge.

Let us take the hypothetical case of a kid with asthma, who experiences physical exertion as dangerous and frightening because it leaves him gasping for air. This bodily experience shapes his sense of himself as sick or disabled, and affects his goals and motivations. He might become particularly motivated by nonphysical pursuits, throwing himself into, say, computer programming. Or, he might work hard to overcome what he sees as a physical disability, and invest extra meaning in his ability to become a long-distance runner. In both cases, the qualities of his body shape his sense of relationship with the world in ways that affect his subsequent attributions, behaviors, and experiences. Moreover, in either scenario the meaning he makes of his bodily qualities ultimately affects those very qualities: becoming a computer programmer probably does nothing to improve his asthma, while becoming a long-distance runner dramatically increases his lung capacity. While this example is exaggerated for effect, it illustrates the basic notion that the qualities of our bodies are both a cause and a consequence of how we use them, and ultimately contribute to the kinds of experiences we have and the kinds of cultural knowledge and skills we embody.

The philosopher Ian Hacking proposed the metaphor of a loop, or "looping" process in the context of a discussion of psychiatric illness, to refer to this kind of circularity. Hacking was theorizing the way in which the social meanings of particular expressions of distress come to reinforce the existence of particular disorders, and ultimately lead to the creation of different categories or "kinds" of people—in this case schizophrenics or depressives, not computer programmers or runners (Hacking 1995). For Hacking, the looping metaphor was a way of transcending debates about whether mental illnesses are "real" or "socially constructed"—he argued that social constructions of mental disorder *become* real through looping. Looping thus provides an excellent model for thinking about how the effects of social and cultural experiences on peoples' bodily states become "real,"[3] and how the qualities of peoples' bodies come to "really" affect their psychological and social states. I borrow Hacking's (1999) term "biolooping," which he uses to refer to the ways in which biological knowledge production helps to create and reinforce different categories of people, but I use it to draw attention to the ways in which embodied processes, including biological ones, are implicated in the continuous and mutually reinforcing relationships among meaning, practice, and experience (Seligman and Kirmayer 2008).

Embodiment can itself be thought of as a product of bio-looping, not reducible to any one of these interacting elements. A bio-looping model can thus help to answer the questions I posed earlier about the mechanisms of embodiment, and how the bodily, practice, and meaning aspects of Candomblé mediumship contribute to the transformations that many mediums experience. In biolooping terms, we can understand the distinctive physiological profiles of mediums that I described earlier as part of the circular process through which bodily qualities feed forward to influence the kinds of experiences that people have and the cultural knowledge and skills they develop. In other words, differences in psychophysiological functioning might be thought of as the kind of bodily quality, like being tall or strong or asthmatic, that shapes and is shaped by experience. These qualities may, under the right circumstances, enhance the capacity to learn and attend to the sensations, meanings, and enactments associated with trance and possession.

Learning, Motivation, and Capacity

The bio-looping model can thus help to explain persistent questions about why some people become mediums and others do not—why only certain individuals are both willing and able to enter trance states and become possessed. Previous anthropological approaches to trance and possession have tended to focus either on its social meaning and communicative functions (Ong 1987; Lambek 1981) or have investigated trance as a biological response to trance induction practices (Lex 1979; Prince 1968, 1982; Rouget 1985; Simons et al. 1988). These approaches have never been integrated to explore how meaning, practice, and biology interact. Moreover, neither type of approach has attended much to the characteristics that individuals bring with them to mediumship, or the role that such characteristics play in the capacity to embody the mediumship role.

Becoming a medium is not simply a matter of motivation—even if an individual wants to take on the role, not every individual is a potential medium. In fact, several of the ogãs and ekédis with whom I worked told stories about how ritual divination had confirmed their mae de santo's intuition that they were meant to become ritual assistants rather than mediums. I was personally told in no uncertain terms by Mae Tiana that I would make a very nice ekédi but did not have what it takes to become a medium. An ogã named Edvaldo even told the story of how his pai de santo thought he had been called to the role of medium, but realized there had been a mistake when Edvaldo failed repeatedly to enter trance during his ensaio—a ritual meant to help preinitiation novices learn to succumb to possession (O'Connor n.d.). A second round of divination revealed that Edvaldo was actually supposed to be an ogã.

Thus, potential mediums must be able to successfully learn the beliefs, practices, and role requirements associated with mediumship, and in particular, they must be able, or must learn to be able, to become possessed. In the context of her work on prayer practices in a contemporary Evangelical church, Tanya Luhrmann (2004; Luhrmann et al. 2010) argues that people differ in their "proclivity" for learning what she refers to as the "metakinetic" aspects of prayer—that is, the embodied dimensions of such practices, associated with things like emotional response and alterations in consciousness. Luhrmann has in fact shown that there are differences between individuals in their capacity for absorption, or deeply focused attention and imaginative experience, and differences in this capacity correspond with differences in the proclivity for achieving vivid, intimate experiences of god through prayer. To use Luhrmann's terms, then, what distinguishes those who become mediums is their proclivity for learning the embodied dimensions of their role. In other words, just as some Evangelicals have a proclivity for absoprtion, those who become mediums may have a proclivity for trance and possession.

In fact, trance and absorption are probably related psychobodily states. Psychologists understand both states to fall under the heading of dissociation. Dissociation is a broad term for experiences involving the separation or partitioning of aspects of one's conscious awareness, memory, behavior, or self-concept (Spiegel and Cardeña 1991). Thus, dissociation encompasses a wide variety of experiences in which consciousness is divided and self-awareness temporarily suspended—ranging from daydreaming, to deep absorption in thoughts and external media like video games, to disorders like dissociative identity disorder (DID) in which individuals experience multiple, relatively nonoverlapping selves or identities (Kihlstrom 2005; Seligman and Kirmayer 2008). Although dissociation often has pathological connotations within psychiatric contexts, experiences that fall under this broad heading can be understood simply as a combined product of an extreme focusing of attention, and the simultaneous inhibition of competing streams of information (Seligman and Kirmayer 2008). Dissociative states like deep absorption or trance thus result from narrowing one's focus so intensely on something internal (thoughts, imaginings, expectations) or external (drums, music, media) that other thoughts or perceptions—including aspects of self-concept, memory, and surroundings—are kept out of awareness.

People learn to dissociate in the kinds of social and cultural situations in which it is a useful and meaningful state to occupy. Such situations include religious contexts in which dissociative states represent important ways of connecting with the divine, and contexts of stress and trauma in which such states represent a way of avoiding awareness of distressing experiences (Seligman and Kirmayer 2008). Dissociation is thus a form of bodily knowledge that is accumulated through particular kinds of experience. Dissociation of all types can therefore be thought of as a product of the kind of biolooping process I have been describing. The proclivity for dissociation of the trance-and-possession variety is intimately related to the bodily knowledge mediums gain through their experiences both before and after their engagement with Candomblé. Thus, in biolooping terms their preinitiation experiences of psychosocial stress and bodily affliction feed forward to shape the particular ways in which prospective mediums engage with the meanings and practices of the religion, creating the motivation and capacity for learning trance and possession.

Jalita and many other Candomblé mediums come to their role with histories of psychosocial and somatic distress, social marginalization, and a disrupted sense of selfhood. In fact, as a group, mediums in my study reported more somatic symptoms like back pain, headaches, and fatigue, than other religious participants.[4] As I discussed in chapter 3, such somatic symptoms are often a consequence of particular kinds of social and cultural experiences—in particular, they are ways of experiencing and expressing distress caused by experiences of social marginalization, inequality, and misfortune (Nichter 1981; Guarnaccia et al. 1996; Dressler 2005; Sweet et al. 2007). But in the case of mediums, somatization also represents a *cause* of social and cultural experiences, since, as we saw in chapter 3, according to their own accounts somatic symptoms served to motivate the religious initiations of many mediums. In other words, for many, this bodily quality or disposition led directly to engagement with the meanings and practices of mediumship.

Moreover, as we have also already seen, previous experiences of distress and affliction shape the way that mediums internalize and identify with the beliefs and meanings of Candomblé. The distressing experiences that many mediums have before initiation can undermine their self-understandings, which in turn affects the way that they take up the religious symbols and meanings of Candomblé. Having been overwhelmed by life transitions, uncontrolled emotions, and unexplained illnesses, Jalita, for instance, was especially primed to learn to understand herself as the victim of spiritual affliction and to embrace the influence of her goddess, Oxum, over her experiences and behaviors. These religious meanings offered a way to understand her sense of deviance and distress as signs of a spiritual calling, and herself as spiritually empowered, rather than ill.

Those with a particular capacity to identify deeply with these religious meanings may also be more likely to become deeply *absorbed* by those meanings and the behavioral enactments that go along with them. For mediums, trance and possession are the ultimate enactments of their belief in the influence of spiritual forces in their lives. Since mediums like Jalita are primed to find this belief particularly personally meaningful, they are also primed to focus intensely on and become deeply absorbed by practices surrounding the enactment of this belief. In particular, this deep personal investment may predispose them to get the most out of the practices associated with trance induction—to focus intensely on the pounding drums, ritual prostrations, and stylized movements of the ritual dances, because these practices are meant to call down the deities. They are also primed to become deeply immersed in a set of expectations about the effects of those practices—effects like the sensations of goosebumps, dizziness, and excitement, as well as the loss of self-awareness and memory known to accompany trance and possession.[5] Because they are motivated to believe in their own spiritual calling as vehicles for the divine, those who become mediums may thus be particularly capable of learning to immerse themselves in rituals of possession—particularly capable, that is, of learning to focus intensely on the sights, sounds, and sensations of these rituals to the exclusion of all other thoughts and perceptions.

Thomas Csordas (2002:244) has talked about such processes in terms of what he calls "somatic modes of attention," which he defines as "culturally elaborated ways of attending to and with one's body." This term is a way of talking about how the body itself attends or acquires knowledge in ways that while preconscious are still inherently cultural and thus shaped by cultural expectations. Certain bodily sensations have particular cultural significance and individuals may therefore develop somatic modes of attention in which those sensations are focal. Dizziness is particularly meaningful in some cultures, heat in others (Hinton et al. 2008). For female refugees from El Salvador, for example, bodily heat holds significance as a symptom of fear, despair, and anger. Salvadoran women are thus likely to pay special attention to sensations of heat, and to attend to and perceive their social environments differently when experiencing such heat (i.e., to perceive the environment as more threatening or oppressive; Jenkins and Valiente 1994).

For middle-aged women in the United States, on the other hand, the association of heat with menopause means that such sensations have an entirely different significance. For many women in their fifties, these sensations may be associated with highly charged meanings about age, femininity, and social role, and these meanings may in turn shape the way that women experience their social worlds—through bodies perceived as aging or aged, or bodies perceived as liberated from certain physical constraints (i.e., menstruation and fertility; Lock 1994). The "somatic modes of attention" concept thus highlights the importance of such nondiscursive forms of bodily knowing and learning.

The somatic mode of attention that many Candomblé mediums occupied prior to their religious involvement was one of affliction. In the absence of religious material to direct and redefine their bodily experiences, the somatic effects of distress became the focus of their attention and the center of meaning. Somatization may thus be the flip side of, or precursor to, the processes that make mediums particularly prone to deeply focus attention on the meanings and sensations associated with mediumship.

Which brings us back again to biolooping and the idea that the ways in which mediums attend to and with their bodies is partly a function of the qualities of their particular bodies—qualities that are created at least in part by their experiences. As we discussed earlier, it is relatively easy to imagine the ways in which physical qualities of bodies like disability, age, height, and weight might mediate the interactions of individuals with social and cultural meanings, and shape their experiences of being in the world—to return to a previous example, doorways mean something different to very tall people. But, as I have already suggested, the bodily qualities that mediate the interactions of individuals with their social and cultural worlds may also include aspects of psychophysiological functioning, including patterns of autonomic nervous system control over heart rate regulation, like those I measured in mediums.

Human Biology, Psychophysiology, and the Mechanics of Embodiment

But what kinds of effects do social and cultural entrainment have on psychophysiological systems? And what are the mechanics of such a process? Psychophysiology, a subfield of psychology focused on investigating the physiological correlates of psychological processes, and human biology, a subfield of anthropology focused on investigating how social and cultural factors interact with and shape human biological variation, each offer important theoretical constructs that can help us address these questions.

Interindividual differences in patterns of physiological arousal are a major focus of psychophysiology research. People differ in both the shape and magnitude of their physiological responses to the stimuli they encounter in their environments. Stimuli consist of almost anything encountered as individuals move through the world—from the sights, sounds, and smells of sensory input and the sensations of physical contact with objects, to social interactions and symbolic transactions. Psychophysiology recognizes a suite of biological systems that tend to be associated with physiological reactions, or arousal to stimuli. These include the neuroendocrine system, particularly the hypothalamic-pituitary-adrenal axis (HPA), which regulates things like your stress hormones; the autonomic nervous system (ANS), which is in charge of things like the activation of the cardiovascular system, including your heart rate and blood pressure; and the feedback and control of various elements of the central nervous system (CNS), which plays a major role in whether you perceive stimuli as threatening, inviting, or neutral.

The activity of these physiological systems often varies widely across individuals, and may also vary independently within individuals—that is, the regulation of your heart rate and blood pressure may or may not follow the same pattern as the regulation of your stress hormone responses. The term "reactivity" has been used to describe characteristic individual patterns of physiological activity and arousability of these various systems in response to stimulation (Rothbart 1989). For example, two individuals might respond to being shouted at by their boss very differently: one might be highly physiologically reactive, responding with dramatically increased heart rate and stress hormone activity, while the other might be less reactive, experiencing little change in physiological functioning. Such differences in reactivity are closely associated with individual differences in stress sensitivity (Boyce et al. 1995; Cacioppo et al. 1995a).

The ability to modulate arousal through state-regulation is the other side of the reactivity coin; state-regulatory capacity affects an individual's control over his or her own level of arousal, including the ability to limit and recover from arousal through the use of behavioral and cognitive mechanisms (Rothbart 1989; Kagan 1994). Individuals who have high state-regulatory capacity may still be highly reactive to stimulation, but able to modulate or recover from their arousal effectively. Those with low state-regulatory capacities may be highly reactive to stimulation and *unable* to modulate their arousal. Hence, variations in reactivity and state regulation are examples of ways in which different bodies bring their own characteristics to interactions with their social and cultural environments.

Physiologists have developed the complementary concepts of "allostasis" and "allostatic load" to capture the idea of a balance between appropriate reactivity to challenge, and potentially maladaptive excessive or chronic responses. Allostasis is defined as the maintenance of physiological stability through dynamic response to demand, or the achievement of "stability through change" (Schulkin et al. 1998; Sterling 2003). The concept of allostasis highlights the important ability of bodies to adjust to shifting contexts through flexibility in regulatory set points of physiological systems, since different kinds of activities and environments make different demands on these systems. For example, lying around on the couch does not require the same amount of energy as strenuous physical activity, so the systems responsible for mobilizing stored energy are capable of up- and down-regulating depending on the situation. Hence, allostasis is about how patterns of physiological response change as needed—how, through regulation of reactivity and state-regulatory mechanisms, our bodies are capable of being highly responsive to our environments. In this view biology is not fixed and homeostatic (always trying to return to the same baseline state), but dynamic and flexible, or "plastic."

The concept of allostasis also draws our attention to the ability of human bodies to anticipate future demands and contexts, and to adjust accordingly through feed-forward regulatory processes (Schulkin 2011). Bodily systems involved in mobilizing energy stores are capable of developing anticipatory patterns of regulation based on our general tendency to engage either in couch-potato behaviors, or strenuous physical activity. If I rarely engage in strenuous physical activity, my body may develop a particular pattern of regulation in anticipation of the fact that I will continue to be a couch potato, by lowering my metabolism for instance. Allostasis is thus a way of thinking about how bodies learn through experience.

The complementary concept of "allostatic load" is defined as "wear and tear on the body and brain arising from attempts to adapt to adversity" (Schulkin et al. 1998:220). The concept of allostatic load is meant to account for the negative health consequences (i.e., cardiovascular disease) of physiological reactivity when it outweighs need, or of responses to stressors that are either chronic or severe and thus impose wear or "load" on multiple physiological systems. Thus, on the one hand allostatic load may result from overactive physiological responses among individuals who are highly reactive but have low self-regulatory capacity—that is, it can result from the qualities of individual bodies. On the other hand, allostatic load may also be seen as the result of the way that bodies respond to social and physical environments that are unremittingly stressful and demanding. In such situations, high reactivity of psychophysiological systems may be appropriate to the individual's situation, but the situation itself is pathological. Allostasis and allostatic load thus both represent processes through which bodies are tuned to their environments, and bodily functioning is shaped by experience.

These processes are mediated in important ways by the kinds of nonconscious, difficult to articulate beliefs and knowledge that I described in chapter 3. Such culturally and socially informed beliefs and knowledge affect how we interpret and make meaning of our experiences, which in turn shapes our learned bodily responses. For example, a woman who has internalized a feminist worldview might have a particularly strong physiological reaction to being yelled at by her male boss because this experience taps into networks of cognitive association linking it to particular social and cultural meanings. In fact, individuals may develop consistent patterns of response to stimuli that are perceived to be the same—a tendency referred to as "response stereotypy" (Krantz et al. 1995; Strelau 1988). This suggests that the meaning of an experience is not necessarily filtered through conscious awareness, but may become a part of an individual's *physical* being through such patterned responses.

Physiological responses are also related to differences in how individuals *attend* to experience—to their "somatic modes of attention" (Csordas 2002). An individual may be more or less likely to focus attention on a particular social stimulus, meaning, or bodily sensation, based not only on its personal and cultural meaning but also on their past and present embodied responses (Challis and Stam 1992). In fact, individuals make attributions about the meaning that particular experiences have for them, based on their bodily response. For instance, if flying on an airplane results in an intense physiological response, including a surge of stress hormones and an increase in heart rate and blood pressure, this will affect the associations an individual has with flying. This is because physiological systems send feedback to the brain that is designed to affect evaluative processing of experience. Thus, we learn to attend differently to experiences based on the way they affect our psychophysiological functioning. Changing the meaning or attributions that an individual makes about his or her bodily responses to an experience therefore has the potential to change the meaning of the experience. Changing the meaning of experience, in turn, has the potential to change patterns of bodily response. Hence, cognitive factors like belief and meaning may play an important role in state-regulation.

Knowledge of psychophysiological processes thus helps to further flesh out the biolooping model, illustrating potential mechanisms through which the effects of experience on bodies, and bodies on experience, are manifest. This is a novel way of theorizing embodiment because it includes a concern with the ways in which *biological* systems are shaped by learning and experience. Thus, instead of talking in broad terms about "bodily ways of knowing," biolooping offers a complex, multilevel understanding of the ways in which bodies are designed to respond dynamically to and integrate social and cultural experience into their functioning.

Psychophysiology of Mediumship

We are now in a position to apply these insights about the psychophysiological mechanisms of embodied learning to the specific case of Candomblé mediumship. How can knowledge about reactivity and state regulation be applied to understanding the bodily learning and experiences of transformation that mediums undergo? And how might something like autonomic nervous system regulation of cardiovascular function affect the proclivity for trance and possession? In order to investigate these questions, I measured aspects of cardiovascular activity among a group of ten mediums and a comparable group of ten non-medium initiates (ogãs and ekédis).[6] Measurements of cardiovascular activity, particularly heart rate (HR) and something called high frequency heart rate variability (HF), have a long history of use in studies of interindividual differences in psychophysiological function (Berntson et al. 1992; Cacioppo 1994; James 1884; Kagan 1994). These measures serve as indicators of how cardiovascular activity is regulated by an individual's autonomic nervous system, and can thus be used as markers of autonomic reactivity and self-regulatory capacity.

A closer look at the biology involved will help demonstrate how this works and what it means for our questions about the embodied dimensions of mediumship. The ANS is divided into two branches, and the heart and other organs are enervated by nerve fibers from both branches. Each branch is associated with different functions: the sympathetic nervous system (SNS) is associated with reactivity— it readies the body for action. SNS nerves act like a gas pedal, speeding up HR when activated, and slowing it down through withdrawal. The parasympathetic nervous system (PNS) is associated with state regulation, conservation, and repair. PNS control over the heart via the vagus nerve acts like a brake, slowing down HR when it is activated, and speeding it up through withdrawal. Past psychophysiology research has focused on the relative balance between the activities of the SNS versus the PNS. More SNS activity meant that an individual was more highly reactive, and this was generally thought to be a bad thing (Uchino and Cacioppo 1995). Greater PNS activity, on the other hand, meant that the individual had higher state-regulatory capacity, and this was generally considered to be a good thing (Porges 1992; Porges et al. 1996).

Mounting evidence suggests, however, that the total regulatory capacity of both subsystems combined may be a particularly meaningful marker of physiological resilience. Tight control over HR activity by both branches means the ability to activate and withdraw dynamically, representing both reactivity and state regulatory capacity. Thus, total regulatory capacity indexes the propensity for a form of allostatic regulation, or the flexible adjustment of physiological function in response to environmental demand (Berntson et al. 2008b). Total regulatory capacity also indexes the ability to respond to stimuli in the environment through cognitive and behavioral channels like attention; in fact, regulation of arousal has been directly correlated with the ability to initiate, sustain, and terminate attention (Hansen et al. 2003; Porges 1992; Richards 1987). Individual differences in total regulatory capacity are thus relevant for understanding variability in the way that bodies respond to their environments, the way that individuals attend to and through their bodies, and the range of effects that experiences have on bodily characteristics.

Psychophysiologists have recently introduced a measure of total regulatory capacity called "Cardiac Autonomic Regulation" (CAR). CAR is calculated by adding together measures of SNS control (HR) and PNS control (HF). Higher scores are associated with a variety of positive outcomes (Berntson et al. 2008b). Individuals with higher CAR appear to be more capable of adjusting their patterns of cardiovascular response to meet the level of demand, and of appropriately matching psychophysiological arousal to circumstance. Individuals with low CAR are more likely to respond disproportionately to challenges or fail to mount adequate responses, leaving them either unable to respond sufficiently or responding excessively, thus damaging their bodies over the long term.

However, such psychophysiological profiles are by no means fixed or static phenomena. Patterns of autonomic nervous system regulation may vary across the life-course, respond to shifts in context, and be moderated by social support, life events, and experience (Alkon et al. 2003; Boyce et al. 1995; de Haan et al. 1998; Gunnar et al. 1996; Meaney 2000; Roy et al. 1998; Singh and Petrides 1999). For example, recent research on loneliness demonstrates that loneliness is associated with low HR and HF—in other words, with low autonomic regulatory control (Hawkley et al. 2003; Norman et al. 2011). Hence, social context, or lack of social engagement, may shape patterns of ANS regulation. Similarly, a number of studies have shown that experiencing negative life events sets up patterns of cardiovascular reactivity, but such patterns can be moderated by social support or enhanced by the experience of additional traumas (Heim et al. 2002; Roy et al. 1998; Uchino et al. 1996).

Demonstrating even more complex interactions among psychophysiological tendencies and environments, studies have also shown that children who have strong psychophysiological reactions to challenges in their environments thrive and in fact do better than other kids if they have very sensitive and supportive care givers, but do worse than other kids in the wrong kind of environment (Boyce and Ellis 2005; Nachmias et al. 1996; Gallagher 2002; Obradović et al. 2010). These data thus suggest that their psychophysiological functioning shapes the meaning of the social environment for these children—lack of sensitivity and support seem to make the environment extra threatening and disruptive, while supportive care seems to create a heightened sense of safety and motivation.

Differences in autonomic regulation have even been linked specifically to participation in religion and spirituality (Bernardi et al. 2001; Lutz et al. 2008; Tartaro et al. 2005). For example, in one recent study, psychophysiology researchers found that a sample of Americans who reported higher levels of spirituality—defined as having a strong sense of relationship with God—also had higher levels of CAR (Berntson et al. 2008a). Thus, while the direction of causality is unclear, these findings suggest that spirituality might contribute to the kinds of experiences that can alter patterns of autonomic nervous system regulation.

I measured CAR for mediums and nonmedium initiates in my study using data from a method called impedance cardiography (see appendix for a detailed description of this method). Along with electrocardiogram data (ECG), impedance can be used to derive measures of HR and HF that can be combined to calculate CAR. I used baseline measurements rather than measurements taken during trance and possession, in part because of methodological and ethical challenges associated with trying to gather such measurements in ritual contexts (see chapter 2 for a full discussion of these issues), but also because I was interested in the bodily capacities or tendencies individuals bring with them to mediumship, not simply the transient effects of trance induction techniques on physiological states. Focus on responses to trance induction alone would not reflect the complexity of the relationships among meaning and practice, expectation and attention, trance and possession that I have been attempting to lay out in this chapter.

What I found is that the baseline CAR scores of mediums were substantially higher than those of nonmedium initiates. Seventy percent of mediums (seven out of ten) had CAR scores above the median for both groups, while 70 percent of the nonmedium initiates had CAR scores that were below the median. Mediums' scores were also less variable, or more similar to one another, than their counterparts' scores (see appendix for additional quantitative details). These data indicate that compared to ogãs and ekédis, the mediums in my study tended to have higher levels of total regulatory control over their cardiovascular function. We know that such control is associated with a greater capacity for dynamic reactivity and state regulation in response to contextual demands.

These findings have a number of implications for our understanding of mediumship, trance, and possession. Most notably, they suggest a link between the proclivity for Candomblé mediumship, and the ability to dynamically regulate arousal. In other words, these data show that the motivation and capacity for mediumship are reflected in the bodily functioning of mediums. This is most compelling in the sense that it documents a connection between a particular kind of religious participation, and particular kinds of bodily qualities among participants. However, because I was unable to collect longitudinal data on the CAR scores of mediums, which would have allowed me to compare their autonomic regulatory capacities before and after initiation, we cannot know with certainty at this time whether this pattern of autonomic control is a cause or effect of the religious embodiment associated with the mediumship role. That is, we cannot be sure whether mediums had higher CAR before becoming mediums, or if they developed higher CAR afterward. Both scenarios suggest interesting and important pathways for how bodily processes and embodied beliefs and practices influence one another and it is worth exploring each in depth.

One possibility is that the psychophysiological profiles of mediums have changed since they became mediums. Under this scenario, mediums would have had lower CAR before initiation, a pattern associated with a lower capacity for state regulation, and developed higher state regulatory capacity through their experiences as mediums. This interpretation is consistent with the life history narratives of mediums, which describe escalating cycles of psychosocial stress, somatic suffering, and disrupted selfhood prior to initiation, followed by the transformation to a state of well-being after initiation.

The somatic suffering prior to initiation and the transformation afterward can both be understood as part of a biolooping process in which the social and cultural experiences of mediums have contributed to shaping their bodily processes, and vice versa. Prior to initiation, experiences associated with poverty, social marginalization, and psychosocial distress may have set up negative patterns of perception, attention, and reactivity. Concepts like allostatis and allostatic load are relevant here to thinking about how their experiences of psychosocial stress could have become embodied as somatic symptoms, through such feed-forward processes.

In such high stress environments people's bodies may come to anticipate stress and arousal, adjusting their patterns of reactivity

through allostatic processes. The chronic nature of such physiological up-regulation contributes to allostatic load or bodily wear and
tear that may cause somatic symptoms. Physiological reactivity and
bodily symptoms are both perceived negatively, and loop back to
reinforce the negative meanings of experiences—making stressful experiences more stressful. Moreover, physiological reactivity
and somatic symptoms shape the way that individuals attend to and
through their bodies. Such states call attention to themselves, and
may promote even greater arousal and more distressing symptoms,
through cycles of attention, negative attribution, and symptom
amplification (cf. Kirmayer and Sartorious 2007). Biolooping would
thus be responsible for creating a stress-sensitive "mode of attention"
(Csordas 2002) among prospective mediums, in which the reactive
qualities of their bodies were a response to the negative qualities of
their social worlds.

However, the relatively high CAR scores of these mediums at
the time that I measured them suggest that the experience of initiation and the practices and meanings associated with mediumship
may have played a role in disrupting or redirecting this looping process. Somatic suffering and physiological arousal have very different
meanings within the context of Candomblé, as indicators of a spiritual calling and material evidence of the work of the orixás in one's
life. As we discussed earlier, changing the meaning or attributions
that individuals make about their bodily responses has the potential to change the meaning of their experience, and changing the
meaning of experience has the potential to change patterns of bodily
response. Hence, patterns of negative reinforcement among stressful
experiences, meanings, and bodily responses are interrupted by the
introduction of a set of religious meanings that make these kinds of
bodily experiences the *basis* for a set of positive expectations and
attributions.

One of the most noteworthy aspects of this biolooping model,
then, is the idea that the same bodily qualities that fed into the negative loop prior to initiation, also feed forward into a positive loop
that is established through religious involvement. In this scenario, the
reactivity that mediums experienced prior to initiation is not extin-
guished after initiation; instead it becomes part of the high level of
total regulatory control established through religious participation.
Engagement with Candomblé simply gives mediums the cognitive
and behavioral tools to increase their state-regulatory capacities. For
example, deep internalization of the meanings associated with possession, combined with the behavioral training of trance induction,

helps filhos learn to manipulate attention and perception in ways that allow them to enhance or inhibit physiological arousal—by focusing narrowly on stimulating sights, sounds, and internal sensations and blocking out nonrelevant input. Such skills may transfer outside the religious context as well, helping mediums to learn to use attention and perception as everyday tools for state-regulation. This interpretation of the data thus suggests that, in much the same way that social support can disrupt patterns of psychophysiological reactivity among people with histories of adversity and a supportive caregiving environment can help reactive children thrive, participation in mediumship may reshape patterns of physiological response in a way that not only allows individuals to induce trance states in appropriate contexts, but may also carry over to help them establish a more general pattern of enhanced state regulation and reduced psychosocial stress.

On the other hand, we must also consider the possibility that mediums already had high CAR prior to initiation. Under this scenario, mediums would have already been both highly reactive to stress and challenge, and highly capable of state regulation, allowing them to recover effectively from their stress responses. This kind of autonomic flexibility is associated with positive health outcomes (Berntson et al. 2008b) but also with high levels of body awareness, and somatic symptom reporting (Zachariae et al. 2000). High CAR may thus have contributed to a high degree of body awareness among mediums—a somatic mode of attention that, in a high stress environment, made them particularly aware of their own bodily responses to stress, and particularly prone to experience and attend to somatic symptoms. This scenario is consistent with the pattern of somatic suffering reported by mediums prior to initiation, and the finding, discussed earlier, that mediums reported higher numbers of somatic symptoms on a psychological inventory. Such tendencies may have been partly responsible for attracting mediums to the behavioral and cognitive tools offered by mediumship, as a way to make meaning of their bodily responses and somatic symptoms.

Having high CAR might also have made it easier for these individuals to induce trance states right from the beginning. Studies have also shown that dissociative states like trance and hypnosis are often characterized by suppression of autonomic arousal (Griffin et al. 1997; Koopman et al. 2004). Researchers have interpreted this suppression of arousal as support for a model of dissociation as the product of top-down inhibitory control within the brain (Sierra and Berrios 1998). Such inhibition functions to control the kinds of information that make it into conscious awareness in particular situations, thus contributing to the pattern of narrowly focused attention and selective awareness that characterize dissociative states. The ability to suppress arousal may be facilitated by high regulatory capacity like that associated with high levels of CAR. In other words, the higher CAR profile may make it easier for mediums to induce trance states by facilitating the situational suppression of autonomic arousal.

In addition, the ability to regulate arousal is directly correlated with attention regulation (Hansen et al. 2003; Porges et al. 1996). In fact, previous research has specifically demonstrated that high autonomic regulatory capacity is associated with the capacity for absorption (Zachariae et al. 2000), or intensely focused attention. This suggests that high CAR among prospective mediums could have made them particularly suited to the techniques of trance induction. In this scenario, a higher capacity to regulate arousal helped make people like Jalita more capable of focusing intense and exclusive attention on the drumming and singing, ritual setting and ritualized actions, meaningful sensations and spiritual significance, of ritual enactments and experiences.

In either scenario, then, the bodily qualities represented by higher levels of CAR are likely to have interacted with meaning and practice to shape filhos' experiences both before and after their engagement with Candomblé. But while these physiological characteristics undoubtedly had important effects on mediums' own experiences, it is also worth considering the possibility that through the performances in which they enable mediums to engage, these qualities also affect other members of the Candomblé community. As I have discussed elsewhere in the book, shared practices are crucial to Candomblé. Mediums play a central role in the religious life of the group by bringing everyone closer to the axé. At the same time, mediums depend on others to coconstruct their revised self-narratives. Thus, there is a reciprocal relationship between mediums and the rest of the community, which may extend to the physiological dimensions of trance and possession as well.

Sociologist Randall Collins (2004: 47) argues that certain kinds of rituals are characterized by "a process in which participants develop a mutual focus of attention and become entrained in each other's bodily micro-rhythms and emotions." What Collins means is that ritual practices serve to synchronize the experiences of the individuals present—creating shared behaviors and emotions that may themselves become the focus of mutual attention. For example, a process of joint attention between mediums and audience members during ritual enactments of trance and possession may result in a kind of coconstruction of the experiences of absorption, physiological arousal, and spiritual transcendence. In other words, I am suggesting the possibility that the processes of mutual entrainment that characterize many rituals may have a psychophysiological dimension. In this case, mutual entrainment, or the synchronization of body and emotion among participants, might include sharing of the autonomic nervous system responses of mediums by others during Candomblé possession rituals. A similar phenomenon was documented during a fire-walking ritual in Spain, in which the pattern of arousal of the ritual participants was mirrored by a similar pattern of arousal among related spectators (Konvalinka et al. 2011).

Thus, the qualities of mediums' bodies that allow them to embody the spirits and deities through possession may also contribute an embodied dimension to the way in which they bring the rest of the community closer to the axé—helping laypeople to really *feel* the presence of this powerful force. Such a phenomenon could contribute to a group level biolooping process, in which joint attention and shared bodily experiences reinforce spiritual meanings for all involved.

Conclusion

The data from my study document a particular pattern of psychophysiological regulation among mediums, a pattern that likely contributes in important ways to the proclivity for mediumship. Even though the study does not allow us to determine whether their enhanced regulatory capacity preceded or followed initiation into mediumship, in either case, these qualities of mediums' bodies interact in a distinctive way with the practices and beliefs of their religious role through a biolooping process.

The biolooping concept helps us to better understand how individuals like Jalita come to embody the role of medium, and how the experiential transformations associated with mediumship might take place. Jalita's experiences prior to initiation primed her to understand her experiences in spiritual terms and to become deeply immersed in and engaged by a set of expectations, meanings, and enactments associated with such understandings. This engagement is transformative for many mediums, and the psychophysiological qualities of their bodies have played an important role as both cause and consequence of this transformation. In the chapter that follows, I further elaborate on the ways in which the process of bodily transformation I have been describing here comes together with the process of narrative transformation discussed in chapter 3, to create the experience of a transformation of the whole self. Building on the model developed here, I make the argument that biolooping effects can create mutually reinforcing, therapeutic changes in bodily and cognitive dimensions of selfhood. By analyzing how the meanings and practices of Candomblé specifically contribute to such an integrated process of self-healing for mediums like Jalita, I begin to demonstrate how biolooping can illuminate processes of self-transformation and the role of meaning and practice in healing more broadly.

Because the interactions of body, meaning, and practice are so highly visible in trance and possession, it in many ways represents an ideal site for examining biolooping processes. But the biolooping model also applies more broadly to many everyday processes of socialization and enculturation. To give just a few examples: the process through which children learn to experience and express socially appropriate emotions (Quinn 2006); learning embodied skills like playing a musical instrument or practicing a martial art (Downey 2010); and the health effects of psychosocial stress can all be understood in terms of biolooping and the feed-forward interactions among experience, physiological response, and meaning. I explore the utility of the biolooping model for thinking about a variety of phenomena that are of anthropological interest, in the final chapter of the book.

Chapter 5
Healing the Embodied Self in Candomblé

Recent focus within anthropology on studies of the body provide an important corrective to earlier research that took a more mentalistic approach, privileging discourse and representation over bodily experience. However, it is important not to throw out the baby (in this case, the mind) with the proverbial bath water. Peoples' experiences are never either mental or bodily. In fact, in some important sense, mental and bodily experiences constitute one another; mental experience is the product of physical, bodily processes, and bodily experience is perceived and attended to via mental processes. Nowhere is this better illustrated than in the exploration of how individuals experience selfhood. As we discussed in chapter 1, self has important social, cognitive-discursive (mental), and bodily dimensions. It consists not only of self-understandings and representations, but also of experiences that are not conscious and not part of language-based self-representation—experiences of occupying a physical body, of perceiving and being in the world.[1]

In the previous chapter, I argued that the embodiment of sociocultural knowledge and experience can be understood as the product of a "biolooping" process in which body, meaning, and practice shape and reinforce one another. Because selves are fundamentally embodied, the notion of biolooping also offers a model for thinking about self—and in particular, about how the embodied and representational aspects of self converge. The major shifts in the experience of self that characterize mediumship make it an ideal domain for the exploration of how self-knowledge is embodied.

The most obvious way in which mediums' selves shift or are altered is through regular engagement with the practice of spirit possession. By definition, spirit possession involves displacement of the conscious, human self by a powerful other (deity, spirit, demon) who temporarily animates the medium's body. As a result, mediums regularly shift from one type of self-experience to another when they become possessed, and the relationship between cognitive and embodied aspects of self—between self-understandings and direct, bodily experiences of being in the world—is deeply implicated in this practice. For example, the understanding of self as a medium between the spiritual and material worlds helps to potentiate the experience of possession, and shifts in bodily states resulting from practices of trance induction help to reinforce understandings of self as a medium between the spiritual and material worlds.

Understandings and experiences of self are not only affected by the shifts in subjectivity associated with trance and possession, however, they are also fundamentally altered by the very process of becoming a medium. By their own accounts, during their initiations mediums often experience their familiar self as distant, suspended, or absent. Many of my informants articulated this experience in terms of being in a constant state of *"transe"* (trance) during their seclusion within the terreiro—sometimes for three or more months. Although trance is probably not literally constant during this time, by referring to constant or prolonged periods of dissociation, initiates communicate an intensely and consistently felt displacement of their taken-for-granted sense of self. This is the sense of liminality—of being socially and psychologically between states—that I discussed in chapter 3.

But mediums' narratives also suggest that by the time they emerge from initiation they have developed a new sense of self—one that differs in important ways from the preinitiation selves they describe. In this chapter I further explore how biolooping in Candomblé mediumship can help us to think about a number of processes related to the embodied experience of self among mediums—how selves are constructed, disrupted, and transformed through feedback and feed-forward influences of multiple processes, including psychophysiological ones.

Embodied Suffering and Otherness

For many mediums, shifts in selfhood actually begin even before they become involved in Candomblé, when illness and affliction create experiences that disrupt both their self-understandings and bodily ways of being. As we have already seen, the mediums in my study describe experiencing simultaneous or consecutive negative life events (e.g., death of a loved one, job loss, financial crisis, and interpersonal problems) before their initiations. Together such experiences have the potential to create feelings of grief, anger, social dislocation, desperation, and an overriding sense of existential distress. The suffering body also figures prominently in these narratives, which include a wide range of physical maladies, from mysterious illnesses resembling tuberculosis, to headaches, dizziness, and skin conditions.

Such experiences of suffering often disrupt an individual's ability to behave in ways that are consistent with the goals and motivations included in his/her self-understandings. Suffering is thus disruptive to self in the sense that it creates a disconnect between lived experience and self-representations (Hollan 2000). For example, there may be a sense of disconnect or conflict for an individual who has embraced the goal of productivity and material success as an integral part of self, but who cannot hold down a job because of chronic health problems. A woman who has embraced the idea of being a mother as a crucial part of self, but who feels so overwhelmed by motherhood that she does not trust herself around her children with a knife (per Jalita's story in chapter 3) will likewise experience such a sense of disconnect. Because the kinds of intrusive psychophysiological responses we discussed in the last chapter are often automatic reactions to psychosocial stress, and not under the control of the conscious self, these responses also may feel deeply disconnected from the intentions and motivations of self. In addition, as I discussed in detail in the previous chapter, attention to physiological symptoms loops back to amplify arousal, ramping up those involuntary bodily responses still further, and in turn enhancing the sense of disconnection and lack of control.

It is often the awareness of a lack of control over thoughts, emotions, bodily responses, and behaviors that lends those processes a quality of "otherness." In other words, the way in which individuals attend to their experiences defines the meaning of those experiences as disconnected from or "other" than self (Csordas 1983, 1993; Seligman and Kirmayer 2008; Shutz 1967).[2] For example, studies of the effects of chronic illness have demonstrated that by drawing intense attention to bodily experience, suffering and disability can heighten people's awareness of their own bodies as objects (Becker 1997; Leventhal et al. 1999). Researchers have shown, for instance, that the need to focus attention on basic physical acts like walking, standing, lifting one's hand, or forming a word with one's mouth creates a sense of self-division within stroke patients—making them feel as if their bodies are things separate from themselves (Ellis-Hill et al. 2000). Similarly, experiences of physiological reactivity may draw mediums' attention to their own bodies in a way that makes their bodies feel distanced from self: my body is not under my control; it is not me; it is other.

Moreover, social marginalization related to race, class, gender, sexual orientation, and/or the failure to fulfill social role expectations (discussed at length in chapter 3) mean that the individuals who become mediums often experience being "other" in a social sense as well. Political, economic, and institutional power structures that shape such experiences of marginalization are thus a critical part of a biolooping process that creates a sense of self-disruption or otherness through feed-forward interactions among embodied suffering, attention, and meaning. And as many students of spirit possession have pointed out, possession practices can serve as a way of articulating the effects of such power structures on the self—of drawing attention to the suffering that accompanies the experience of otherness in many social and political contexts.

The self-alienating quality of such experiences lends itself to interpretation as interference in one's life by powerful "others" (spirits and deities) (cf. Csordas 1983). If my experiences feel out of my control, it might be because they are under the control of some other power or force; if my body is behaving in ways that do not feel volitional, a spirit or deity could be responsible. As Michael Lambek (1996: 239) puts it, "Spirits often specifically represent a difference that has invaded the self and that has become personally problematic...they are an expression of the other within oneself." In fact, some scholars have even argued that the powerful "others" by whom individuals become possessed—the spirits, gods, demons, or ancestors—can be understood as *internalizations* of the external power structures that shape and constrain the lives of these individuals (Boddy 1989; Comaroff and Comaroff 1993; Mageo 1996; Ong 1988).

But thematizing the experience of otherness as the work of the spirits is not merely a way for Candomblé mediums to express and draw attention to the predicaments in which they find themselves, it is way of transforming those predicaments. That is, involvement in Candomblé and the opportunities for expressing and rethematizing suffering that it affords, become part of a biolooping process through which mediums' selves are actually transformed. Recognizing the work of powerful others in one's life is the first step in this larger process.

Suffering and the Body in Candomblé Belief and Practice

As I discussed in chapter 3, Candomblé cosmology includes the idea that the head of every human being is "owned" by a particular orixá, along with a *juntó*, or second-in-command. The idiom of "owner-ship" underscores the belief that the personalities of these two orixás are part of the true nature of the individual whose head they own. Moreover, the owners of an individual's head by definition exert a fair amount of control over his or her fate. Failure to acknowledge one's orixás is thus understood to lead to disturbances in life, trouble with interpersonal relationships or jobs, and even health problems. In other words, it can lead to various forms of "suffering"—suffering which can in turn contribute to a feeling of otherness that lends itself to interpretation as the influence of the spirits over an individual's life.

In order to identify their orixás, individuals must have a divina-tion, like the one I described in chapter 1, performed by a mae or pai de santo. As the account of my own divination experience dem-onstrates, by identifying the orixás who own an individual's head, a spiritual leader identifies and highlights key aspects of that individu-al's self. This identification is significant in the context of Candomblé because it is an active component of a system that encourages indi-viduals to accept that some fundamental part of their self (the orixá part) is not under their direct control—it is in some respect "other." By linking an individual's traits and behaviors to the orixás, this pro-cess thus points to the degree to which they are not responsible for their own destinies, and yet it puts their destinies into the hands of known entities rather than random forces. Hence, this system also encourages each individual to know and respect the orixá elements of self and in this way, paradoxically, to exercise a certain amount of control over them. Spiritual leaders I interviewed emphasized that individuals must engage in appropriate practices to "*cuidar*," or care for, indulge, and accommodate the qualities, motivations, and desires of their orixás, and by extension, the orixá characteristics of them-selves. These aspects of self become understood as simultaneously me and not me, self and not self.

Identification of an individual's orixás thus encourages the kind of redirection of attention that helps to reshape the meaning of experi-ence and behavior. The way that mediums talked about their rela-tionships to their orixás suggests that for many, identification of the orixás focused their attention on aspects of self to be understood as fundamental. In other words, knowledge of their orixás' character-istics served to increase mediums' awareness of those characteristics as important aspects of themselves. Discovering that Oxum is the owner of their heads, for example, might lead mediums to attend more to the gentle, nurturing qualities of themselves. For others, identification with the orixás highlights an aspect of self that has been overattended to, or impossible to ignore, and convinces them that they are not its agent. For instance, discovering that their heads are owned by Xangó helps individuals to make sense of a tendency toward stubbornness and inflexibility. In such cases, mediums learn to attend to certain characteristics or behaviors in a way that enhances the sense of otherness—distancing themselves still further from these aspects of self. Overall, this process enables individuals to attend to, and even cultivate, different aspects of their cognitive and emotional repertoires—adding to, or subtracting from, their previous self-understandings.

What is more, the process of identifying with the orixás motivates mediums to develop distinct agentive stances toward their own experiences and behaviors. By opening up the possibility for sanctioned divisions of subjectivity, Candomblé participation makes it intelligible that some aspects of experience and behavior are both one's own and not one's own—that is, it allows for the possibility that not all aspects of what a person feels or does are under the control of a single, coherent consciousness. This is underscored by the widely shared belief that human individuals are totally unaware of what their bodies do while possessed, and have amnesia for the entire period during which they are in trance. Candomblé thus allows for psychologically and socially ambiguous forms of agency. Behaviors, thoughts, emotions, and even bodily characteristics like weight gain, new tastes, or food aversions may be adopted both within and outside the ritual setting. These can then be claimed or disavowed as products of the self, through their attribution to forces outside the realm of *human* agency altogether.

The process of identification thus allows individuals to reshape their core sense of selfhood, to escape ownership of or responsibility for previous suffering, to reorient toward new or different characteristics, and even at times to separate themselves entirely from self-awareness and from their own behaviors and bodily characteristics. Hence, built into this religious system is a logic or model of selfhood that takes for granted that individuals may experience discontinuities in the embodied and representational dimensions of self. In other words, the logic of self in Candomblé accounts not just for *ideas* about what selves are in general, or who particular individuals understand themselves to be, but for the *experiential* dimensions of selfhood as well—for behaviors and bodily responses.

In fact, as many observers have noted, Candomblé is above all a religion of the body, of embodiment. There is an emphasis among spiritual leaders and adherents alike on the importance of practice—on what adherents *do* in their ritual performances and everyday lives (Johnson 2002). Practices revolve around axé, or the life force of the universe, the accumulation and depletion of which are fundamentally embodied processes. Mae Tiana and the other spiritual leaders I interviewed emphasized that all areas of life, especially bodily well-being, suffer when one's axé is depleted. Spiritual crisis, or the failure to cuidar one's orixás, depletes axé and is manifest as the social and emotional suffering described earlier, culminating for many in some form of bodily suffering.

The affliction or well-being of the body is therefore viewed as an obvious material indicator of spiritual well-being, or a lack thereof. Thus, in addition to the ability of somatic crisis to motivate individuals to cross the threshold into Candomblé, discussed in chapter 3, such crises are the most frequent catalysts for initiation because an understanding of disruptions of self and spirit as fundamentally embodied processes is built into the logic of the religion. It should not be surprising, then, that many of the practices that serve to bolster axé involve the body—such practices range from everyday acts of devotion, like wearing sacred beads symbolic of one's orixás, to more specialized acts including making sacrifices, consuming sacred food and feasting, rituals of cleansing, ritualized movements and physical acts of devotion (prostration, for example), and, of course, trance and possession.

Possession, or the notion of control or animation of the body by forces other than the individual's mind or will, metaphorically links the lack of control that individuals feel over their lives, to the need or desire to relinquish control to the gods, via the dysfunctional body. In other words, the body mediates, both symbolically and experientially, between the suffering of the individual and the work of the orixás in their lives. Developing a relationship with the gods as their medium thus serves to both normalize and formalize the experience of otherness that embodied suffering has already created in mediums—it normalizes by attributing otherness to the gods, and it formalizes by building-in the experience of otherness, in the form of trance and possession, as a central part of the embodied practice of the religion.

The process of becoming a medium also includes an embodied logic. It is understood in Candomblé that in order to resolve their bodily afflictions, individuals who experience the kinds of somatic suffering that I have described must be formally initiated. From a spiritual perspective, initiation is understood as the means through which mediums learn to cuidar (care for or look after) their orixás, opening and preparing their bodies and minds for possession and other forms of devotion. Thus, learning to take spiritual care involves bodily practices, but it is the spiritual function of these practices that leads to healing.

From a biolooping perspective, techniques of religious formation can be understood as a means for intervening in existing loops of influence among body, meaning, and practice. The processes of initiation and ongoing devotion in Candomblé contribute to internalization of bodily knowledge, which in turn creates new patterns of bodily response and reshapes the embodied dimensions of self (cf. Lester 2005). The complex and unique ways in which initiation and ongoing practices of mediumship bring together embodied self-experience with self-understandings are thus what ultimately leads to experiences of healing self-transformation.

Initiation and the Unmaking of Self

As I mentioned earlier, embodied disruptions of self and spirit are addressed in Candomblé through their formalization—or the way in which such discontinuities become ritualized as part of Candomblé practice—and through their normalization—or the way in which they are assigned new meaning. This process, which helps to bring together embodied self-experience and self-understandings, takes place first during initiation and continues in subsequent devotional practices, especially those involving trance and possession.

The initiation process itself is referred to as *fazer o santo* (to make the saint), and as a result, the process of becoming a medium is commonly abbreviated as being feito or "made." Mediums talked about their spiritual life histories in terms of when they were made, they frequently referenced the terreiro where they were made, they tracked their own and others' spiritual genealogies in terms of who made whom, and the internal hierarchy within the terreiro was based on spiritual age, or the amount of time since each individual was made.

The implications of this idiom have to do not only with formal installation of the orixá into the initiate's head, but also with the unmaking and making of *self* that takes place before and during the initiation. Students of ritual dating back to Arnold Van Gennep (1960) have understood such rites of passage as a means to deconstruct existing selves so that they may be reconstructed in a new form. But as I discussed earlier, potential mediums arrive at Candomblé with selves that have already been divided by the experience of suffering and conflict. Thus initiation serves first to reinforce the breakdown or deconstruction of the extant self. In other words, the self must be officially unmade before it can be *feito*.

Candomblé initiations traditionally involve extended periods of seclusion within the terreiro, during which spiritual leaders and other adepts model proper ritual behavior for the initiate who is simultaneously learning of ritual secrets and obligations. This includes learning songs, prayers, myths, and dances; eating and coming to recognize ritual foods; identifying medicinal herbs and learning healing practices; and participating in bodily transformations such as head shaving (*raspagem*) and ritual incision of the head. The self is unmade during this process in both symbolic and embodied ways, through practices meant to suppress elements of the old self—distancing individuals from their everyday social roles, for instance, by isolating them within the terreiro, where they temporarily cease to be wife, mother, friend, or manicurist. They are also prevented from engaging in many of their familiar everyday practices while in seclusion—practices that may influence how they understand themselves. For instance, initiates often go for long periods without being allowed to bathe or groom themselves. Given the emphasis on personal hygiene in mainstream Brazilian culture (discussed in chapter 2), for many initiates the inability to engage in this practice is likely to accentuate the sense of distance from their taken-for-granted self.

Such practices also serve to manipulate the initiate's attention, directing it away from self-conscious awareness, and by extension, away from their experiences of suffering. This is a particularly potent way in which practices of initiation can help to disrupt patterns of bodily response previously entrained in mediums through the interactions of their particular bodies with their social worlds. Manipulation of attention is accomplished in two main ways during initiation: first, by directing the initiate's attention *onto* new experiences, many of which resemble the individual's former suffering in their intensity, but because they are spiritually significant, do not have the same negative valence. Such experiences include sleeping on the floor, being isolated from friends and family, eating only ritual foods, itchiness and discomfort resulting from having blood and other substances applied to the body but not being able to wash them off (Wafer 1991), having one's head shaved, having one's head incised, participating in novel and elaborate rituals, and learning trance induction techniques that encourage intense focus on rhythmic and repetitive stimuli like dancing, singing/chanting, and drumming—all of which symbolically clear the way to the ownership of the head by the orixás, but also change the way the individual looks and feels.

The second way this is accomplished is by directing the individual's attention *away* from old suffering, using techniques like seclusion from the everyday world and immersion in a different setting and living conditions. Thus, the same practices that help to unmake or disassemble the existing self also direct attention away from that self and its experiences of suffering. Even the intense boredom that comes from spending long periods in isolation can serve to direct attention away from self-conscious awareness (Johnson 2002). The initiation experience thus disrupts old looping patterns among negative experiences, bodily responses, and self-implicating meanings, by distancing initiates from those stressful experiences while at the same time creating new networks of association among ritual situations and behaviors, nonself-implicating meanings, and new patterns of response.

As a result of such practices, mediums describe spending months in an altered state of consciousness during initiation, their everyday sense of selfhood suspended. By their own accounts, initiates are most often possessed by their erê, or child orixás during this time, suggesting that the adult self, with its life history, goals, and responsibilities, is largely absent. Instead, the initiate possesses (or is possessed by) a childlike or proto-self who is immersed in the immediacy of the initiation experience. Self must therefore also be remade or reestablished before the medium can emerge from initiation. This remaking also takes place through the combined work of meaning and practice.

Biolooping in the Healing and Remaking of Self

The remaking of self in Candomblé initiation takes place through both mental and bodily channels. As discussed earlier, identification of an individual's orixás helps to shape and contextualize cognitive and emotional aspects of self. But initiates also learn to understand and experience the body not simply as a neutral and stable container occupied by different spirits, but as itself a dynamic medium which may display changes and discontinuities at the physiological level when animated by a different consciousness.

These shifts in the characteristics of the body can be seen in the movements of the possession dance. For instance, when possessed by Oxalá,[3] the most senior orixá, mediums dance with the hunched posture and slow deliberate movements of a wizened old man. This creates a focus on, and embodiment of, the orixá's characteristics. Mediums told me of other dramatic changes in bodily characteristics associated with possession as well, such as relief from physical disability when possessed by a nondisabled orixá, or the ability to consume alcohol in one who normally could not tolerate it, when possessed by her caboclo (indigenous South American spirit). Such experiences further reinforce the notion that qualities of the body may be disconnected from the agency of the individual, and may not correspond to his/her prior self-concept.

Consequently, while possession by the orixás may reinforce the experience of one's body as a foreign object, this experience ceases to undermine the continuity of self. This is a key point for understanding how biolooping can contribute to self-transformation. The meaning of nonvolitional or unfamiliar bodily responses is entirely altered by mediumship when it becomes interpreted as the embodiment of the orixás. This change in meaning fundamentally alters the way such bodily responses are perceived and attended to. Just as rapid heart rate and a jolt of adrenaline can easily be perceived as sexual arousal or fear depending on whether one is facing down a lion or an attractive human being (Dutton and Aron 1974), so too can the sense of uncontrol associated with exaggerated, attention-dominating psychophysiological arousal go from alienating to spiritually meaningful in the context of possession instead of stressful experience. Moreover, the connection of autonomic nervous system responses and characteristics to spirituality means that even outside the ritual context, the individual may be less likely to associate such arousal with a stressful stimulus and to negatively evaluate it.

Embedding potentially alienating bodily experience in a meaningful context is thus a fundamental part of the biolooping process through which the bodies and selves of mediums become healed. Not only does reinterpretation of bodily experience allow it to be reconciled with self-representations, but it affects those bodily experiences themselves by shaping patterns of attention that in turn affect what information is processed. Rather than being reinforced, escalated, and continuing to dominate awareness, such experiences become part of the background again. Hence, internalization of a new way of attributing meaning to embodied experience becomes a tool for the self-regulation of arousal.

Evidence for a distinctive psychophysiological profile among mediums (discussed in depth in chapter 4) supports the notion that immersion into this spiritual system may aid in the self-regulation of arousal, since the pattern of autonomic control they display is typically associated with a heightened capacity for self-regulation. Immersion into Candomblé belief and practice may thus promote healing of embodied selves in part by changing patterns and perceptions of psychophysiological arousal. Such an interpretation is supported by the way mediums describe recovering from the somatic ills that caused them to become initiated in the first place. In addition to immediate recovery, mediums also consistently express never suffering from such somatic crises again. For example, Ana, who sought help from Candomblé for a medically unexplained rash covering her whole body, stated unequivocally, "My life changed plenty [since initiation]…I don't have illness any more."

The narratives of mediums thus seem to describe healing in fairly absolute terms. Yet in his seminal work on spiritual healing, Thomas Csordas (1983) has argued that this kind of healing is often incremental—taking place little by little. While mediumship narratives were overwhelmingly narratives of recovery—in their accounts, initiation healed them and prevented the recurrence of such illness—these accounts do not indicate that once initiated these mediums never got sick again or even that the healing was total. In fact, it was not uncommon for mediums to discuss current problems and even illnesses. It would seem, then, that this narrative practice is not intended to communicate that a medium's *body* was healed of a particular illness at a particular time, or that it has become immune to illness. Rather it is a statement of the broad healing or reparation of the embodied *self*. It is a way of talking about becoming a different kind of person—one who sometimes becomes ill or experiences misfortunes, but is no longer chronically afflicted. In other words, these narratives are about healing at a more fundamental level, and this form of healing serves to reframe all subsequent suffering in relation to a new kind of subjectivity.

The healing mediums experience is constituted in large part through a reorientation toward symptoms and experiences. In this sense it is likely to be, as Csordas (1983) argues, incremental, since it involves an ongoing process of interpretation and reinterpretation. Mediums may gradually become more adept at interpreting new experiences in religious terms, or their ability to do so may be uneven. Yet access to a religious frame within which they can interpret subsequent suffering means that such suffering is less likely to radically undermine the sense of self and cause a distressing sense of division as it did before initiation. New physical or existential ills become part of an ongoing concern with fulfilling ritual obligations. They are a source of concern and attention as symptoms or signs of the orixás' displeasure, but they can be addressed through religious practice, and mediums feel empowered to carry out such remediation. Thus, embodied knowledge of, and engagement with, a range of ritual practices also helps to prevent the recreation of old patterns of suffering. Such practice has the effect of diverting attention from symptoms or misfortunes, interrupting cycles of symptom amplification, and retuning physiological arousal.

The Cases of Lucia and Pedro: Revisited

Not only is self-healing an incremental process, but it is also a variable one—both in terms of how it exerts its effects, and also the degree to which it is efficacious for each individual. While there is a general pattern of transformation through which Candomblé participation acts to heal conflicted and divided selves, the system is also immensely flexible and its effects idiosyncratic and person-specific.[4] This flexibility means that the self-healing process adapts to the idiosyncrasies of each person's life, their particular experiences and characteristics, and the forms of suffering that bring them to be initiated.

The result is a different kind of fit between the needs of each individual, and the structure and content of the religion. Some people are particularly motivated by identification with their orixás to cultivate new kinds of behaviors and characteristics. For others it is more important to objectify certain aspects of existing personality, and separate them from self—to avoid the experience of dissonance brought on by unwanted thoughts and behaviors, by attributing them to the agency of their orixás. Yet for each individual it is the balance of meaning and practice that creates the kind of biolooping effect among mind, body, individual, and society that I have been describing.

By revisiting two of the cases discussed in chapter three,[5] I illustrate both the regularities and individual differences in how Candomblé meaning and practice contribute to a biolooping process, and how this process helps to heal each individual's self.

Lucia

Like most mediumship narratives I collected, Lucia's centered around the suffering she experienced prior to becoming initiated. The particular forms of suffering Lucia recounted consisted especially of anxiety, guilt, and emotional instability which she attributed to two main causes: terror related to her own political activism during the military dictatorship; and her emotional response to the death of her father.

Her experience of extreme fear and anxiety around being caught by the military police caused her to be, in her own words, *traumatizada* (traumatized), with the life-(and self-)altering effect of causing her to drop out of college. Her feelings of grief and guilt in relation to her father's death caused her to become more and more emotionally unstable. She became paranoid, suffered delusions, went into rages in which she threw things at her mother. Psychiatric medication did not control her emotional volatility and Lucia feared she would be committed and/or commit suicide. Lucia ended up seeking help in Candomblé at the suggestion of a friend. She was eventually initiated at the terreiro where she remains a *filha de santo* today. She believes her initiation transformed her into someone "tranquil."

Prior to their initiations, many mediums are vulnerable to the negative cycles of psychosocial stress, attention, somatic distress, and corporeal alienation described earlier in this chapter. In Lucia's case the intrusive effects of her anxiety prevented her from being able to concentrate on her studies, causing her to drop out of college. Dropping out of college undermined her sense of self by violating her own goals and expectations as well as those of others in her social context. This is particularly so because Lucia also failed to follow the alternative track for women in her social group, to get married and have children. And although she did not talk about it explicitly, it is likely that she was left unable to bear children by the condition that caused her to have uterine surgery during this same period.

At the same time, the feedback between anxiety and physiological response sensitized Lucia to other stressors, making her especially vulnerable to the trauma of losing her father. As Lucia puts it, the trauma of her father's death had a particularly strong effect on her because of "the type of person" she was at the time: "sensitive." Moreover, the experience of losing her father and feeling responsible for his death also powerfully undermined her sense of self: according to Lucia, "*a partir daquele momento eu não fui mais a mesma pessoa*" ("from that moment I was not the same person anymore").

The somatic effects and sense of alienation from body that Lucia experienced as a result of her stressful and traumatic experiences are apparent in her recollection of how she responded to the headaches she commonly suffered at the time. She told me: "I just remember that I had a headache, that when it started to hurt I banged my head into the wall, and when I heard my head pound as it hit the wall, I said "let's see if she breaks it today." She was so distanced from herself that she describes banging her head into a wall, listening to the sound it made, and wondering about its effects on her body in the third person. Through this anecdote Lucia thus captures a powerful sense of otherness.

The sense of otherness and disruption of self that Lucia experienced is also underscored by the fact that during this preinitiation period she spontaneously dissociated (in her words, "went into trance") while in a high stress situation—when she was about to undergo uterine surgery. Though she has since made spiritual meaning of this dissociative experience, at the time Lucia did not have the frame of reference necessary to symbolically 'smooth over' the experience with religious attributions (Kirmayer 1994). The fact that this spontaneous episode of dissociation did not have symbolic meaning for her at the time supports the idea that it was a response to acute anxiety—in other words, it occurred as part of a larger pattern of self-fragmentation or disintegration.

In summary, Lucia's expectations, goals, and desires and her ability to conform to social expectations were derailed by multiple acutely stressful life events, which ultimately resulted in severe embodied suffering. Her profound suffering led Lucia to experience a sense of alienation from her life, her mood, and her behavior, none of which matched her self-concept or self-expectations. She became a foreign person to herself, someone who was, in her words, "not normal."

Lucia thus entered her initiation process with a self already deeply divided by the experience of suffering. Initiation further disrupted her ties to the taken-for-granted elements of her personhood, including relationships (she left her mother and siblings), setting/context (she not only entered the terreiro for a period of isolation, but uprooted herself further by moving from Rio to Salvador for her initiation) and goals (she abandoned her job, her hopes for university). Like many other mediums, Lucia's articulation of the liminality of this period included an account of an extended episode of trance: as she put it, "I stayed in *erê*-trance almost a full month."

The initiation process and internalization of the logic of self in Candomblé contributed to the re-making and healing of Lucia's self, through multiple channels. First, identification of Oxalá, the oldest and wisest of the orixás, as the owner of her head gave Lucia the opportunity to identify with his calmness, wisdom, kindness, and tranquility. Though it seems as though it would have been hard for a young woman to identify with and adopt the characteristics of the oldest of the orixás, Lucia describes her transformation as immediate. Prior to her initiation, she identified herself as high-strung, sensitive, and emotionally volatile; afterward, she says she became "tranquil." Her initiation thus figures as an emotional turning point in her self-narrative and though her account is retrospective, as I argued in chapter 3, behavioral transformations of the kind Lucia describes are potentiated by new self-understandings like those articulated in her narrative. Lucia comes across as exceptionally calm and deliberate, peaceful and wise—thus the personality she projects matches the sense of her own characteristics articulated in her self-narrative. In other words, her behaviors coincide with her self-understandings. This idea is underscored by the way in which Lucia's self has transformed in a social sense as well. With 30 years as a medium at her terreiro and an influential (though not particularly lucrative)[6] job at a museum related to Afro-Brazilian culture, Lucia has positioned herself as both a religious and cultural expert and spends a good deal of time mentoring younger spiritual adepts. In this sense, she embodies in her social identity the qualities of Oxalá as well—particularly his wise and paternal nature.

Mediumship thus helped Lucia to restructure aspects of her personality and social role, by giving her the characteristics of her orixá on which to anchor and around which to construct a new self-narrative. All of the suffering and emotional volatility she experienced prior to initiation she now sees as symptoms of her spiritual affliction, rather than as characteristics of her true self. As she puts it, "After I was made, I became a different person—no longer the same. Really I went through a process of [self] recognition." Her suffering and the "sensitive" nature she describes prior to initiation can thus be understood as having contributed to a cognitive and emotional proclivity for the meaning content and practices of the religion.

At the same time, mediumship also transformed the qualities of Lucia's body. Through initiation and ongoing devotion, Lucia learned to embody the physical characteristics of her primary deity: she learned the stooped posture and slow deliberate movements of Oxalá, which she took on whenever she was possessed. But Lucia seems to embody Oxalá even when she is not possessed, with her slow deliberate movements, her careful speech, and her eternally calm demeanor. Moreover, aging has further reinforced Lucia's identification with the senior deity. For example, as a result of arthritis she has developed a somewhat hunched posture and walks with a slow, shuffling gait and a slight limp, even when she is not possessed. Oxalá does not eat foods containing salt or sugar, and Lucia explained to me that she is unable to eat salt or sugar because she suffers from both diabetes and hypertension. Though she understands her diabetes and hypertension as hereditary, she views them not as illness or affliction, but rather as physical manifestations of her connection to her orixá. This belief helps prevent her from feeling a renewed sense of alienation from her body that could result from these chronic conditions, and protects her from having to struggle to incorporate illness or a "sick role" into her self-understandings. In addition, while these ailments demand her focus and attention to her body at times, they do not do so in ways that undermine her normal patterns of self-awareness. This is because her self-awareness as a medium is already punctuated by moments of embodied identification with her orixá, of which her illnesses have now simply become a part.

Similarly, internalization of the idea that body and self may be detached has also allowed Lucia to detach from her distressing psychophysiological responses by attending to them differently. Moreover, the practice elements of Candomblé help to structure her attention in such a way that they may help avert cycles of symptom amplification in the first place. For Lucia, Candomblé devotion means daily practice: when I knew her, she lived in a small building on the grounds of her terreiro, and was responsible for tending the terreiro's shrine to Oxalá. She made frequent offerings to Oxalá as well as other deities, and not simply to petition them for help with a particular problem, but as acts of regular maintenance to her relationship with the gods.

I witnessed the painstaking, methodical, attention Lucia committed to such acts of devotion, and her absorption in the knowledge surrounding them, when she helped a friend and me to create an offering for one of our orixás. She seemed to relish the process of traveling to different stores to buy the items we needed for our offering, moving from place to place with a sense of transcendent purpose. She talked quietly to us, and herself, as she methodically assembled the items in a basket, describing the meaning and value of each item included in the offering. She spoke with a quiet intensity as she instructed us on how to communicate our petition to the orixá, how to imbue the offering with our needs and desires before giving it over to the deity. Her regular offerings and maintenance of the shrine to Oxalá at her terreiro were undertaken with the same focus, the same methodical attention and sense of purpose. The degree of absorption she demonstrated in these ritual processes suggests that tuning in to these practices with such intensity was especially therapeutic for her. Moreover, as I discussed in chapter 4, the proclivity for the meanings and practices of Candomblé likely also contributed to her capacity for deeply focused attention, absorption, and dissociation.

Trance induction training, which involves learning to narrowly concentrate attention on the music and movements of possession rituals, and hence to dissociate in response to specific cues, also helped Lucia learn to control and manipulate her own attention, arousal, and awareness, while making the distancing of self from body meaningful, predictable, and contextual. My psychophysiological data, discussed in depth in the last chapter, suggest that the effects of this spiritual system on self may include the retuning of cardiac autonomic processes, such that practicing mediums like Lucia end up with a distinctive capacity to self-regulate their psychophysiological arousal.

Hence, for Lucia becoming a medium initiated a biolooping process in which mutual influences among meaning, body, and practice served to transform both the representational and embodied dimensions of herself. In other words, the way Lucia thinks about herself and the meanings she attributes to her own experiences has shaped and been shaped by embodied learning. Thus, being "made" has helped Lucia to put herself back together again, healing and recohering her previously damaged, divided self.

Pedro

Like Lucia, Pedro narrated his spiritual life history in terms of a pattern of suffering, and yet his suffering was very different from hers. Pedro is an Afro-Brazilian, homosexual man, whose suffering was likely related to his status in such a marginalized group. On the surface, this suffering was characterized by drinking, fighting, and drifting (between places, religions, and occupations)—all of which were symptoms of a broader condition of alienation and existential distress.

Pedro's narrative centers in particular around his inability to find and keep a job. He describes in exhaustive detail the circumstances of his dismissals, the unfairness, the demoralization he experienced. The emotional toll this took on him—both because of its practical effects (he was forced to move back in with his parents) as well as its symbolic ones—especially in one case in which he was accused of misconduct—are palpable. He describes channeling his energies and frustrations into street and beach life, expressing his alienation through self-destructive embodied behaviors—in particular alcohol abuse and aggression—trapping him in a negative cycle.

His dissatisfaction with his life and the conflict he experienced during this time were demonstrated by his restless search for greater fulfillment, in the form of different jobs, moving to a different city (Rio) and back, and serial participation in different religions. His story also documents a prolonged period of approach and with-drawal from Candomblé, drifting back to drinking and fighting, being fired from additional jobs, before he finally became initiated. Each time he approached Candomblé, he would, in his own terms, *passar mal* (become sick), fainting on several different occasions.[7] A number of maes de santo informed him that he must be made, but for some time he resisted.

It is not uncommon for mediums to speak of their initial resistance to becoming initiated. But unlike most other narratives I collected, Pedro described being miserable during his initiation. Yet Pedro's narrative ends with the same subjective experience of healing and transformation. While he has continued to drift somewhat in terms of his vocation, he no longer describes feeling a sense of dissatisfaction and existential crisis, and communicates no longer falling into the negative patterns of behavior he had engaged in prior to initiation. As he put it, "In terms of fighting, today I am a more tranquil person. I am calm, very calm…I understand fights, I also try to make peace. But when I see that peace is not going to reign in that moment, I prefer to remove myself." He is able to resist acting on anger, finding peace and tranquility where previously there was none. Like Lucia, he has developed a new way of being in the world.

For Pedro, the way that this self-transformation was effected dif-fers in important ways from Lucia. Pedro's identification of his pri-mary orixá, the warrior god Ogum, provided a model for making attributions about already present personality traits rather than a model around which to thoroughly reshape his personality. As Pedro now understands it, Ogum is responsible for his aggression and fight-ing, and his attraction to the street life. Hence, identification with the orixá has given him a way to distance himself from problematic char-acteristics and behaviors, which prior to initiation had "invaded" his self and created a sense of otherness. Yet he has also resisted certain elements of this model, stating, for example:

> My mae de santo says that people of Ogum like to work in the street, work as vendors, but I think that…the orixá in one is a protection, the orixá in one is peace and equilibrium, so I don't think that I have to take part in everything of the orixá, that…because the orixá likes this I have to be vending something.

Instead, he expressed a sense of certainty that he could become some kind of professional, and certainty that he would find the right pro-fession. In fact, when I conducted a follow-up interview with him a year later, Pedro was taking a course to be a medical assistant. Thus, he distinguished between the orixá elements of self—those aspects of self responsible for his previous bad behavior and alienation—and other elements of self: "This is a thing I want to do, a thing I like, it is a thing that is mine." Yet rather than creating a greater sense of division, distancing from some aspects of his former self and behavior has helped to reduce Pedro's experience of dissonance.

Moreover, this has been a useful way for Pedro to represent himself socially as well—as in control of some aspects of his destiny, yet not responsible for others. This position is particularly empowering for Pedro in the sense that the negative aspects of his personality, because they are attributed to the orixás, actually function as signs of his spiritual legitimacy, thus allowing him to occupy a prominent and respected role within the religious community.

Hence, while Pedro's self-transformation has above all been a behavioral transformation—he has stopped his heavy drinking and brawling—this behavioral transformation has been facilitated by shifts in cognition, attention, and social feedback. Attributing his negative tendencies to the characteristics of his orixá allows Pedro to accept these characteristics and to place them in a spiritual context. But it also serves to further objectify them: they become at once self and not-self. This process of objectification in turn allows Pedro to gain some emotional distance as well as cognitive and behavioral control over these previously automatic and embodied, yet dissonant, aspects of self. As he stated, he still understands fighting—he can see how reactive responses to situations occur, and can relate to the anger and aggression that result—but he is now capable of trying to make peace instead. In other words, there is now enough cognitive control, and built-in attribution to the orixá, that allow him to attend to his own embodied responses differently, and to avoid reactive and aggressive behaviors. The spiritual meaning he has made of his self-destructive behaviors has thus enhanced Pedro's capacity for self-regulation.

Although in Pedro's story the embodied elements of suffering and self-conflict are less obvious than in some others, they are important all the same. Pedro's very existential suffering had its sources in aspects of his embodied self, in the sense that his blackness and homosexuality were almost certainly factors in his employment problems. The sense that these embodied aspects of self-represented obstacles to his ability to find a vocation likely contributed to an underlying sense of self-conflict. In addition, Pedro's story is about experiencing a lack of control over self, and as I discussed earlier, it is often the experience of a lack of control over thoughts, emotions, and behaviors that makes individuals feel "other." Pedro's lack of control was expressed through out-of-control embodied behaviors like drinking and fighting, and his description of his descent into such behaviors indicates that his emotions and actions during that period felt other—that these embodied aspects of self did not feel integrated with, and were not under the control of, his cognized self. Thus, while somatization (in the sense of unexplained illness) was not a source of self-disruption for Pedro, his existential suffering nevertheless had important embodied dimensions.

Interestingly, Pedro also associates with his spiritual calling an experience of extreme physical suffering (an abscessed tooth) he endured years before his initiation. His inclusion of this story in his mediumship narrative, in spite of the fact that this problem was probably healed by the antibiotics he was prescribed by a dentist and not by his initiation as a medium, suggests that Pedro experienced this physical suffering as part of his larger experience of existential distress, embodied suffering, and dissonance—all of which he now understands as symptoms of his spiritual calling.[8]

Because of these embodied dimensions of his suffering and self-disruption, the practice elements of Candomblé were central to Pedro's transformation as well. It is clear from interacting with him that Pedro has an enormous amount of cognitive and physical energy. As a result of his inability to find and keep a satisfying job prior to his initiation, much of Pedro's energy was channeled into self-destructive behaviors. The practice elements of Candomblé give Pedro an alternative outlet into which he can channel his energies and his attention. They give him something to do when he feels like drinking, a form of action in which to engage when he feels angry or aggressive. Because he interprets such feelings as the work of his orixá, this serves to reinforce the idea that ritual practices, like making offerings or attending festas, are an appropriate response—they not only appease his feelings and urges, they appease Ogum. It is noteworthy that Pedro attends more festas at different terreiros than any other medium I know, suggesting that he finds the ritual practices involved to be particularly attractive, and perhaps therapeutic. Especially in light of his history of problems with alcohol abuse, his attendance at festas all over the city is somewhat reminiscent of an alcoholic who searches out AA meetings whenever he gets the urge to drink.

This may be partly because, by embodying the characteristics of his orixá while possessed, Pedro has the opportunity to enact the powerful, aggressive qualities of his warrior god; in other words, he is given the opportunity to transform into the great and savage Ogum. This opportunity allows Pedro to direct his aggressive tendencies and energies into his ritual performances. Pedro may also seek out the social feedback at such festas, which reinforces his understanding of himself as spiritually empowered and reminds him that he is no longer the beach brawling former self, but the filho of Ogum.

It is worth noting that Pedro's unsatisfying experience with another religion, Mesa Branca, is probably related to his need for more active, embodied practices. Pedro complained that Mesa Branca was "like going to a meeting—you just sat there and had a meeting and then went away." His need for a more embodied religious experience was vividly demonstrated by his powerful embodied response to Candomblé—every time he approached the religion prior to becoming initiated he became sick or fainted.

Yet unlike Lucia, Pedro's preinitiation suffering was of a more continuous, low-grade nature, rather than an acute crisis. This suggests that despite his inability to reach his goals, his inability to exercise control over certain elements of his embodied reactions to situations, and his ensuing alienation from elements of his personality and behavior, Pedro may not have come to his initiation as fragmented as did Lucia. This could help to explain his unusually negative experience with initiation; his existing self may have required more dismantling through initiation, before it could be rebuilt and reintegrated.

Like most mediums, as part of the initiation process Pedro was separated from his friends and family—a fact that he mentioned repeatedly in his narrative, describing in particular his misery at not being able to see his mother and father. Pedro also had to undergo the physical rigors of initiation like sleeping on the floor, eating only ritual foods, having his head shaved. Given that he had experienced less somatic suffering prior to his initiation, these rigors may have been more difficult for Pedro to endure. He describes trying to escape his initiation on more than one occasion, running out into the street where he fainted and was brought back into the barracão. He also describes being "caught" or "picked up" by his orixá repeatedly during initiation, every time he behaved or thought "wrong." Unlike Lucia's story, in which the familiar self was displaced for a prolonged period during constant erê trance, Pedro's description suggests more of a struggle. He details a prolonged process in which elements of his old, damaged self reemerged and had to be displaced by his orixá self.

The differences in the subjective state of each individual at the time of initiation relate to other differences in the process of transformation as well. Lucia has internalized and identified with everything about

Oxalá, and reshaped her personality around the characteristics of her orixá. Pedro, on the other hand, identifies with elements of Ogum, and this identification has shifted the way he attends to those elements of himself, but he rejects other parts of the connection to his deity.

Thus, these different people came to the religion in different states of disrepair, having experienced distinct forms of suffering and different threats to their subjectivity, and the logic of Candomblé helped to heal them in somewhat different ways. Yet for both mediums, the convergence of meaning and practice has played an important role in transforming their patterns of attention and behavior, providing both a key outlet and explanation for their embodied tendencies, and facilitating their transformation.

Conclusion

The selves of Lucia and Pedro were threatened and disrupted via embodied processes. Their experiences of suffering not only undermined their cognized senses of self, but also set up for each of them a learned, negative pattern of attention, arousal, and attribution, affecting multiple levels of self-experience. It would seem, therefore, that any process of self-healing would have to address not just cognitive aspects of self, but act to reshape body, behavior, and meaning all together. In other words, the healing of selves must involve a form of embodied learning—or relearning.

Through a particular set of beliefs and practices that offer alternative forms of selfhood and agency with a distinctive embodied logic, becoming a Candomblé medium encompasses such a process of embodied relearning. Candomblé religious formation appears to initiate new patterns of attention, arousal, and attribution, resetting what I have referred to as the "biolooping process" at the heart of social and cultural entrainment. This process is a fundamentally social process as well, as individuals come to embody shared cultural meanings, and take on embodied roles that are socially significant and play an important part in the life of the community. By revealing the details of how such a process works, close examination of healing self-transformation in Candomblé also sheds light on the complex and layered nature of selves and the vital involvement of mind, body, and sociocultural context in embodied learning.

Chapter 6
Conclusion: Stepping Back

The title of the introduction to this book, "Stepping into This Supernatural World," was borrowed from a quotation by one of the mediums with whom I spent a good deal of time, as she talked about the factors that lead to mediumship. As the title of the opening chapter, the phrase was meant to refer not only to how people come to participate in spirit possession, but also to serve as a metaphor for my own entry, and that of the reader, into the very different world of meaning within Candomblé. The partial inversion of the phrase here is meant to signal that in conclusion my goal is to step back from the specificity of Candomblé mediumship, in order to demonstrate how the ideas generated through this analysis also have utility *outside* that "supernatural world."

For one of the central claims I made at the start of this book was that spirit possession can be a lens through which to examine certain fundamental aspects of our shared human experience. While spirit possession appears to involve radical transformations of subjectivity that on the surface may seem foreign to many, I have tried to show how in the case of Brazilian Candomblé such transformations are both a product of a very particular social and ontological context, and at the same time representative of a more general set of crucially important, though relatively commonplace, processes linking together minds and bodies, individuals and cultures.

Yet the way that mediums *become* their deities—Jalita's eye-rolling, quivering entry into trance, and her stereotyped, frenetic dancing after being possessed by Oxum, for example, or Lucia's post-initiation development of the stooped posture, shuffling gait, and beatific demeanor of Oxála—will hardly seem commonplace to many Americans. However, we can understand these transformations of subjectivity in more general terms, as a result of the way that the symbols and meanings, structures and practices to which people are exposed and/or with which they actively engage shape both their bodily dispositions and cognitive understandings of self. In other words, such transformations result from the way the embodied self is shaped by social and cultural experience. I have demonstrated that the internalization of knowledge, engagement in bodily practices, and entrainment of physiological systems that come together in the process help explain how people come to experience themselves as possessed by powerful spiritual others. But the combined effects of these factors also contribute to many other kinds of phenomena.

In Candomblé two types of learning—embodied and discursive—combine to foster a form of self-transformation that transcends the temporary shifts in subjectivity that occur during possession. The more enduring transformations that mediums experience contribute to healing and, because they involve simultaneous changes in both conceptual and embodied dimensions of self that affect well-being, such transformations can contribute to healing not only social and emotional forms of distress, but bodily afflictions as well. While spirit possession mediumship represents a relatively dramatic example of the synergistic effects of these kinds of learning on selfhood and well-being, such bidirectional influences between meaning and embodied experience are ubiquitous. Their effects can be subtle (i.e., the way one responds to social challenge) or dramatic (i.e., the recovery from disease) and can take place within a variety of contexts, including not only the supernatural or religious, but also the social, medical, athletic, or musical, among others.

Biolooping as a Tool for Social Science

Within the larger set of processes I have described, one of the most striking things about Candomblé mediumship is that it allows us to see how meanings and attributions, bodily practices and experiences, work to reinforce one another. Transformations of bodily experience affect the way that mediums think about and reflect on themselves, at the same time that self-understandings influence bodily states, experiences, and behaviors. Mediumship also draws attention to the developmental trajectory of embodiment; that is, the ways in which the shaping of bodily and representational aspects of self through experience is in turn influenced by capacities, including culturally entrained patterns of physiological response, and motivations that particular people bring with them to their roles and experiences. In theoretical terms, I have proposed that we understand the circularity of these influences as a kind of looping process. Borrowing from Ian Hacking, I developed the concept of "biolooping," intended to capture both the mutually reinforcing interactions and effects of embodied and discursive forms of learning, and the feed-forward loops through which the qualities of culturally entrained bodies constrain and potentiate the embodiment of new forms of experiential knowledge.

I have shown that within Candomblé, suffering is what often brings people to mediumship. Such suffering is a form of embodied learning that creates patterns of cognitive and bodily response. Especially when it comes to disrupt taken-for-granted ways of being in the world, this embodied learning has the potential to threaten or disrupt peoples' selves. But I proposed that such embodied learning can also serve as a source of motivation and capacity for the role of spirit possession medium. The interactions of experience, motivation, and capacity are well demonstrated by the stories of Lucia and Pedro, each of whom experienced histories of negative experience and suffering prior to initiation. But the healing transformations they experienced through their religious formation were also *enabled* by their prior experiences of suffering. In other words, I demonstrated how the patterns of cognitive and bodily response, including patterns of autonomic function, that people bring to their role contribute to their capacity to experience the embodied learning associated with the meanings and practices of mediumship.

The biolooping model is thus an attempt to capture how this kind of bidirectional influence between mind and body within each individual intersects with the loops of influence that connect particular individuals to their sociocultural contexts. Hence, this concept can help us to think about enduring anthropological questions relating to the ways in which individuals differentially engage with, utilize, internalize, embody, contest, and transform the symbolic and material substance of their social and cultural worlds (Obeyesekere 1981; Stromberg 1985). Moreover, by providing a model for the way that effects on our bodies shape how we experience our selves, and conversely, effects on our self-understandings shape our bodies and bodily processes, this concept draws our attention to the position of the self as the locus of interaction between mind and body, individual and context.

The biolooping concept can also help us, therefore, to understand how phenomena like illness, physical training, weight gain and loss, which reshape or transform the body, simultaneously act to transform the way self is represented inwardly and outwardly. A wealth of medical anthropology has documented, for instance, how disease can result in "biographical disruption," meaning that the suffering and disability that result from becoming ill can threaten deeply held self-understandings and undermine expectations and goals (Becker 1997; Hunt 2000). Being diagnosed with diabetes, for instance, in addition to all of the ways in which it limits people behaviorally, can also, because of its association with morally loaded risk factors like engagement in a "deleterious lifestyle" (i.e., overeating and lack of exercise), undermine an individual's understanding of him/ herself as a virtuous person (Seligman 2014). What is more, disease forces the body into awareness, and when the body is no longer the taken-for-granted medium of experience, it can become a disconcerting obstacle to be overcome. Ellis-Hill and colleagues (2000) have demonstrated, for example, how the need to focus attention on basic physical acts, like walking, undermines the sense of self-coherence in stroke patients.

The concept of biolooping can similarly help us to understand how changes in self-understanding, like those that might accompany the experience of social discrimination or being diagnosed with a mental illness, can transform not only the way the body is experienced, but the way it functions—influencing physiological state and phenomenology at once. Adopting or being assigned a new social identity may also cause a shift in self-understanding with bodily consequences. After reading one of my articles about Candomblé mediums, an undergraduate student in one of my classes wrote a paper comparing "coming out" as gay to becoming a medium, convincing me that this could be an instructive example for exploring the process of biolooping. While sexual identities are increasingly understood to be diverse, complex, and fluid (Savin-Williams 2011), my student noted that for some individuals in the United States, the process of "coming out" means embracing a new self-representation that taps into an existing cultural model—in much the same way that mediums tap into the cultural model for mediumship. This process often involves reinterpretation of past experiences and characteristics in new terms involving the once hidden but newly embraced sexual identity, in a way that resembles mediums' rescripting of self-narratives around the notion of spiritual calling. Previous distress, for example, may come to be understood as the cost of suppressing one's "true" or essential sexuality (Atkins 1998; Epstein 1992).[1]

The resulting transformation of self may for some also entail bodily and behavioral transformations, like the adoption of different kinds of dress and physical mannerisms that match the new self-understanding, or even changes in the bodily consequences of desire (Atkins 1998; Morris 1995). We might speculate, for instance, that being attracted to members of the same sex could precipitate a physiological stress response when it conflicts with self-understanding or generates stigma, but a biolooping process might dampen such responses if attraction comes to take on a more positive meaning, and becomes part of a new self-understanding in the context of a supportive community. Arousal itself may also be subject to biolooping effects. For instance, coming out as gay could make one attend more to feelings of attraction to members of the same sex, as the identity, performance, and bodily aspects of being openly gay come to reinforce one another in the context of a queer community (Rivera-Severa 2012). In this way self-understandings can shape and reinforce bodily experience and function, and vice versa.

In addition, the biolooping concept can help us to think about the developmental trajectory of embodied selves; that is, the way that particular embodied selves, shaped through experience, may in turn be predisposed to particular kinds of experience. Histories of embodied learning may make some people particularly vulnerable to certain kinds of mental and physical illnesses, for example. The idea of biolooping may thus illuminate enduring questions in psychology and anthropology about why, all other things being more or less equal, some people are more vulnerable to depression, alcoholism, or post-traumatic stress disorder (PTSD). Moreover, since biolooping is fundamentally based on a notion of biological plasticity, bringing this concept to bear on such questions helps us resist more reductionist approaches that would answer such questions in terms of genetics.

The ideas captured by biolooping may even be applicable to questions in the health sciences about why certain kinds of mental and physical comorbidities exist. The concept could help explain, for instance, why there is a twofold higher chance of being depressed if one suffers from diabetes, and vice versa (Anderson et al. 2001; De Groot et al. 2006). Loops between illness identities, behaviors, and physiological processes associated with each of these illnesses may prime individuals for the other. Depressed individuals, for example, may have negative self-understandings and feelings of worthlessness and hopelessness that cause them to neglect self-care, or engage in negative health behaviors that make them vulnerable to diabetes (Lloyd et al. 2010). Feelings of lethargy, sleeplessness, sleepiness, and pain that accompany depression may reinforce lack of activity and motivation. These bodily symptoms of depression are also instantiated in altered neurochemistry, which in repeated episodes of major depression is itself a product of a form of bodily entrainment referred to as "kindling." In each depressive episode the kinds of neurochemical responses associated with depression become increasingly easy to produce, with less and less environmental provocation, as certain pathways in the brain become established. There is evidence that these neurochemical changes may also affect metabolism (Ismail 2010; Kendler et al. 2000; Monroe and Harkness 2005). Patterns of behavioral and physiological response associated with depression thus prime individuals for diabetes through multiple channels, so that in effect, one form of embodiment potentiates another.

Just as biolooping can help us think about differences in individual vulnerability to certain kinds of mental and physical illness, it can also help us understand why some people may, through their histories of embodied learning, be particularly responsive to certain kinds of therapeutic practices—like yoga, acupuncture, and mindfulness based meditation. The developmental looping of embodiment is also relevant to understanding religious participation other than Candomblé. Such developmental trajectories may make some people particularly amenable to the rhetorical and practice-based persuasions of contemporary forms of Evangelical Christianity, for example. Tanya Luhrmann (2012) has shown, for instance, that some individuals have a proclivity for absorption that allows them to have the kind of sensory experiences of God embraced by their religious traditions. Engagement in such prayer practices may simply reinforce innate tendencies, but Luhrmann's research suggests that absorption is also amenable to training. The capacity for absorption that some individuals bring with them to these religious practices may therefore be the result of prior forms of embodied learning—experiences earlier in life that have shaped or reinforced the need or desire to become deeply absorbed. Experiences like the avoidance of unpleasant situations, for example (Seligman and Kirmayer 2008), or positive experiences in imaginative play and engagement with media (Stromberg 2009).

Moreover, such capacity may also be potentiated by particular bodily qualities that people bring with them to these situations—for example, as I discussed in earlier chapters, the capacity for high levels of autonomic self-regulation is associated with the ability to narrowly focus attention, and may thus contribute to absorption (Hansen et al. 2003; Zachariae et al. 2000). Such physiological capacities may in turn be further reinforced and entrained by engagement in absorptive practices. Thus, biolooping of embodied knowledge may feed back to potentiate subsequent forms of embodied learning in a variety of contexts.

There are many other examples that clearly illustrate the way that the two levels of biolooping—the loops of interaction between the mind and body, and between the individual and his/her sociocultural context—intersect. How bidirectional influences of discursive and embodied learning create specific capacities, vulnerabilities, and motivations that selves bring with them to subsequent social and cultural experience is nicely illustrated by the case of addiction, for one. It is well documented that exposure to certain kinds of experiences (especially family dysfunction and modeling of addictive behavior, but also things like lack of success, negative or traumatic life events) make some individuals especially vulnerable to addiction (Kilpatrick et al. 2000). We can understand this in terms of the way that such experiences shape self-understandings and moral personhood, and contribute to particular bodily ways of being that help make these selves particularly prone to drug and alcohol dependence. Such dependence in turn shapes self-understandings (Quintero and Nichter 1996) and entrains bodily systems (Hyman et al. 2006) in ways that are mutually reinforcing—the physical desire for the drug shapes a self that is oriented more and more toward the need for the drug and the drug as a goal (Lende 2005). This in turn further reinforces drug use and physiological dependence, which feed forward to strengthen the goals, desires, and expectations contained within self-understandings.

These examples are meant to demonstrate that the concept of biolooping has potential application to a variety of problems and questions of interest not only within anthropology, but within the social sciences more broadly. The utility of this concept lies especially in its ability to help scholars think in nonreductive and nonessentializing ways about the relationships among social, psychological, and embodied processes. This concept was born out of a nontraditional, integrative research project, and its application to other research problems may also require the use of multimethod, transdisciplinary approaches. Particularly for anthropologists interested in questions related to embodied learning, mind–body interaction, and embodied selfhood, such approaches hold great potential to advance our understanding. It is my hope that the model provided by my research on Candomblé spirit possession mediumship can serve as a guide to others interested in pursuing their own forms of integrative research.

Appendix: Methods

Study Design

In order to investigate the social and emotional contexts occupied by mediums and the phenomenology of mediumship, this study used traditional ethnographic methods of participant observation and both formal and informal interviewing. In addition, to test the hypothesis that mediums differ in systematic ways from others in terms of their psychological and psychophysiological characteristics, this study used a cross-sectional, comparative design to compare mediums to other Candomblé participants and comparable individuals outside of the Candomblé community. This comparative design is essentially a "natural" experiment, following the logic of John Stuart Mill's (1856) classic "method of differences."

Participants and Sampling

Five groups were used in the cross-sectional study design. Comparison groups were based on natural groups within the religion itself, with the addition of two control groups. The religious comparison groups were created around the different levels of participation in the religion: those who are initiated and who become possessed formed the "mediums" group; the ogãs and ekédis, who are initiated but cannot become possessed formed the "nonmedium initiates" group; and uninitiated, lay religious participants made up the "frequenters" group.

Religious participants were obtained through convenience sampling. Participant observation at two main terreiros allowed access to two different religious populations from which all religious participants were drawn. All individuals from these populations who were interested in participating in the study were recruited. Since it is well known that Candomblé mediums are disproportionately female, the group of mediums recruited reflect this gender bias: two men and nine women were recruited for participation. Also, as the other religious groups do not, in general, have such a disproportionate participation by one sex or the other, equal numbers of males and females were selected for participation from these groups.

The participants in control group one were selected to match the religious frequenters in terms of socioeconomic status (SES) in an effort to control for the effects of SES. As the study progressed it became apparent that SES needed to be considered as an independent variable, and a high-SES control group was added. Control individuals were drawn from a convenience sample, and were recruited to the first control group if their SES matched that of the religious frequenters (overwhelmingly from the lowest SES strata). SES was determined by occupation and level of education. In both groups, 80 percent of participants were unskilled laborers. Control participants in the SES-matched group were also drawn from the same age range as the religious frequenters (over 18 and under 65), and the sample was deliberately divided equally across sexes. Control participants in the group not matched for SES were selected from a higher income group, but were also drawn from the same age range and divided equally by sex.

Basic demographic data were gathered from individuals in both control groups, in addition to a very short interview regarding their views on Candomblé, and application of all of the psychological inventories. Religious frequenters participated in semistructured interviews and psychological inventories, but not psychophysiological measurement. Individuals in the medium and nonmedium initiates group were given the full "case study" protocol, consisting of detailed semistructured interviews, psychological inventories, and psychophysiological measurement. In addition, a subgroup of mediums was asked to take part in life history interviews.

Research Instruments

Data from preliminary participant observation were used for the development, in Portuguese, of a series of semistructured interviews for use with the three religious comparison groups, and the translation and back-translation of several standardized psychological inventories. Formal interviews using these instruments were accompanied by continued participant observation, including informal conversations and interviews with Candomblé participants.

Semistructured Interviews

The semistructured interviews were designed to collect a range of information, from background and demographic data, to information about the individual's social support and religious experience. The interviews used open-ended questions designed to allow the interviewee the freedom to answer with as much or as little detail as they wished. Follow-up probes were used to prompt additional information. Data from these interviews were recorded in several manners: the interviews were tape-recorded and fully transcribed, and in addition, a paper record of each interview was kept. The semistructured interviews were first piloted with several individuals to make sure that all of the questions made linguistic and cultural sense, before being used for data collection. Some of the questions in these interviews ended up being relatively useless (i.e., questions about locus of control), while others proved surprisingly important (i.e., have you ever visited a mental health professional?).

Life History Interviews

Toward the end of the research, a subgroup of mediums was asked to participate in life history interviews. A total of six individuals were interviewed, and interviews were both audio- and videotaped with the permission of the participants. Open-ended questions were used, to the extent necessary, to keep participants on track. The interviews were designed to elicit a kind of "spiritual life history" of each medium. Interviews lasted from one and a half to three hours.

Psychological Inventories

The psychological inventories I used were selected on the basis of content, psychometric properties, and the potential for comparison. Two of the instruments, the State Trait Anxiety Inventory (STAI) and the Dissociative Experiences Scale (DES), are standardized instruments that have been used widely in Euro-American research, but neither had been previously validated for use in the Brazilian context. Both instruments were carefully translated and back-translated, and the translation evaluated for linguistic and cultural accuracy by local experts. However, the adapted versions were not extensively piloted, nor were their validity and reliability formally established. The third inventory selected for the research, the *Questionário de Morbidade Psiquiátrica do Adulto* (adult psychiatric morbidity questionnaire or

QMPA), is a Brazilian instrument used widely within Brazil for studies of psychiatric epidemiology (Almeida-Filho et al. 1997; Santana 1982). This instrument was selected because of its status as a locally validated instrument.

Impedance Cardiography

The impedance cardiography method was selected because, combined with ECG data, it allows derivation of two separate measures of heart rate function that together create a picture of autonomic balance, or the relative dominance of the parasympathetic versus the sympathetic nervous system. Impedance cardiography works by measuring electrical impedance in the thoracic region of the body (between the neck and the diaphragm), in response to low-energy, high-frequency alternating current. Changes in the impedance of the thorax in response to applied electrical current result from mechanical events in the cardiac cycle (Papillo and Shapiro 1990). In other words, electrodes applied to the participant's chest create an electrical circuit, and by sending extremely low voltage electricity through this circuit the machine is able to detect differences in the opposition encountered, which are associated with changes in parameters such as blood volume and contractility occurring as the heart pumps. Impedance can be used in conjunction with electrocardiogram (ECG) to derive a number of indices of cardiac function, including stroke volume, cardiac output, myocardial contractility, and systolic time intervals (ibid.).

The gold standard (at the time) in instrumentation for impedance cardiography, the Minnesota Instruments Impedance Cardiograph model HIC 2000, was used for this research. The HIC 2000 system uses four wire leads with alligator clips that attach to electrodes on the research participant's body. I chose to use band electrodes because this was the type of electrode most commonly used for impedance cardiography. Band electrodes consist of rolls of disposable adhesive tape that contain a strip of aluminum-coated mylar in the center that acts as the electrode. Two bands were placed around the skin of the neck, and two around the chest of each participant. The outer two bands (referred to as "current electrodes") are designed to send alternating current through the thoracic region, while the inner bands (the "voltage electrodes"), positioned inside the current path, record the resulting changes in impedance (Sherwood et al. 1990). To maximize recording, the lower band was placed at the base of the neck, with the upper band three centimeters above, while the bands on the chest were positioned so that the upper band covered the xyphis-ternal junction, with the lower band three centimeters beneath. The alligator clips were then attached to the ends of the band electrodes, and recording begun.[1]

Impedance recordings generate both the raw impedance sig-nal (delta-Z) as well as the first derivative of the impedance signal, known as dZ/dt. An ECG signal may also be derived from the raw impedance signal. Together, the dZ/dt and ECG waves can be used to derive measures of both sympathetic nervous system control over cardiac activity as well as parasympathetic activation. Specifically, the two waves allow the calculation of pre-ejection period (PEP) and respiratory sinus arrhythmia (RSA). PEP refers to the time between the onset of left ventricular depolarization and the opening of the semilunar valves. PEP is the result of variations in the conduction time from the atria to the ventricles, and research has shown that control of the conductivity of this area of the myocardium is car-ried out primarily through sympathetic innervation (Berntson et al. 1997; Papillo and Shapiro 1990). Thus, PEP is considered a relatively sensitive index of sympathetic nervous system control over the heart. RSA, otherwise known as high frequency heart rate variability (HF HRV), refers to regular variation in heart rate resulting from respira-tion (acceleration on the inhale, deceleration on the exhale), which is dependent primarily on parasympathetic innervation of the heart via the vagus nerve. Thus, RSA represents an important noninvasive marker of PNS control over the heart.

Custom software (Mindware, Gahanna, Ohio, United States) was used to edit and summarize the impedance and ECG data. Mindware uses ensemble averaging of the ECG and impedance waveforms for each minute of data to produce and estimate PEP for each partici-pant. PEP was calculated by measuring the interval (in milliseconds) between the onset of the Q-wave of the ECG signal, and the B-point, or the point preceding the greatest change in slope, of the dZ/dt waveform. Minute by minute means were then averaged over the three-minute baseline period at the beginning of the recording, and two–three additional baseline minutes at the end of the session, for each participant.

RSA was calculated using spectral analysis on the ECG signal derived from the impedance recordings. Spectral analysis refers to the statistical method by which the variance associated with RSA is partitioned from the total heart rate variance (Berntson et al. 1997). Heart rate variability is separated into its component frequencies and the spectral densities for just the frequencies associated with normal respiration (between .12 and .40 Hz) are summed. The sum of these spectral densities represents a measure of high frequency heart rate variability, which reflects the degree of PNS control of the heart. I used a well-validated procedure created by Berntson et al. to perform the analyses (Fast Fourier transform, Mindware, Gahanna, Ohio, United States; Berntson et al. 1997).

Data Analysis

Traditional anthropological methods were used for coding and analyzing ethnographic data (field notes and formal and informal interviews). In particular, I employed a grounded theory approach, meaning that I created codes gradually through a careful reading and rereading of these texts in search of emergent themes. For example, as I studied the spiritual life history narratives of mediums, the theme of transformation and a particular set of conceptual categories and properties associated with it emerged as central to the experiences and representations of mediumship. Several of the semistructured interview questions were quantified and used to generate descriptive statistics for comparison across groups. The questions about motivation for participating in Candomblé and about past experience with mental health care revealed significant differences between groups (i.e., 63 percent of filhos were motivated to participate in Candomblé by illness, versus 10 percent of nonmedium initiates and 5 percent of frequenters).

Data from the three psychological inventories were entered into SPSS (Statistical Package for the Social Sciences) for data analysis. I conducted statistical analyses (primarily ANOVA) comparing the results from the psychological questionnaires across all of the groups. Analyses of the standardized inventory on anxiety (the STAI) did not reveal particularly compelling results across groups (although the majority of low SES participants did have higher trait anxiety scores than those found in a normative US sample). Similarly, while all religious participants together had higher scores on the dissociative disorders screening questionnaire (DES) than nonreligious participants, mediums' scores were not higher than those of other religious participants, except on a question related to memory and absorption. The question was: "Have you ever remembered an experience so vividly that you felt you were reliving it at that moment?" Filhos' mean for this item was 43.64 (*SD* 39.3), compared to 23.67 (*SD* 26.5) for all other groups, significant at the p < .1 level.

The only psychological instrument to reveal more robust results was the Brazilian screening instrument for anxiety and depression, the QMPA. This instrument showed significant differences between low and high SES study participants (M 11.6 compared to 4.6 p < .05). In addition, this instrument revealed differences between mediums and other comparison groups in terms of numbers of somatic symptoms, although these differences are no longer significant if the high SES group is removed from the analysis. I defined as "somatic" any symptom or set of symptoms on the QMPA involving a form of bodily distress. Results from ANOVA show a significant difference when the mean number of somatic symptoms for filhos, 4.0 (SD 1.5), is compared to the combined mean for all other comparison groups, 2.7 (SD 2.3), p < .05. However, when the high SES group (mean .8, SD 1.14) is removed from the analysis, the between groups difference is no longer significant, though mediums still show somewhat higher numbers of somatic symptoms: filhos 4.0 (SD 1.48), ogãs 3.7 (SD 2.11), *frequentadors* 3.2 (SD 2.46), SES-matched controls, 2.75 (SD 2.27). Analyses also showed a significant difference between the mean number of somatic symptoms for all religious participants (M 3.54) compared to the mean for the two control groups (M 2.1 p < .01). These results are discussed briefly in chapters 1 and 4.

In analyzing the psychophysiology data, I conducted numerous analyses including comparison of mediums and nonmedium initiates in terms of their cardiovascular responses to the interview, and to a particularly "stressful" question within the interview ("Can you tell me about the worst thing that has happened in your life?"). I did not find significant differences between the groups in terms of the autonomic origins of cardiac function for either of these analyses. Following a recent innovation in psychophysiology (Berntson et al. 2008b), however, I also conducted an analysis examining something called "Cardiac Autonomic Regulation" (CAR), for which I did find more compelling differences between groups. CAR, which is the sum of both SNS and PNS influence over cardiac function, is considered an index of an individual's total autonomic regulatory capacity, or the capacity of their ANS to respond dynamically to challenges and stimuli (Berntson et al. 2008a and b).

Parasympathetic (RSA) and sympathetic measures (PEP) from baseline recordings taken both before and after the interview were aggregated and following Berntson et al. (2008a and b), the data were normalized. Normalization was necessary because of the large differences in means between RSA and PEP. Normalization entailed transforming values to z scores so that the values are expressed as standard deviations relative to the population means. Because PEP values have an inverse relationship to sympathetic control (i.e., lower PEP equals higher sympathetic activation) absolute PEP values were used in order to facilitate use in conjunction with RSA values (which do not have an inverse relationship with parasympathetic control). Normalized and inverted values for PEP were then summed with RSA to create a CAR score for each participant (Berntson et al. 2008b). CAR scores were then compared by group membership using ANOVA, and results indicated a trend in the differences between mediums and nonmedium initiates: baseline CAR scores of mediums were a half a standard deviation higher than those of nonmedium initiates. However, these findings were not technically significant (i.e., the analyses did not have $p < .05$).

In a later set of analyses, I used a nonparametric statistical test to compare results by group membership because such tests are well suited to small samples with unequal variances. Median CAR scores were compared across medium and nonmedium initiates using the K-Sample equality of medians test. The median CAR value for mediums (.52) was substantially higher than that of nonmedium initiates (-.47) ($p = .074$). Moreover, when split at the median, 70 percent of mediums had CAR scores above the median, and 70 percent of the nonmedium initiates had CAR scores below the median.

Notes

1 Introduction: Stepping into the "Supernatural World" of Candomblé

1. I met with a female Candomblé leader, known as a *mae de santo* or "mother of saint," whom I would later get to know very well.
2. I later learned that Iansã is also associated with some less desirable traits, such as a tendency to make trouble and fly off the handle.
3. See Seligman and Kirmayer (2008) for a comprehensive discussion of the issue of dissociation in spirit possession.
4. In fact, critics have pointed out that preoccupation with the material dimensions of this process (i.e., the "placebo" itself is credited with causing the effect) exemplifies the failure to appreciate the effects of *meaning* (Moerman and Jonas 2002).
5. There is a well-known stereotype that male Candomblé mediums are gay. This is certainly not always true, though in the case of the male mediums with whom I worked closely, it happened to be the case.
6. Some social theorist have argued that the idea of self as an internal seat of experience and personhood is an illusion perpetuated by power to convince us that we are the authors of our own motivations and desires. While I accept the idea that the content of motivation and desire is deeply social and cultural, and as such is heavily influenced by power, this should not be used as an excuse to dismiss as unimportant the fact that human self-awareness allows us to be both subjects and objects to ourselves. It allows us to reflect upon and evaluate our own experiences, and to develop an enduring sense of being, even if this sense is largely constructed.
7. The notion that our behaviors and experiences are influenced by implicit or procedural memories is further supported by evidence from a variety of sources demonstrating that deficits in the ability to form or access autobiographical memories do not necessarily affect the ability to access and form these other kinds of memories (cf. Kontos [2006] on embodied memory in Alzheimer's patients and Suzanne Corkin [2013] on the formation of procedural memory in an amnesic neurological patient).
8. The term "entrainment" is typically used to refer to the synchronization of patterns of behavior among members of the same species or social group (Kinsbourne 2005). Here I use it to refer to a kind of synchronization of patterns of physiological response with the demands of the sociocultural and physical environment.

9. This process is also beautifully described in a paper by Kathleen O'Connor (2013) on the "*ensaio*," or ritual practice of teaching new initiates to enter a trance state.

10. Attaching "bio" to terms (i.e., bio-power, bio-politics) has become a fashionable way of critiquing the power dynamics and politics inherent in the biomedical discourses and practices that are so pervasive in the contemporary world. With my use of "biolooping," which calls to mind these other "bio" terms, I do want to acknowledge that even as I attempt to bridge biological and cultural understandings of embodiment, I remain cognizant of the ways in which biological knowledge is conditioned by social and political dynamics. But I suggest that being critical of such bio-politics does not have to mean that we dismiss entirely the utility of understanding biological mechanisms, particularly in light of contemporary understandings of biological systems as plastic and responsive, rather than fixed and primary.

11. I have put many of the more technical details about research instruments, study design, and analysis into an appendix. This information is not relegated to the back of the book because I think these details are unimportant, but because they will not have the same importance to all readers. For many, such details will seem dry and uninteresting—the kind of information they have to skip through in order to get to the part they find really interesting. For others, these details will be key pieces of information upon which to evaluate the merits of my study, or to model their own research. Thus, for those in the latter group, I have made this information available while sparing the rest.

12. This is true throughout Candomblé.

13. Precise current numbers are very difficult to come by. A recent project of the Centro de Estudos Afro-Orientais of the Federal University of Bahia called the "Mapeamento dos terreiros de Salvador" has attempted to document the name, location, and "*naçao*" of each terreiro in the city. They estimate that there are currently 1,165 terreiros in Salvador. However, there are likely to be many terreiros that have still not been documented. Furthermore, as far as I know there is no existing documentation of the sizes of individual terreiros.

14. The ways in which these ideas are the result of the uptake of research by scholars of Candomblé, particularly anthropologists, is fascinating, but beyond the scope of this book. For a detailed discussion of these issues see Selka (2007); Capone (2010); Matory (2005).

15. Protection of such rituals from the gaze of the uninitiated also has to do with the need to safeguard ritual secrets, which are the source of initiated participants' spiritual and social power (Johnson 2002).

16. Uninitiated individuals may occasionally go into trance at public festas, but this is considered unsafe. Since the uninitiated individual is not experienced with or trained for possession, the trance may be violent and uncontrolled.

17. Spiritism is not African-derived. It grew out of the writings of Allan Kardec and first developed in the United States.
18. See Rapoza (2012).
19. In particular, "Africanness" has become a central trope of the black movement, and participation in the Afro-Brazilian religions, especially Candomblé, has become equated with Africanness (Capone 2010) and antiracist sentiment (Selka 2007). The relative Africanness of particular Candomblé "nacoes" has consequently become a point of contention within the broader Candomblé community (ibid.). The two small terreiros through which I did most of my research identified themselves as "*Nagô*," the nação most closely associated with "pure" Yoruba tradition. Nagô is typically not associated with the hybrid practices of caboclo worship or Catholic syncretism, yet the two terreiros in which I conducted my research included both forms of worship in spite of their identification with this nação, suggesting at the very least some variability within the "naçoes." It may also be that the notion of Yoruba purity was not something Mae Tiana and Pai João were aware of, or it may be that they claimed Nagô identity in order to align themselves with this valued notion of purity, in spite of their more hybrid practices. It is also important to note that, as Selka has established in his work on religion and ethnic identity in Bahia, there are many competing versions of Afro-Brazilian identity in contemporary Bahia, some of which are linked to religious traditions other than Candomblé.
20. It should also be noted that in recent years participation in the religion by non-Afro-Brazilians has increased substantially. Yet its political and social significance have thus far remained largely unchanged.
21. Spiritism tends to attract a more middle class demographic, but in recent years an economic "squeeze" on the middle class may be making it more difficult for these individuals to meet social expectations as well (cf. Dressler et al. [2005]).
22. While my argument revolves around the idea that such practices are often extremely beneficial for individuals, I think the question of whether, in the grand scheme of things, these kinds of cultural and spiritual interventions have ultimately been a source of liberation for Afro-Brazilians, or contributed to their continued oppression—in a Marxist "opiate of the masses" sense—probably deserves consideration. It is, however, beyond the scope of this book.

2   Reflections on the Challenges and Rewards of Integrative Research

1. There are undoubtedly others in the field currently engaged in research that could be labeled "biocultural ethnography," and my hope is that

this book will inspire more junior researchers to take on the challenges of such an approach.

2. This is a good argument for thoroughly piloting methods within the study population, which is not something I was able to do with the impedance method in Brazil, due to limited time and limits on the ability to recruit participants for this part of the study.

3. Other kinds of recruitment strategies, like those typically used in large survey studies (i.e., advertisement), were thus not well suited to soliciting participation within this religious community.

4. However, just how far to take participant observation in the context of a religion like Candomblé was also at issue. This is a religion in which many anthropologists have upped the ante considerably in the area of participation by becoming devotees and even full-blown initiates. Some of these anthropologists would undoubtedly argue that my role as a regular observer and occasional participant positioned me too far outside the religion to gain true insight, and may even have prevented me from accessing important religious information. But I doubted that such an intimate level of participation would have allowed me to maintain the special liminal position that I think is central to being both participant and observer, and which seemed especially important to straddling the dual role of scientific fieldworker and ethnographer.

5. In fact, ambulatory impedance cardiography units now exist (i.e., the Mindware Ambulatory Impedance Cardiograph MW1000A) suggesting that if I had waited several years some of the problems I encountered would have been solved by improvements in the technology.

6. In light of Tanya Luhrmann's (2012) fascinating findings on the relationship between absorption and prayer, I do wish I had tried using the Tellegen Absorption Scale (University of Minnesota Press 2011) among Candomblé mediums.

7. However, findings like those from Luhrmann's recent study on prayer practices suggest that it is entirely possible that people bring important differences in capacity—like the differences in absorptive capacity that she found. Such differences could include variability in ANS function, and might, because their interaction with religious practices is reinforcing, cause individuals like these to score higher on measures of "religiosity" and "spirituality." There is, therefore, a potent argument to be made for the other direction of causality as well.

3 Sometimes Affliction Is the Door: Healing and Transformation in Narratives of Mediumship

1. This concept is most often invoked in the contexts of illness and religion.

2. The kind of encompassing transformation I am referring to here is similar to what A. F. C. Wallace means when he talks about changes to, or revitalization of, a person's "mazeway" (Wallace 1955, 1956).

3. This understanding of conversion assumes an agent who is compelled to conversion by some combination of individual psychological need and divine intervention. But conversion can also be forced on an individual or group by other more powerful humans—as was the case with conversion to Christianity in Brazil and countless other colonial settings.

4. Typically terreiros that identify with the Nagô nação do not worship the lesser spirits, though the terreiros in which I worked claimed to be Nagô and still included worship of these spirits. This disparity is evidence not only that such categorizations are ideals that do not entirely reflect the reality of identification and practice on the ground, but also reflects the fact that there are potent political motivations for terreiros to identify as Nagô.

5. Successful human interaction with the orixás must take into account knowledge of such characteristics if the deity is to be kept happy. Therefore, interactions with Oxum typically involve offerings of perfume, flowers, or make-up, as well as praise of her beauty, grace, and benevolence through song and prayer.

6. I use the two terms more or less interchangeably from here forward in order to underscore their equivalence.

7. Interestingly, the dichotomy between mind and body is a perfect example of the kind of idea or belief I am talking about. While people influenced by normative Western culture may be able to articulate the idea that mind and body are separate (and to be fair, many would also say that they do not believe this to be the case), nevertheless, this belief is so pervasively present and influences so much of the way that our institutions (especially the medical ones) and even our language are structured that many people have a deeply intuitive sense that the mind is somehow distinct from the body.

8. Tanya Luhrmann's (2012) recent work with Evangelical Christians suggests that even within this brand of Christianity, where the notion of earning an intimate relationship with God through devotional practices is strongly held, there is also an awareness of individual differences in the capacity to "hear God."

4   Looking Inside: Biological Mechanisms and Embodiment in Candomblé Trance and Possession

1. This trembling makes the onset of trance look something like a mild seizure, which has led some to speculate about the relationship of trance states to epilepsy.

2. The group of mediums from whom I collected psychophysiology measurements overlapped with, but was not identical to, the group of filhos dancing in the roda at Pai João's festa for Oxum.

3. Biolooping is thus analogous to bio-feedback in the sense that both refer to the way in which changes at the cognitive level can affect physiological states.

4. Mediums had a mean of 4 somatic symptoms on a psychological inventory, compared to a mean of 3.3 for the other participants. This difference was significant at the $p = .05$ level when the control groups were included in the analysis, but not when the high SES control group was removed.

5. The notion that belief in possession is fundamentally implicated in the capacity to experience trance suggests that earlier theories distinguishing between trance as a biological state, and possession as a set of beliefs about trance (Bourguignon 1979), may have been misleading.

6. Ogãs and ekédis make an excellent comparison group because they are similar to mediums in their level of dedication to and responsibility within the religion. Like mediums, they go through an initiation process (though not as prolonged or intensive) and afterward are given access to secret ritual knowledge while taking on important ritual responsibilities. However, they differ fundamentally from mediums in that they do not become possessed or enter trance states.

5   Healing the Embodied Self in Candomblé

1. Other important work on this topic includes Csordas (1994); Hallowell (1954); Hollan (2000, 2004); and Lester (2005).

2. This idea resembles what Elias (1956) refers to as the way of "detachment" as opposed to "involvement."

3. This elderly Oxalá is just one of many variants of this deity found within the Nagô sect of Candomblé. However, my informants, despite considering themselves part of the Nagô nação, actually practiced a more syncretic form of Candomblé and did not identify multiple variants of each orixá.

4. It should also be noted that this process is unlikely to work for everyone. Those for whom it does not work are likely to drop out, and I was not able to recruit any such individuals into my study.

5. More detailed accounts of Lucia and Pedro's narratives are presented in chapter 3.

6. I never asked Lucia what her income was, but her living conditions were consistent with working class status.

7. Fainting by the uninitiated at Candomblé rituals is typically interpreted as *bolar no santo* or rolling to the saint, a sign that one needs to be initiated (Van de Port 2005).

8. Inclusion of this experience also serves the instrumental purpose of fitting Pedro's story to the conventions of mediumship narratives and legitimizing it as a narrative of affliction as discussed in chapter 3 (see also Seligman 2005b).

6   Conclusion: Stepping Back

1. It is also worth noting that this teleological American model of coming out, and coming out narratives, is not necessarily shared across social and cultural contexts (Blackwood 2010).

Appendix: Methods

1. I was trained in the application of the electrodes and use of the impedance cardiograph by a well-established researcher in the field of psychophysiology several months before leaving for the field, and along with a colleague, designed and executed a small pilot study using impedance methods with college undergraduates at our university.

Glossary of Candomblé Terms

Axé	The vital force that animates all things in the Candomblé cosmology. Present especially in sacred objects, the term can also be used to refer to the objects themselves as well as to the general spiritual power of the religion.
Barracão	The central space of a terreiro in which public events and rituals take place.
Bolação	A special state of trance that people fall into before being initiated. Typically involves falling to the floor in a fixed position during a public festa.
Caboclo	Indigenous South American spirit.
Consulta	A spiritual consultation with a Candomblé practitioner—either a mae or pai de santo, or with a medium possessed by a spirit.
Cuidar	Literally, to care for or look after. Used to refer to practices and behaviors necessary to maintain a good relationship with one's orixás.
Ekédi	Female initiate who acts as a ritual assistant within the terreiro. Ekédis do not go into trance and become possessed.
Erê	Spirit who is a child version of an orixá.
Exú	Lesser spirit who acts as a go between for the orixás and humans. A trickster character who is often petitioned for practical help.
Fazer o santo	Literally, to make the saint. Refers to act of being initiated into mediumship.
Feito	To be "made," or initiated into mediumship.
Festa	Public ritual held at a terreiro in honor of a particular orixá.
Filho/a de santo	Literally, son or daughter of saint. The term is used to refer to an initiated medium.
Iansã	Female warrior orixá associated with lightning and storms.
Iemanja	Female orixá associated with the sea.

Iaô	A junior initiate.
Juntó Orixá	The second-in-command of an individual's head.
Mae de Santo	Literally, mother of saint, a female spiritual leader within Candomblé.
Ogã	Male initiate who acts as a ritual assistant and dignitary of the terreiro, but who cannot go into trance or become possessed.
Ogum	Male warrior orixá associated with iron and fire.
Orixá	One of the pantheon of deities within the Candomblé religion.
Oxalá	Most senior male orixá often thought of as the father of the other gods. Associated with wisdom.
Oxum	Female orixá associated with sweet or fresh water.
Pai de Santo	Literally, father of saint, a male spiritual leader within Candomblé.
Pai/Mae Pequenã/o	Senior male or female initiate of the terreiro who acts as a second-in-command to the spiritual leader.
Roda	Circular dance for the orixás, which moves counterclockwise.
Saida	The ceremony in which a new initiate is first presented to the community.
Terreiro	Literally, sacred ground; refers to a Candomblé house or center both in terms of the physical space and the institution.
Xangô	Male warrior orixá associated with thunder and lightning.

References

Alkon, Abbey, Lauren H. Goldstein, Nancy Smider, Marilyn J. Essex, David J. Kupfer, and W. Thomas Boyce (2003) Developmental and contextual influences on autonomic reactivity in young children. *Developmental Psychobiology* 42: 64–78.

Almeida-Filho, Naomar, Carlos Caruso, Nubia Rodrigues, E. Corin, and Gilles Bibeau (1997) When healing is prevention: Afro-Brazilian religious practices related to mental disorders and associated stigma in Bahia, Brazil. *Curare Journal of Ethnomedicine* 12: 195–214.

Anderson Ryan J., Kenneth E. Freedland, Ray E. Clouse, and Patrick J. Lustman (2001) The prevalence of comorbid depression in adults with diabetes. *Diabetes Care* 24: 1069–1078.

Asad, Talal (1993) *Genealogies of Religion: Disciplines and Reasons of Power in Christianity and Islam.* Baltimore, MD: Johns Hopkins University Press.

Atkins, Dawn, ed. (1998) *Looking Queer: Body Image and Identity in Lesbian, Bisexual, Gay and Transgender Communities.* New York: Haworth Press.

Austin Broos, Diane (2003) The anthropology of conversion: An introduction. In *The Anthropology of Religious Conversion.* Andrew Bucksier and Stephen D. Glaser, eds. Pp. 1–12. New York: Rowan and Littlefield.

Baer, Werner (2002) *The Brazilian Economy.* New York: Praeger.

Bargh, John A., and Kimberly Barndollar (1996) Automaticity in action: The unconscious as repository of chronic goals and motives. In *The Psychology of Action: Linking Cognition and Motivation to Behavior.* P. M. Gollwitzer and John A. Bargh, eds. Pp. 457–481. New York: Guilford Press.

Barsalou, Lawrence, Aron K. Barbey, W. Kyle Simmons, and Ava Santos (2004) Embodiment in religious knowledge. *Journal of Cognition and Culture* 5: 14–49.

Bastide, Roger (2001) *O Candomblé da Bahia.* Sao Paulo, Brazil: Companhia das Letras.

Becker, Gaylene (1997) *Disrupted Lives: How People Create Meaning in a Chaotic World.* Berkeley: University of California Press.

Beets, Michael W., and Erin Mitchell (2010) Effects of yoga on stress, depression, and health-related quality of life in a nonclinical, bi-ethnic sample of adolescents: A pilot study. *Hispanic Health Care International* 8(1): 47–53.

Bernardi, Luciano, Peter Sleight, Gabriele Bandinelli, Simone Cencetti, Lamberto Fattorini, Johanna Wdowczyc-Szulc, and Alfonso Lagi (2001) Effect of rosary prayer and yoga mantras on autonomic cardiovascular rhythms: Comparative study. *British Medical Journal* 323: 1446–1449.

Berntson, Gary G., Greg J. Norman, Louise C. Hawkley, and John T. Cacioppo (2008a) Spirituality and autonomic cardiac control. *Annals of Behavioral Medicine* 35(2): 198–208.

—— (2008b) Cardiac autonomic balance versus cardiac regulatory capacity. *Psychophysiology* 45: 643–652.

Berntson, Gary G., J. Thomas Bigger, Dwain L. Eckberg, Paul Grossman, Peter G. Kaufmann, Marek Malik, Haikady N. Nagaraja, Stephen W. Porges, J. Philip Saul, Peter H. Stone, and Maurits W. van der Molen (1997) Heart rate variability: Origins, methods, and interpretive caveats. *Psychophysiology* 34: 623–648.

Berntson, Gary G., John T. Cacioppo, and Annette Fieldstone (1996) Illusions, arithmetic, and the bidirectional modulation of vagal control of the heart. *Biological Psychology* 44: 1–17.

Berntson, Gary G., Sarah T. Boysen and John T. Cacioppo (1992) Cardiac orienting and defensive responses: Potential origins in autonomic space. In *Attention and Information Processing in Infants and Adults*. Byron A. Campbell, Harlene Hayne, and Rick Richardson, eds. Pp. 163–200. Hillsdale, NJ: Erlbaum.

Biederman, Joseph, Jerrold F. Rosenbaum, Elizabeth A. Bolduc-Murphy, Stephen V. Faraone, Jonathan Chaloff, Dina R. Hirshfeld, and Jerome Kagan (1995) Behavioral inhibition as a temperamental risk factor for anxiety disorders. *Child and Adolescent Psychiatric Clinics of North America* 2: 667–683.

Biehl, Joao, Byron Good, and Arthur Kleinman, eds. (2007) *Subjectivity: Ethnographic Investigation*. Berkeley: University of California Press.

Blackwood, Evelyn (2010) *Falling into the Lesbi World: Desire and Difference in Indonesia*. Honolulu: University of Hawaii Press.

—— (2011) (Trans)gender: Tomboi embodiment. In *A Companion to the Anthropology of the Body and Embodiment*. Frances E. Mascia-Lees, ed. Pp. 207–222. West Sussex, UK: Blackwell Publishing, Ltd.

Boddy, Janice (1989) *Wombs and Alien Spirits: Women, Men, and the Zar Cult in Northern Sudan*. Madison: University of Wisconsin Press.

—— (1993) Subversive kinship: The role of spirit possession in negotiation social place in rural northern Sudan. *PoLAR: Political and Legal Anthropology Review* 16(2): 29–38.

—— (1994) Spirit possession revisited: Beyond instrumentality. *Annual Review of Anthropology* 23: 407–434.

Bourdieu, Pierre (1984) The habitus and the space of life-styles. In *Distinction: A Social Critique of the Judgements of Taste*. Pierre Bourdieu, ed. Pp. 169–225. Abingdon: Routledge Kegan & Paul.

—— (1990) Structures, habitus, practices. In *The Logic of Practice*. Pierre Bourdieu, ed. Pp. 52–65. Stanford, CA: Stanford University Press.

Bourguignon, Erika (1979) *Psychological Anthropology: An Introduction to Human Nature and Cultural Differences*. New York: Holt, Rinehart and Winston.

—— (1989) Multiple personality, possession trance, and the psychic unity of mankind. *Ethos* 17: 371–384.

Boyce, W. Thomas, Abbey Alkon, Jeanne M. Tschann, Margaret A. Chesney, and Bruce S. Alpert (1995) Dimensions of psychobiologic reactivity: Cardiovascular responses to laboratory stressors in preschool children. *Annals of Behavioral Medicine* 17: 315–323.

Boyce, W. Thomas, and Bruce J. Ellis (2005) Biological sensitivity to context: I. An evolutionary-developmental theory of the origins and functions of stress reactivity. *Development and Psychopathology* 17(2): 271–301.

Brown, Diana (1986) *Umbanda Religion and Politics in Brazil*. Ann Arbor: University of Michigan.

Bruner, Jerome S. (1987) Life as narrative. *Social Research* 54: 11–32.

———— (1994) The "remembered" self. In *The Remembering Self: Construction and Accuracy in the Self-Narrative*. Ulric Neisser and Robyn Fivush, eds. Pp. 41–54. Cambridge: Cambridge University Press.

Bury, Michael (1982) Chronic illness as biographical disruption. *Sociology of Health* 4(2): 167–182.

Butler, Kim D. (1998a) *Freedoms Given, Freedoms Won: Afro-Brazilians in Post-Abolition Sao Paulo and Salvador*. New Brunswick, NJ: Rutgers University Press.

———— (1998b) Ginga Bahiana: The politics of race, class, culture and power in Salvador, Bahia. In *Afro-Brazilian Culture and Politics*. Hendrik Kraay, ed. Armonk, NY: M.E. Sharpe.

Cacioppo, John T. (1994) Social neuroscience: Autonomic, neuroendocrine, and immune responses to brief psychological stress. *Psychophysiology* 31: 113–128.

Cacioppo, John T., Bert N. Uchino, William Malarkey, and Ronald Glaser (1995a) Individual differences in cardiac sympathetic control predict endocrine and immune responses to acute stress. *Journal of Personality and Social Psychology* 69(4): 736–743.

———— (1995b) Heterogeneity in neuroendocrine and immune responses to brief psychological stressors as a function of autonomic cardiac activation. *Psychosomatic Medicine* 57: 154–164.

———— (1998) Autonomic, neuroendocrine, and immune responses to acute psychological stress: The reactivity hypothesis. *Annals of the NY Academy of Sciences* 840: 664–673.

Cacioppo, John T., John M. Ernst, Mary H. Burleson, Martha K. McClintock, William B. Malarkey, Louise C. Hawkley, Ray B. Kowalski, Alisa Paulsen, J. Allan Hobson, Kenneth Hugdahl, David Spiegel, and Gary G. Berntson (2000) Lonely traits and concomitant physiological processes: The MacArthur social neuroscience studies. *International Journal of Psychobiology* 35(2): 143–145.

Cacioppo, John T., Louise C. Hawkley, Edith M. Rickett, and Christopher M. Masi (2005) Sociality, spirituality, and meaning-making: Chicago health, aging, and social relations study (CHASRS). *Review of General Psychology* 9: 143–155.

Cain, Carole (1991) Personal stories: Identity acquisition and self-understanding in alcoholics anonymous. *Ethos* 19: 210–253.

Canino, Glorisa, Roberto Lewis-Fernandez, and Milagros Bravo (1997) Methodological challenges in cross-cultural mental health research. *Transcultural Psychiatry* 34: 163–184.

Capone, Stefania (2010) *Searching for Africa in Brazil: Power and Tradition in Candomblé*. Durham, NC: Duke University Press.

Cardeña, Etzel (1992) Trance and possession as dissociative disorders. *Transcultural Psychiatric Research Review* 29(4): 287–300.

Challis, Gary B., and Henderikus J. Stam (1992) A longitudinal study of the development of anticipatory nausea and vomiting in cancer chemotherapy patients: The role of absorption and autonomic perception. *Health Psychology* 11(3): 181–189.

Coe, Christopher L., Gabriele R. Lubach, Mary L. Schneider, Donald J. Dierschke, and William B. Ershler (1992) Early rearing conditions alter immune responses in the developing infant primate. *Pediatrics* 90(3): 505–509.

Cohen, Sheldon, David A. J. Tyrrell, and Andrew P. Smith (1991) Psychological stress and susceptibility to the common cold. *New England Journal of Medicine* 325(9): 606–612.

Collins, Randall (2004) *Interaction Ritual Chains*. Princeton, NJ: Princeton University Press.

Comaroff, Jean, and John L. Comaroff, eds. (1993) *Modernity and Its Malcontents: Ritual and Power in Postcolonial Africa*. Chicago: University of Chicago Press.

Connerton, Paul (1995) *How Societies Remember*. Cambridge: Cambridge University Press.

Cooper, Marc, and Tim Frasca (2003) "Lula's Moment." *The Nation*, March 10, pp. 11–15.

Corder, Gregory W., and Dale I. Foreman (2009) Nonparametric statistics for non-statisticians: A step-by-step approach. Hoboken, NJ: John Wiley & Sons.

Corkin, Suzanne (2013) *Permanent Present Tense: The Unforgettable Life of the Amnesic Patient, H. M.* New York: Basic Books.

Cromby, John (2005) Theorizing embodied subjectivity. *International Journal of Critical Psychology* 15: 133–150.

Csordas, Thomas (1983) The rhetoric of transformation in ritual healing. *Culture, Medicine, and Psychiatry* 7(4): 333–375.

——— (1990) Embodiment as a paradigm for anthropology. *Ethos* 18: 5–47.

——— (1993) Somatic modes of attention. *Cultural Anthropology* 8(2): 135–156.

——— (1994) *The Sacred Self*. Berkeley: University of California Press.

——— (2002) *Body, Meaning, Healing*. New York: Palgrave MacMillan.

D'Andrade, Roy G. (1992) Schemas and motivation. In *Human Motives and Cultural Models*. Roy G. D'Andrade, Claudia Strauss, and Naomi Quinn, eds. Pp. 23–44. Cambridge, MA: Cambridge University Press.

De Castro, Eduardo Viveiros (2004) Exchanging perspectives: The transformation of objects into subjects in Amerindian ontologies. *Common Knowledge* 10(3): 463–484.

De Groot, Mary, Julie Wagner, Brenda Pinkerman, and Erin Hockman (2006) Depression treatment and satisfaction in a multicultural sample of type 1 and type 2 diabetic patients. *Diabetes Care* 29(3): 549–553.

de Haan, Michelle, Megan R. Gunnar, Kathryn Tout, Jordan Hart, and Kathy Stansbury (1998) Familiar and novel contexts yield different associations between cortisol and behavior among 2-yr-old children. *Developmental Psychobiology* 33: 93–101.

Dow, James (1986) Universal aspects of symbolic healing: A theoretical synthesis. *American Anthropologist* 88: 56–69.

Downey, Greg (2010) 'Practice without theory': A neuroanthropological perspective on embodied learning. *Journal of the Royal Anthropological Institute* S22–S40.

Dressler, William, Mauro C. Balieiro, and Jose Ernesto dos Santos (1998) Culture, socioeconomic status, and physical and mental health in Brazil. *Medical Anthropology Quarterly* 12(4): 424–446.

Dressler, William, Mauro C. Balieiro, Rosane P. Riberio, and Jose Ernesto dos Santos (2005) Cultural consonance and arterial blood pressure in urban Brazil. *Social Science and Medicine* 61(3): 527–540.

Dressler, William, and James R. Bindon (2000) The health consequences of cultural consonance: Cultural dimensions of lifestyle, social support, and arterial blood pressure in an African American community. *American Anthropologist* 102(2): 244–260.

Dumit, Joseph (2003) Is it me or my brain? Depression and neuroscientific facts. *Journal of Medical Humanities* 24(1/2): 35–47.

Dutton, Donald G., and Arthur P. Aron (1974) Some evidence for heightened sexual attraction under conditions of high anxiety. *Journal of Personality and Social Psychology* 30(4): 510.

Elias, Norbert (1939) *The Civilizing Process: Sociogenetic and Psychogenetic Investigations*, trans. Edmund Jephcott, Malden, MA: Blackwell Publishers.

——— (1956) Problems of involvement and detachment. *The British Journal of Sociology* 7(3): 226–252.

Ellis-Hill, Caroline S., Sheila Payne, and Christopher Ward (2000) Self-Body split: Issues of identity in physical recovery following a stroke. *Disability and Rehabilitation* 22(16): 725–733.

Epstein, Steven (1992) Gay politics, ethnic identity: The limits of social constructionism. In *Forms of Desire: Sexual Orientation and the Social Constructionist Controversy*. Edward Stein, ed. Pp. 239–293. New York: Routledge.

Evans-Pritchard, Edward Evan (1956) *Nuer Religion*. Oxford: Clarendon Press.

Ewart, Craig K., and Kenneth B. Kolodner (1991) Social competence interview for assessing physiological reactivity in adolescents. *Psychosomatic Medicine* 53: 289–304.

Ewing, Katherine P. (1990) The illusion of wholeness: Culture, self, and the experience of inconsistency. *Ethos* 18(3): 251–278.

Freeman, Chris (2011) Neoliberalism: Embodying and affecting neoliberalism. In *A Companion to the Anthropology of the Body and Embodiment*. Frances E. Mascia-Lees, ed. Pp. 353–369. West Sussex, UK: Blackwell Publishing, Ltd.

Gallagher, Kathleen Cranley (2002) Does child temperament moderate the influence of parenting on adjustment? *Developmental Review* 22(4): 623–643.

Gardner, Wendi L., Shira Gabriel, and Angela Y. Lee (1999) "I" value freedom, but "we" value relationships: Self-construal priming mirrors cultural differences in judgment. *Psychological Science* 10(4): 321–326.

Gergen, Kenneth (1991) *The Saturated Self: Dilemmas of Identity in Cotemporary Life*. New York: Basic Books.

Good, Byron (1994) Medical anthropology and the problem of belief. In *Medicine, Rationality and Experience*. Byron Good, ed. Pp. 1–24. Cambridge, MA: Cambridge University Press.

Goodman, Felicitas D. (1988) *Ecstasy, Ritual and Alternate Reality*. Bloomington: Indiana University Press.

Gravlee, Clarence C., William Dressler, and H. Russell Bernard (2005) Skin color, social classification, and blood pressure in southeastern Puerto Rico. *American Journal of Public Health* 95(12): 2191–2197.

Greenfield, Sidney M., and Russell Prust (1990) Popular religion, patronage, and resource distribution in Brazil: A model of a hypothesis for the survival of the economically marginal. In *Perspectives on the Informal Economy*. M. Estelle Smith, ed. Pp. 123–146. Lanham, MD: University Press of America.

Gregg, Jessica L. (2003) *Virtually Virgins: Sexual Strategies and Cervical Cancer in Recife, Brazil*. Stanford, CA: Stanford University Press.

Griffin, Michael, Patricia A. Resick, and Mindy B. Mechanic (1997) Objective assessment of peritraumatic dissociation: Psychophysiological indicators. *American Journal of Psychiatry* 154(8): 1081–1088.

Guarnaccia, Peter J., Melissa Rivera, Felipe Franco, and Charlie Neighbors (1996) The experiences of ataques de nervios: Towards an anthropology of emotions in Puerto Rico. *Culture, Medicine, and Psychiatry* 20(3): 343–367.

Gunnar, Megan R., Laurie Brodersen, Melissa Nachmias, Kristin Buss, and Joseph Rigatuso (1996) Stress reactivity and attachment security. *Developmental Psychobiology* 29: 191–204.

Hacking, Ian (1995) *Rewriting the Soul: Multiple Personality and the Science of Memory*. Princeton, NJ: Princeton University Press.

——— (1999) *The Social Construction of What?* Cambridge, MA: Harvard University Press.

Hallowell, Alfred Iriving (1955) The self and its behavioral environment. In *Culture and Experience*. Alfred Irving Hallowell, ed. Pp. 75–110. Philadelphia: University of Pennsylvania Press.

Halloy, Arnaud (2012) Gods in the flesh: Learning emotions in the Xangô possession cult (Brazil). *Ethnos* 77(2): 177–202.

Halloy, Arnaud, and Vlad Naumescu (2012) Learning spirit possession: An introduction. *Ethnos* 77(2): 155–176.

Hanchard, Michael (1999) *Racial Politics in Contemporary Brazil.* Durham, NC: Duke University Press.

Hansen, Anita Lill, Bjørn Helge Johnsen, and Julian F. Thayer (2003) Vagal influence on working memory and attention. *International Journal of Psychophysiology* 48(3): 263–274.

Harding, Rachel E. (2000) *A Refuge in Thunder: Candomblé and the Creation of Black Identity in Nineteenth-Century Bahia.* Bloomington: Indiana University Press.

Harding, Susan F. (1987) Convicted by the Holy Spirit: The rhetoric of fundamental Baptist conversion. *American Ethnologist* 14: 167–181.

Hawkley, Louise C., Mary H. Burleson, Gary G. Bernston, and John T. Cacioppo (2003) Loneliness in everyday life: Cardiovascular activity, psychosocial context, and health behaviors. *Journal of Personality and Social Psychology* 85: 105–120.

Hay, M. Cameron (2010) Suffering in a productive world: Chronic illness, visibility, and the space beyond agency. *American Ethnologist* 37(2): 259–274.

Heim, Christine D., Jeffrey Newport, Dieter Wagner, Molly M. Wilcox, Andrew H. Miller, and Charles B. Nemeroff (2002) The role of early adverse experience and adulthood stress in the prediction of neuroendocrine stress reactivity in women: A multiple regression analysis. *Depression and Anxiety* 15(3): 117–125.

Hinton, Devon E., David Howes, and Laurence J. Kirmayer (2008) Toward a medical anthropology of sensations: Definitions and research agenda. *Transcultural Psychiatry* 45(2): 142–162.

Hollan, Douglas (1992) Cross-cultural differences in the self. *Journal of Anthropological Research* 48(4): 283–300.

——— (2000) Constructivist models of mind, contemporary psychoanalysis, and the development of culture theory. *American Anthropologist* 102(3): 538–550.

——— (2004) Self systems, cultural idioms of distress, and the psychobodily consequences of childhood suffering. *Transcultural Psychiatry* 41: 62–79.

Holland, Dorothy, and Kevin Leander (2004) Ethnographic studies of positioning and subjectivity: An introduction. *Ethos* 3(2): 127–139.

Hunt, Linda (2000) Strategic suffering. In *Narrative and the Cultural Construction of Illness and Healing.* Cheryl Mattingly and Linda C. Garro, eds. Pp. 88–107. Berkeley: University of California Press.

Hyman, Steven E., Robert C. Malenka, and Eric J. Nestler (2006) Neural mechanisms of addiction: The role of reward-related learning and memory. *Annual Review of Neuroscience* 29: 565–598.

Ismail, Khalida (2010) Unraveling the pathogenesis of the depression diabetes link. In *Depression and Diabetes.* Wayne Katon, Mario Maj, and Norman Sartorius, eds. Pp. 29–62. Chichester, UK: John Wiley & Sons.

Ivry, Tsipy (2009) *Embodying Culture: Pregnancy in Japan and Israel.* New Brunswick, NJ: Rutgers University Press.

Jackson, Michael (1983) Knowledge of the body. *Man* 18: 327–345.

James, William (1884) What is an emotion? *Mind* 9: 188–205.

———— (1885) *The Varieties of Religious Experience.* Cambridge, MA: Harvard University Press.

Jenkins, Janis H., and Martha Valiente (1994) Bodily transactions of the passions: El calor among Salvadoran women refugees. In *Embodiment and Experience: The Existential Ground of Culture and Self.* Thomas J. Csordas, ed. Pp. 163–182. Cambridge: Cambridge University Press.

Johnson, Paul C. (2002) *Secrets, Gossip, and Gods.* Oxford: Oxford University Press.

Kagan, Jerome (1994) *Galen's Prophecy.* New York: Basic Books.

Kapferer, Bruce (1979) Mind, self, and other in demonic illness: The negotiation and reconstruction of self. *American Ethnologist* 6: 110–133.

Keller, Mary (2002) *The Hammer and the Flute.* Baltimore, MD: Johns Hopkins University Press.

Kendler, Kenneth S., Laura M. Thornton, and Charles O. Gardener (2000) Stressful life events and previous episodes in the etiology of major depression in women: An evaluation of the "kindling" hypothesis. *The American Journal of Psychiatry* 157(8): 1243–1251.

Kihlstrom, John F. (2005) Dissociative disorders. *Annual Review of Clinical Psychology* 1: 227–253.

Kilpatrick, Dean G., Ron Acierno, Benjamin Saunders, Heidi S. Resnick, Connie L. Best, and Paula P. Schnurr (2000) Risk factors for adolescent substance abuse and dependence: Data from a national sample. *Journal of Consulting and Clinical Psychology* 68: 19–30.

Kinsbourne, Marcel (2005) Imitation as entrainment: Brain mechanisms and social consequences. In *Perspectives on Imitation: From Neuroscience to Social Science 2.* Susan Hurley and Nick Chater, eds. Pp. 163–172. Cambridge, MA: MIT Press.

Kirmayer, Laurence J. (1994) Pacing the void: Social and cultural dimensions of dissociation. In *Dissociation: Culture, Mind, and Body.* David Spiegel, ed. Pp. 91–122. Washington: American Psychiatric Press.

———— (2000) Broken narratives: Clinical encounters and the poetics of illness experience. In *Narrative and the Cultural Construction of Illness and Healing.* Cheryl Mattingly and Linda C. Garro, eds. Pp. 153–180. Berkeley: University of California Press.

———— (2004) The cultural diversity of healing: Meaning, metaphor and mechanism. *British Medical Bulletin* 69: 33–48.

Kirmayer, Laurence J., and Allan Young (1998) Culture and somatization: Clinical, epidemiological, and ethnographic perspectives. *Psychosomatic Medicine* 60(4): 420–430.

Kirmayer, Laurence J., and Norman Sartorius (2007) Cultural models and somatic syndromes. *Psychosomatic Medicine* 69: 832–840.

Kontos, Pia C. (2006) Embodied selfhood: An ethnographic exploration of Alzheimer's disease. In *Thinking about Dementia: Culture, Loss, and the Anthropology of Senility.* Annette Leibing and Lawrence Cohen, eds. Pp. 195–217. New Brunswick: Rutgers University Press.

Konvalinka, Ivana, Dimitris Xygalatas, Joseph Bulbulia, Uffe Schjødt, Else-Marie Jegindø, Sebastian Wallot, Guy Van Orden, and Andreas Roepstorff (2011) Synchronized arousal between performers and related spectators in a fire-walking ritual. *PNAS* 108(20): 8514–8519.

Koopman, Cheryl, Victor Carrion, Lisa D. Butler, Shiv Sudhakar, Laura Palmer, and Hans Steiner (2004) Relationships of dissociation and childhood abuse and neglect with heart rate in delinquent adolescents. *Journal of Traumatic Stress* 17: 47–54.

Krantz, David S., and Jennifer J. Falconer (1995) Using cardiovascular measures in stress research: An introduction. In *Measuring Stress: A Guide for Health and Social Scientists.* Sheldon Cohen, Ronald C. Kessler, and Lynn Underwood Gordon, eds. Pp. 202–209. Oxford: Oxford University Press.

Kusserow, Adrie (2004) *American Individualisms: Child Rearing and Social Class in Three Neighborhoods.* New York: Palgrave Macmillan.

Kuzawa, Christopher, Pedro Hallal, Linda Adair, Santosh Bhargava, Caroline Fall, Nanette Lee, et al. (2012). Birth weight, postnatal weight gain, and adult body composition in five low and middle income countries. *American Journal of Human Biology*, 24(1): 5–13.

Lakoff, George (1993) The contemporary theory of metaphor. *Metaphor and Thought* 2: 202–251.

Lakoff, George, and Mark Johnson (1999) *Philosophy in the Flesh: The Embodied Mind and Its Challenge to Western Thought.* New York: Basic.

Lambek, Michael (1981) *Human Spirits: A Cultural Account of Trance in Mayotte.* Cambridge: Cambridge University Press.

—— (1989) From disease to discourse: Remarks on the conceptualization of trance and spirit possession. In *Altered States of Consciousness and Mental Health.* Colleen Ward, ed. Pp. 36–61. London: Sage Publications.

—— (1996) Afterword: Spirits and their histories. In *Spirits in Culture, History, and Mind.* Jeanette Marie Mageo and Alan Howard, eds. Pp. 237–250. London: Routledge.

Lende, Daniel H. (2005) Wanting and drug use: A biocultural approach to the analysis of addiction. *Ethos* 33: 100–124.

Lester, Rebecca J. (2005) *Jesus in Our Wombs: Embodying Modernity in a Mexican Convent.* Berkeley: University of California Press.

Leventhal, Howard, Ellen L. Idler, and Elaine A. Leventhal (1999) The impact of chronic illness on the self system. In *Self, Social Identity, and Physical Health.* Richard J. Contrada and Richard D. Ashmore, eds. Pp. 185–208. New York: Oxford University Press.

Levine, Robert M. (1999) How Brazil works. In *The Brazil Reader: History, Culture, Politics.* Robert M. Levine and John J. Crocitti, eds. Pp. 402–407. Raleigh, NC: Duke University Press.

Lévi-Strauss, Claude (1963) The effectiveness of symbols. *Structural Anthropology* 1: 186–205.

Lewis, Ioan Myrddin (1971) *Ecstatic Religion*. London: Routledge.

Lex, Barbara (1979) Neurobiology of ritual trance. In *The Spectrum of Ritual: A Biogenetic Structural Analysis*. Eugene G. d'Aquili, Charles D. Laughlin, and John McManus, eds. Pp. 117–151. New York: Columbia University Press.

Liang, Sai-Woon, John M. Jemerin, Jeanne M. Tschann, Diane W. Wara, and W. Thomas Boyce (1997) Life events, frontal electroencephalogram laterality, and functional immune status after acute psychological stressors in adolescents. *Psychosomatic Medicine* 59: 178–186.

Lin, Kuan-Yin, Yu-Ting Hu, K. J. Chang, H. F. Lin, and Jau-Yih Tsauo (2011) Effects of yoga on psychological health, quality of life, and physical health of patients with cancer: A meta-analysis. *Evidence-Based Complementary and Alternative Medicine*, Article ID 659876: 1–12. doi:10.1155/2011/659876.

Lloyd, Cathy E., Norbert Hermanns, Arie Nouwen, Frans Pouwer, Leigh Underwood, and Kirsty Winkley (2010) The epidemiology of depression and diabetes. In *Depression and Diabetes*. Wayne Katon, Mario M. Maj, and Norman Sartorius, eds. Pp. 1–27. Chichester, UK: John Wiley & Sons.

Lock, Margaret (1994) *Encounters with Aging: Mythologies of Menopause in Japan and North America*. Los Angeles, Berkeley: University of California Press.

Lovell, Peggy (1994) Race, gender, and development in Brazil. *Latin American Research Review* 29(3): 7–35.

——— (2000) Race, gender and regional labor market inequalities in Brazil. *Review of Social Economy* 58(3): 277–293.

Luhrmann, Tanya (2004) Metakinesis: How God becomes intimate in contemporary U.S. Christianity. *American Anthropologist* 106(3): 518–528.

——— (2012) *When God Talks Back: Understanding the American Evangelical Relationship with God*. New York: Vintage Books.

Luhrmann, Tanya, Howard Nusbaum, and Ronald Thisted (2010) The absorption hypothesis: Learning to hear God in Evangelical Christianity. *American Anthropologist* 112: 66–78.

Lutz, Antoine, Julie Brefczynski-Lewis, Tom Johnstone, and Richard J. Davidson (2008) Regulation of the neural circuitry of emotion by compassion meditation: Effects of meditative expertise. *PLoS ONE* 3(3)

Mageo, Jeannette Marie (1996) Continuity and shape shifting: Samoan spirits in culture history. In *Spirits in Culture, History, and Mind*. Jeanette Marie Mageo and Alan Howard, eds. Pp. 29–54. London: Routledge.

Mahmood, Saba (2001) Feminist theory, embodiment, and the docile agent: Some reflections on the Egyptian Islamic revival. *Cultural Anthropology* 16(2): 202–236.

Marmot, Michael (2005) Social determinants of health inequalities. *The Lancet* 365(9464): 1099–1104.

Mascia-Lees, Frances E. (2011a) Introduction. In *A Companion to the Anthropology of the Body and Embodiment*. Chichester: Wiley-Blackwell.

—— (2011b) Aesthetics: Aesthetic embodiment and commodity capitalism. In *A Companion to the Anthropology of the Body and Embodiment*. Frances E. Mascia-Lees, ed. Pp. 3–23. West Sussex, UK: Blackwell Publishing, Ltd.

Matory, J. Lorand (2005) *Black Atlantic Religion: Tradition, Transnationalism, and Matriarchy in Afro-Brazilian Candomblé*. Princeton, NJ: Princeton University Press.

Mauss, Marcel (1934) The technology of the body. In *Incorporations*. Jonathan Crary and Sanford Kwinter, eds. Pp. 455–477. New York: Zone.

McAdams, Dan P. (1989) The development of narrative identity. In *Personality Psychology: Recent Trends and Emerging Directions*. David M. Buss and Nancy Cantor, eds. Pp. 160–174. New York: Springer-Verlag.

—— (1993) *The Stories We Live By: Personal Myths and the Making of the Self*. New York: Guilford Press.

McDade, Thomas W. (2002) Status incongruity in Samoan youth: A biocultural analysis of culture change, stress, and immune function. *Medical Anthropology Quarterly* 16(2): 123–150.

—— (2003) Life history theory and the immune system: Steps toward a human ecological immunology. *American Journal of Physical Anthropology* 122: 100–125.

Meaney, M. (2000) Neonatal maternal nurturing reduces adult reactivity in a rat model. Annual Meeting of the American Psychosomatic Society, Savannah, Georgia.

Mill, John Stuart (1856) *A System of Logic, Ratiocinative and Inductive* (4th ed.). London: Parker.

Miller, P. (1994) Narrative practices: Their role in socialization and self-construction. In *The Remembered Self: Construction and Accuracy in the Self Narrative*. Ulric Neisser and Robyn Fivush, eds. Pp. 158–179. Cambridge: Cambridge University Press.

Miller, William R., and Carl E. Thoresen (2003) Spirituality, religion, and health. An emerging research field. *American Psychologist* 58: 24–35.

Moerman, Daniel E., and Wayne B. Jonas (2002) Deconstructing the placebo effect and finding the meaning response. *Annals of Internal Medicine* 136(6): 471–476.

Monroe, Scott M., and Kate L. Harkness (2005) Life stress, the "kindling" hypothesis, and the recurrence of depression: Considerations from a life stress perspective. *Psychological Review* 112(2): 417–445.

Morris, Rosalind C. (1995) All dressed up: Performance theory and the new anthropology of sex and gender. *Annual Review of Anthropology* 24: 567–592.

Muggah, Robert (2014) How to end Brazil's homicide epidemic. *Huffington Post*.

Mulligan, Neil W., and Miri Besken (2013) Implicit memory. In *The Oxford Handbook of Cognitive Psychology*. Daniel Reisberg, ed. Pp. 220–231. Oxford: Oxford University Press.

Nachmias, Melissa, Megan Gunnar, Sarah Mangelsdorf, Robin Hornik Parritz, and Kristin Buss (1996) Behavioral inhibition and stress reactivity: The moderating role of attachment security. *Child Development* 67(2): 508–522.

Nations, Marilyn K., and Cristina M. G. Monte (1996) "I'm not dog, no!" Cries of resistance against cholera control campaigns. *Social Science and Medicine* 43(6): 1007–1024.

Nehamas, Nicholas, and Jose Luiz Brufatto de Oliveira (2012) What the U.S. can learn from Brazil's epidemic of gun violence. *Latitude News*.

Nichter, Mark (1981) Idioms of distress: Alternatives in the expression of psychosocial distress: A case study from South India. *Culture, Medicine, and Psychiatry* 5(4): 379–408.

Norman, Greg J., John T. Cacioppo, John S. Morris, William B. Malarkey, Gary G. Bernston, and A. Courtney DeVries (2011) Oxytocin increases autonomic cardiac control: Moderation by loneliness. *Biological Psychology* 86: 174–180.

Nuckolls, Charles W. (1991) Deciding how to decide: Possession-mediumship in Jalari divination. *Medical Anthropology* 13(1–2): 57–82.

Obeyesekere, Gananath (1981) *Medusa's Hair*. Chicago, IL: University of Chicago Press.

——— (1990) *The Work of Culture*. Chicago, IL: University of Chicago Press.

Obradović, Jelena, Nicole R. Bush, Juliet Stamperdahl, Nancy E. Adler, and W. Thomas Boyce (2010) Biological sensitivity to context: The interactive effects of stress reactivity and family adversity on socioemotional behavior and school readiness. *Child Development* 81(1): 270–289.

Ochs, Elinor, and Lisa Capps (1996) Narrating the self. *Annual Review of Anthropology* 25: 19–43.

O'Connor, Kathleen (2013) Trance Training: The *Ensaio* in Candomblé Initiatic Ritual. Unpublished paper given at the 2014 Meeting of the American Anthropological Association. Chicago, IL.

Ong, Aiwa (1987) *Spirits of Resistance and Capitalist Discipline: Factory Women in Malaysia*. Albany: State University of New York Press.

——— (1988) The production of possession: Spirits and the multinational corporation in Malaysia. *American Ethnologist* 15(1): 28–42.

Ortner, Sherry B. (2005) Subjectivity and cultural critique. *Anthropological Theory* 5(1): 31–52.

Oyserman, Daphna, and Spike W. S. Lee (2008) Does culture influence what and how we think? Effects of priming individualism and collectivism. *Psychological Bulletin* 134(2): 311.

Papillo, J., and D. Shapiro (1990) The cardiovascular system. In *Principles of Psychobiology: Physical, Social and Inferential Elements*. J. T. Cacioppo and L. G. Tassinary, eds. Pp. 456–512. Cambridge: Cambridge University Press.

Penedo, Frank J., Lara Traeger, Jason Dahn, Ivan Molton, Jeffrey S. Gonzalez, Neil Schneiderman, and Michael H. Antoni (2007) Cognitive behavioral stress management intervention improves quality of life in Spanish monolingual Hispanic men treated for localized prostate cancer: Results of a randomized controlled trial. *International Journal of Behavioral Medicine* 14(3): 164–172.

Pett, Marjorie A. (1997) *Nonparametric Statistics in Health Care Research: Statistics for Small Samples and Unusual Distributions.* London: Sage Publications.

Porges, Stephen W. (1992) Vagal tone: A physiological marker of stress vulnerability. *Pediatrics* 90: 498–504.

Porges, Stephen W., Jane A. Doussard-Roosevelt, and Amitesh Maiti (1996) Vagal tone and the physiological regulation of emotion. In *Emotion Regulation: Behavioral and Biological Considerations. Monographs of the Society for Research in Child Development* 59(2–3): 167–186.

Prandi, Reginaldo (2001) *Mitologia Dos Orixás.* São Paulo, Brazil: Companhia Das Letras.

Prince, Raymond H. (1968) *Trance and Possession States.* Montreal: RM Bucke Memorial.

——— (1982) Shamanism and endorphins: Hypotheses for a synthesis. *Ethos* 10: 409–425.

Quinn, Naomi (2003) Cultural selves. *Annals of the New York Academy of Sciences* 1001: 145–176.

——— (2006) The self. *Anthropological Theory* 6(3): 362–384.

Quintero, Gilbert, and Mark Nichter (1996) The Semantics of addiction: Moving beyond expert models to lay understandings. *Journal of Psychoactive Drugs* 28(3): 219–228.

Rapoza, Kenneth (2012) *In Brazil: The Poor Get Richer Faster.* Forbes. www.forbes.com/sites/kenrapoza/2012/09/25/in-brazil-the-poor-get-richer-faster/.

Richards, Jane E. (1987) Infant visual attention and respiratory sinus arrhythmia. *Child Development* 58: 488–496.

Richardson, James T. (1985) The active vs. passive convert: Paradigm conflict in conversion/recruitment research. *Journal for the Scientific Study of Religion* 24(2): 163–179.

Ricoeur, Paul (1992) *Oneself as Another.* Chicago, IL: University of Chicago Press.

Rivera-Servera, Ramon (2012) *Performing Queer Latinidad: Dance, Sexuality, Politics.* Ann Arbor: University of Michigan Press.

Roediger, Henry L. (1990) Implicit memory: Retention without remembering. *American Psychologist* 45(9): 1043–1056.

Rose, Nicholas (1998) *Inventing Our Selves: Psychology, Power, and Personhood.* Cambridge, MA: Cambridge University Press.

Rothbart Mary K. (1989) Biological processes in temperament. In *Temperament in Childhood.* Gedolph A. Kohnstamm and Mary K. Rothbart, eds. Pp. 77–110. New York: John Wiley & Sons.

Rouget, Gilbert (1985) *Music and Trance: A Theory of the Relations between Music and Possession*. Chicago, IL: University of Chicago Press.

Roy, Mark P., Andrew Steptoe, and Clemens Kirschbaum (1998) Life events and social support as moderators of individual differences in cardiovascular and cortisol reactivity. *Journal of Personality and Social Psychology* 75(5): 1273–1281.

Sansone, Livio (2003) *Blackness without Ethnicity*. New York: Palgrave MacMillan.

Santana, Vilma Sousa (1982) Estudo epidemiologico as doencas mentais em um Bairro de Salvador. *Serie de Estudo em Saude* 3: 122.

Savin-Williams, Ritch (2011) Identity development among sexual minority youth. In *Handbook of Identity Theory and Research*, S. J. Schwartz et al., eds. Pp. 671–692. New York: Springer.

Scheper-Hughes, Nancy, and Margaret M. Lock (1987) The mindful body: A prolegomenon to future work in medical anthropology. *Medical Anthropology Quarterly* 1: 6–41.

Schieffelin, Edward L. (1985) Performance and the cultural construction of reality. *American Ethnologist* 12(4): 707–724.

Schulkin, Jay (2011) Social allostasis: Anticipatory regulation of the internal milieu. *Frontiers in Evolutionary Neuroscience* 2:1–15.

Schulkin Jay, Philip W. Gold, and Bruce S. McEwen (1998) Induction of corticotropin-releasing hormone gene expression by glucocorticoids: Implication for understanding the states of fear and anxiety and allostatic load. *Psychoneuroendocrinology* 23: 219–243.

Schwartz, Carl E., Nancy Snidman, and Jerome Kagan (1999) Adolescent social anxiety as an outcome of inhibited temperament in childhood. *Journal of the American Academy of Child & Adolescent Psychiatry* 38(8): 1008–1015.

Seligman, Rebecca (2005a) Distress, dissociation, and embodied experience: Reconsidering the pathways to mediumship and mental health. *Ethos* 33: 71–99.

——— (2005b) From affliction to affirmation. *Transcultural Psychiatry* 42(2): 272–294.

——— (2010) The unmaking and making of self: Embodied suffering and mind-body healing in Brazilian Candomble. *Ethos* 38(3): 297–320.

Seligman, Rebecca, Emily Mendenhall, Maria Valdovinos, Alicia Fernandez, and Elizabeth Jacobs (2014) Self care and subjectivity among Mexican diabetes patients in the U.S. *Medical Anthropology Quarterly*. DOI: 10.1111/maq.12107.

Seligman, Rebecca, and Ryan A. Brown (2010) Theory and method at the intersection of anthropology and cultural neuroscience. *Social Cognitive and Affective Neuroscience* 5(2–3): 130–137.

Seligman, Rebecca, and Laurence J. Kirmayer (2008) Dissociative experience and cultural neuroscience: Narrative, metaphor and mechanism. *Culture, Medicine, Psychiatry* 32: 31–64.

Selka, Stephen L. (2005) Ethnoreligious identity politics in Bahia, Brazil. *Latin American Perspectives* 32: 72–94.

——— (2007) *Religion and the Politics of Ethnic Identity in Bahia, Brazil.* Gainesville: University of Florida Press.

Sherwood, Andrew, Michael T. Allen, Jochen Fahrenberg, Robert M. Kelsey, William R. Lovallo, and Lorenz J. P. Van Doornen (1990) Methodological guidelines for impedance cardiography. *Psychophysiology* 27: 1–23.

Shore, Bradd (1996) *Culture in Mind.* Oxford: Oxford University Press.

Shutz, Alfred (1967) *The Phenomenology of the Social World.* Evanston, IL: Northwestern University Press.

Shweder, Richard A., and E. Bourne (1981) Does the concept of the person vary cross culturally? In *Cultural Conceptions of Mental Health and Therapy.* A. Marsella and G. White, eds. Pp. 158–199. Boston: Reidel.

Sierra, Mauricio, and German E. Berrios (1998) Depersonalization: Neurobiological perspectives. *Biological Psychiatry* 44: 898–908.

Simons, Ronald C., Frank R. Ervin, and Raymond H. Prince (1988) The psychobiology of trance I: Training for Thaipusam. *Transcultural Psychiatry* 25(4): 249–266.

Singh, A., and J. Petrides (1999) Differential hypothalamic-pituitary-adrenal axis reactivity to psychological and physical stress. *Journal of Clinical Endocrinological Metabolism* 84: 1944–1948.

Skidmore, Thomas (1999) *Brazil: Five Centuries of Change.* New York: Oxford University Press.

Snodgrass, Jeffrey G., Michael G. Lacy, H. J. Francois Denagh II, Jesse Fagan, and David E. Most (2011) Magical flight and monstrous stress: Technologies of absorption and mental illness in Azeroth. *Culture, Medicine, and Psychiatry* 35(1): 26–62.

Spiegel, David, and Etzel Cardeña (1991) Disintegrated experience: The dissociative disorders revisited. *Journal of Abnormal Psychology* 100(3): 366–378.

Spiro, Melford E. (1965) Religious systems as culturally constituted defense mechanisms. In *Context and Meaning in Cultural Anthropology.* Melford E. Spiro, ed. Pp. 100–113. New York: The Free Press.

Sterling, Peter (2003) Principles of allostasis: Optimal design, predictive regulation, pathophysiology and rational therapeutics. In *Allostasis, Homeostasis, and the Costs of Adaptation.* Jay Shulkin, ed. Pp. 17–64. Cambridge, MA: MIT Press.

Stoller, Paul (1992) Embodying cultural memory in Songhay spirit possession. *Archives de Sciences Sociales de Religions* 79: 53–68.

Strathern, Andrew (1996) *Body Thoughts.* Ann Arbor: University of Michigan.

Strauss, Claudia (1992) What makes Tony run? In *Human Motives and Cultural Models.* R. D'Andrade, Claudia Strauss, and Naomi Quinn, eds. Pp. 197–224. Cambridge: Cambridge University Press.

Strelau, Jan (1988) Temperamental dimensions as co-determinants of resistance to stress. In *Individual Differences, Stress, and Health Psychology.* Michael Pierre Janisse, ed. New York: Springer-Verlag.

Stromberg, Peter G. (1985) The impression point: Synthesis of symbol and self. *Ethos* 13: 56–74.

———— (1993) *Language and Self-Transformation: A Study of the Christian Conversion Narrative.* Publications of the Society for Psychological Anthropology. Cambridge & New York: Cambridge University Press.

Stromberg, Peter G. (2009) *Caught in Play.* Stanford, CA: Stanford University Press.

Suomi, Stephen J. (1991) Early stress and adult emotional reactivity in rhesus monkeys. In *The Childhood Environment and Adult Disease.* CIBA Foundation Symposium, eds. Pp. 171–188. West Sussex: John Wiley & Sons, Ltd.

Sweet, Elizabeth, Thomas W. McDade, Catarina I. Kiefe, and Kiang Liu (2007) Relationships between skin color, income, and blood pressure among African Americans in the CARDIA study. *American Journal of Public Health* 97(12): 2253–2259.

Tartaro, Jessica, Linda J. Luecken, and Heather E. Gunn (2005) Exploring heart and soul: Effects of religiosity/spirituality and gender on blood pressure and cortisol stress responses. *Journal of Health Psychology* 10: 753–766.

Taves, Ann (2009) *Religious Experience Reconsidered: A Building-Block Approach to the Study of Religion and Other Special Things.* Princeton, NJ: Princeton University Press.

———— (2010) Experience as site of contested meaning and value: The attributional dog and its special tail. *Religion* 40(4): 317–323.

Turner, Terence (1995) Social body and embodied subject: Bodiliness, subjectivity, and sociality among the Kayapo. *Cultural Anthropology* 10(2): 143–170.

Turner, Victor (1969) *The Ritual Process.* Ithaca, NY: Cornell University Press.

Uchino, Bert N., and John T. Cacioppo (1995) Individual differences in cardiac sympathetic control predict endocrine and immune responses to acute psychological stress. *Journal of Personality and Social Psychology* 69: 736–743.

Uchino, Bert N., John T. Cacioppo, and Janice K. Kiecolt-Glaser (1996) The relationship between social support and physiological processes: A review with emphasis on underlying mechanisms and implications for health. *Psychological Bulletin* 119(3): 488.

Van de Port, Mattijs (2005) Candomble´ in pink, green, and black: Rescripting the Afro-Brazilian heritage in the public sphere of Salvador, Bahia. *Social Anthropology* 13(1): 3–26.

Van Gennep, Arnold (1960) *The Rites of Passage.* Chicago, IL: University of Chicago Press.

Van Wolputte, Steven (2004) Hang on to your self: Of bodies, embodiment, and selves. *Annual Review of Anthropology*: 251–269.

Verger, Pierre (1981) *Orixa's: Deuses Ioruba's na Africa e no Novo Mundo.* Salvador, Brazil: Corrupio.

Voeks, Robert A. (1997) *Sacred Leaves of Candomblé*. Austin: University of Texas Press.

Wafer, James (1991) *The Taste of Blood*. Philadelphia: University of Pennsylvania Press.

Walker, Sheila S. (1990) Everyday and esoteric reality in the Afro-Brazilian Candomblé. In *History of Religions* 30(2): 103–128.

Wallace, Anthony F. C. (1955) The disruption of the individual's identification with his culture in disasters and other extreme situations. Paper read at the National Research Council, Committee on Disaster Studies, Conference on Theories of Human Behavior in Extreme Situations, Vassar College.

——— (1956) Revitalization movements. *American Anthropologist* 58(2): 264–281.

Ward, Colleen (1989a) Possession and exorcism: Psychopathology and psychotherapy in a magico-religious context. In *Altered States of Consciousness and Mental Health*. Colleen Ward, ed. Pp. 125–144. London: Sage Publications.

——— (1989b) The cross-cultural study of altered states of consciousness. In *Altered States of Consciousness and Mental Health*. Colleen Ward, ed. Pp. 15–35. London: Sage Publications.

Weisner, Thomas S. (2012) Mixed methods should be a valued practice in anthropology. *Anthropology News* 53(5): 3–4.

Westen, Drew (2001) Beyond the binary opposition in psychological anthropology: Integrating contemporary psychoanalysis and cognitive science. In *The Psychology of Cultural Experience*. Carmella Moore and Holly Matthews, eds. Pp. 21–47. Cambridge: Cambridge University Press.

Weyer, Christian, Richard E. Pratley, Robert S. Lindsay, and P. Antonio Tataranni (2000) Relationship between birth weight and body composition, energy metabolism, and sympathetic nervous system activity later in life. *Obesity Research* 8(8): 559–565.

Wiley, Andrea S. (2004) *An Ecology of High-Altitude Infancy: A Biocultural Perspective*. Cambridge: Cambridge University Press.

Witztum, Eliezer, and Yehuda Goodman (1999) Narrative construction of distress and therapy: A model based on work with Ultra-Orthodox Jews. *Transcultural Psychiatry* 36: 403–436.

Yoshikawa, Hirokazu, Thomas S. Weisner, Ariel Khalil, and Niobe Way (2008) Mixing qualitative and quantitative research in developmental science: Uses and methodological choices. *Developmental Psychology* 44(2): 344–354.

Zachariae, Robert, Michael M. Jorgenson, Peter Bjerring, and Gunner Svendsen (2000) Autonomic and psychological responses to an acute psychological stressor and relaxation: The influence of hypnotizability and absorption. *Clinical and Experimental Hypnosis* 48(4): 388–403.

Index

Building Dreams

A Movie-Making Adventure

by

Rick Ingalsbe

Foreword by
Patrick Read Johnson,
Writer & Director of the film

5-25-77

www.RickIngalsbeStudio.com

Contents

Acknowledgements

I want to express my gratitude to everyone with whom I worked on *5-25-77*. Thank you for accepting me as one of your own. I can't begin to express how grateful I am to all the people who were instrumental in making this dream of mine come true:

My good friend Charles Adams, thank you for posting photos of my models on your website, which started it all.

Scott Alexander for being a friend and a mentor. Thank you!

Leigh Jones, I enjoyed working with you, and appreciate our continued friendship.

Rob Proce, my 'partner' on set. I couldn't have done it without you.

Jay William Stephen, thanks for the pictures.

Lorne Peterson, I am grateful to you for so much, not the least of which is for being so incredibly awesome!

Ron Burton a special thanks to my long-time friend for convincing me to write this book.

Patrick Read Johnson, the man who invited me to be a part of his incredible movie. You were in the beginning a 'larger-than-life' filmmaker to me. Now I am proud to simply call you my good friend.

Tina, my incredible wife. You are my world! Thank

you for all your encouragement, support, and for believing in me even when I doubt myself. When a man's wife is his number one fan, he can accomplish ANYTHING. I love you with all my heart!

Finally, I give thanks to God of whom it is written, "Take delight in the Lord, and he will give you the desires of your heart." (Psalm 37:4)

Foreword

BY PATRICK READ JOHNSON

A long time ago... In a galaxy just off the Illinois Tollway...

I was given the gift of "opportunity".

The opportunity in question was thrilling, to be sure. But it was equally *intimidating.* Because what I did with it would determine the course of the rest of my life. If I took the risk, it was possible that the great and powerful wizards behind the Hollywood curtain might show me how their magic was made. And if that happened, then maybe, just maybe, one day, if I was brave, lucky, clever, and endearing enough, they might even give ME a chance to pull the levers myself! And if THAT happened— Well...what might come NEXT was too scary to even contemplate.

But there was one thing that was even more terrifying. The thought of what would become of me if I DIDN'T take the chance. Living the rest of my life with a hole in my heart the shape and size of my wildest dream.

Since then, even in the worst of times, I have never once regretted my ultimate decision.

And because simply thanking the special people who gave me that first opportunity can never fully repay its value, I have done all I can to create opportunities for others with dreams of their own.

To those that are standing on the edge of the cliff, looking out across the infinite undiscovered country of their future, I say what Ray Bradbury once said to me...

"Jump! Build your wings on the way down!"

Rick Ingalsbe did... I asked him to jump off a cliff. And the wings he built not only lifted him higher than he could have imagined—they also saved *my* film.

But this is his story... I'll let him tell it...

—Patrick Read Johnson

Introduction

One day in 2005, I was flipping through the pages of a movie magazine when I found an article that featured people involved with the original *Star Wars* trilogy. Written as a "then and now" piece, it briefly described their current projects. I found the name Gary Kurtz, the producer of both *Star Wars* and *The Empire Strikes Back*, with the statement, "Producing a 1977-set comedy about a kid trying to see *Star Wars*." This intrigued me because at that time it would have been the first movie involving *Star Wars* that wasn't an actual *Star Wars* movie. I put the magazine down thinking that I would love to go see that movie when it is finished. There was no way of knowing then that I would end up contributing to the making of that film in multiple ways. There was no reason to even imagine that this could happen, as I had no movie-making experience. But not long after reading that article, everything was about to change.

CHAPTER ONE

An Indelible Impression

I was just a little boy sitting in a large movie theater with great anticipation. It was 1977, and I was about to see *Star Wars* for the first time. We didn't go to movies much at all when I was a kid. In fact, this was only the second time I had ever been to the cinema in my early life. But for a young sci-fi fan caught up in television shows like *Star Trek (the original series), Lost in Space,* and *The Twilight Zone*, my mother knew how important it was for me to see this new movie, which instantly became a cultural phenomenon.

I'll never forget that day. Our family station wagon was full with my mom driving, my little sister and grandmother next to her, my older brother and two of his friends in the back seat, and my best friend and me stuffed way in the back.

It was quite an event in those days to see *Star Wars* when it was new. It was like going on a wild ride at Disney World right in your home town. It was a magical experience that spilled over into popular culture like no other movie had done before. When the film began with its dramatic, symphonic theme and opening crawl, I knew we were in for a fun adventure, but when I saw that huge Star Destroyer fly overhead for the first time, my jaw dropped. My best friend and I looked at each other like this was the coolest thing we'd ever seen in all our 11 years!

Up until that time, the word 'starship' conjured up images of smooth-bodied, saucer-shaped vehicles. But then came this new definition, unlike anything I had seen before, projected on a screen so large it enveloped my entire field of vision, as well as my imagination. As the Star Destroyer—or Imperial Cruiser—made its first dramatic appearance, it moved through space with power and authority. Its size and angular shape were menacing, yet majestic, a presence that caused all other ships near it to beware. Like all the wondrous machinery in *Star Wars*, the Imperial Cruiser was a total departure from what I was used to seeing.

In 1978, *The Making of Star Wars* television special aired. That's when I learned that the Star Destroyer and all those incredible spaceships were actually models made by artists at a place called Industrial Light & Magic (ILM). The fact that the spaceships were models may have been obvious to some, but I was just a kid with no concept of how movies were made. This was a fascinating revelation to me, and I was hooked on everything "special effects."

After that, I became an even bigger fan of those who made *Star Wars* than I was of the movie itself. People like Dennis Muren, Phil Tippett, Joe Johnston, John Dykstra, Lorne Peterson, Steve Gawley, and everyone connected with Industrial Light & Magic became my childhood heroes.

Not long after in my fifth grade art class, the teacher

put a variety of different materials in the middle of the room. She instructed us each to make something out of this pile of junk. I'll never forget the impression this made on me, this pile of raw materials for whatever the imagination could do with it. I grabbed a bunch of wood pieces of all shapes and sizes, the largest being a triangular wedge. I glued them up to be my very first, very crude rendition of a Star Destroyer. This inspired me to go home and build a bigger one out of cardboard and Scotch tape. It was flimsy and didn't last long, but it was made out of a desire that was dissatisfied by just having pictures of the Star Destroyer in books, posters, and bubblegum cards. I wanted to see it for real, unlimited by the fixed, 2-dimensional views in pictures. I went nuts when my mom bought me the toy when it came out. As much as I loved it, though, it was not much bigger than 7-inches. A Star Destroyer is supposed to be BIG!

Meanwhile, I began to learn as much about moviemaking, visual effects, and all the goings on at ILM as I could. Then, to my great surprise, my grandfather gave me an 8mm movie camera with stop-motion capabilities on my 12th birthday. I was always a dreamer, dreaming mostly about what it was like to be one of those guys at ILM making *Star Wars*. With this movie camera, my basement became my own ILM studio, as I made my version of a *Star Wars* movie. Of course, my new toy Star Destroyer played a very prominent role in it. Deep down, my dream was that I could someday be involved with real moviemaking. Like many young dreamers, I didn't know where to begin.

From where I grew up near Buffalo, New York,

Hollywood might just as well have been located on Mars. There was no one around who understood me and my 'weird' interests. It didn't help that I was debilitatingly shy, and found it difficult to communicate. I had been—with all the best of intentions—encouraged to use my artistic abilities for a more 'realistic' career path. I carried on with my dreams suppressed... but not completely. As the years went by, I had learned a lot about movie-making. I honestly believed that, if given half a chance on a movie set, I could show what I am really capable of doing. Realistically, though, it didn't seem likely that chance would ever come.

CHAPTER TWO

As Fate Would Have It

In 2003, after six years of working in advertising as a graphic designer for one of the largest companies in my area, my department became the victim of corporate downsizing. I was out of work for a total of six months. One day, growing tired of hours of sending out resumes, I decided I needed a break. For fun, I did a search that led me to a website called Starshipbuilder.com, a site about making models for movies and as a hobby. Suddenly, there it was!

Photos were taken by a fan of the Imperial Star Destroyer on display in a museum. Here were photos of my favorite filming model like I had never seen before. Instead of the far away, grainy images, which were all that was available for years, these were closeup details from different angles. I had a lot of time on my hands and I was looking for a creative outlet. I always wanted to try scratch-building a studio-scale model. I felt inspired by those photos. As I stared I said, "I think I can do this."

In hindsight, though, I was incredibly naive! I had never tried scratch-building a studio-scale model before, yet after seeing those pictures, I became convinced I could. I reasoned that I would never get the chance to see the real thing, so I might as well make one myself. After researching, it seemed experienced hobbyists were scratch-building everything *but* Star Destroyers. So I couldn't learn from what others had done. I was on my own.

It was a risky thing to do when unemployed. I spent hundreds out of our savings on materials to make something that could very well have ended up being an unrecognizable disaster! But my understanding and supportive wife Tina was all right with this, because she saw that this creative diversion kept my spirits up during a difficult time.

My first replica was truly a crash course in studio-scale model-making. All the books and documentaries I'd read or seen always referred to the filming model as "the 3-footer." Naturally, that's where I began—at 3-feet long (1 meter). It has a foam core inner frame (I had no woodworking tools yet), a Plexiglas hull, and styrene superstructure. An aluminum tube runs through the middle engine that acts as the one and only mounting point.

Then it came time to cover it with kitbashed details (a technique whereby pieces of commercial model kits are used to add details to a filming model). As a kid, I was only interested in building spaceship model kits. Therefore, I knew nothing about all the battleships, tanks, cars, trucks, or any other kits that were used to detail the Star Destroyer. My only solution was to make up my own details. After all, I reasoned, every rendition of the Star Destroyer built by ILM had different details, one from another, so why couldn't mine?

Once again I was incredibly naive to think I could just go to the hobby store and buy five or six kits of battleships and tanks, come home, and cover my model with the pieces inside. What a rude awakening that was! There must have been pieces from a ridiculous number of kits covering the filming model!

Lacking the money to spend on more kits—and wanting to finish what I started—I quickly learned how to replicate parts in resin.

I love the 'found objects' approach to scratch-building—the idea that anything that looks right can end up as a part of a model. I found these wonderful egg-shaped candy containers to use for the three main engines. Wooden checkers were used as my four secondary engines. Finally, I sprayed the model with white paint, drew all the panel lines in pencil, and after two months of intense work, my first Star Destroyer replica was finished. It didn't turn out as bad as I had feared. Not perfect, but not bad.

Months later, after vowing I'd never do it again, I changed my mind and decided that I could use my experience to build an even better Star Destroyer... and the process began again! It also took two months to build. The final piece was much improved from the first attempt. It was a cleaner build with better proportions (though still not quite right). I bought a band saw so I could make a proper wooden frame. The rest was pretty much constructed like the first, except I used Sintra (a lightweight yet rigid PVC board) for the hull of the ship instead of Plexiglas. Cyanoacrylate (CA, or super glue) seems made for this material. It also made panel lines easy to scribe, as I didn't want to simply draw them on like the first one.

By this time I was working full time again, so I could afford to buy more kits for detailing. However, I still did not know what parts from what kits were used on the real thing. Once again, very little of its details were accurate. That was fine, because the proportions were more important to me.

It was Tina that first urged me to send pictures of my models to someone in Hollywood. She saw how much I loved building them and knew about my dream to work in movies someday. Why is it, when we are faced with the very thing we want more than anything else, we are sometimes taken over by self-doubt? Maybe it was simply fear. Maybe it's because I had a lifetime of being convinced you can't get there from here, but for some reason I told Tina that, as a beginner, my model-making skills couldn't possibly be good enough.

Knowing me better than anyone, she continued urging me on and hoping, even praying, that if I wouldn't try contacting someone in the movie industry that someone in the industry would try contacting me. I did, however, take several photos of both models and submitted some of them to Charles Adams, the owner of the Starshipbuilder.com website.

He asked me if it would be all right to post them on his site for the entire world to see. As I gave him permission, I remembered thinking it doesn't get much better than that!

It didn't take long before I began receiving numerous e-mails from all over asking me about my replicas. One of them seemed so unbelievable that I almost deleted it. With my finger on the button, I paused thinking, "What if this is real?"

It turned out that the writer was from the Chicago

Museum of Science and Industry. He said that he was the manager of a touring exhibit called *Action! An Adventure in Movie-Making*. They had a collection of models, props, costumes and makeups from some of the most famous movies of our time—and they had the original Imperial Cruiser filming model—at least for a while. He explained that Lucasfilm, Ltd. decided to remove the model from that exhibit for use in another one. The Star Destroyer was the center piece of the exhibit, so this left him in a quandary. His solution was to receive permission from Lucasfilm and ILM to locate and use a fan-made replica as a replacement. He saw the recently posted photos of mine online and contacted me right away.

This was the chance of a lifetime, especially for a beginning model-maker like me. What an honor to have something I built alongside actual movie icons from some of my most favorite movies! It doesn't get any better than that!

Immediately, I did a write up for Starship-builder.com about it. I submitted photos sent to me by the exhibit manager of my model in the very display case that once held the original. Charles Adams was happy to post them on his site.

My model was with the museum tour from 2005 through 2009. The *Action!* exhibit began at the Chicago Museum of Science and Industry with the original Star Destroyer filming model. My replica replaced it for the tour that traveled to the Liberty Science Center in Liberty State Park, New Jersey; the Carnegie Science Center in Pittsburgh, Pennsylvania; and Discovery Place in Charlotte, North Carolina.

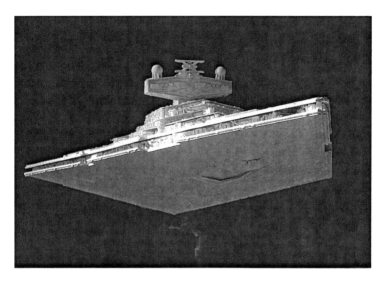

My first attempt at scratch-building a Star Destroyer replica.

*My second attempt at this difficult subject. This one replaced
the real filming model in the museum tour.*

Action! An Adventure in Movie-Making exhibit.

I remember the day when Charles (I now consider him a good friend) posted that museum article. It was early in July 2005. When it was online, my wife and I talked about how wonderful it would be if something bigger happened as a result of someone reading my article. Of course, I was dreaming again. Not wanting to build up false hopes, I had to consider the most likely scenario: that nothing would happen at all.

As fate would have it, though, my article had only been online for a mere five hours when I received an e-mail from a familiar name—Scott Alexander (also known as the legendary "Captain Cardboard"). Like many people in model-building circles, I had heard of Scott and knew of his outstanding work. Because it came so soon after the museum article was posted, I thought his e-mail must have been because of the article. What I didn't know was that his e-mail was about to change my life.

At first, Scott said he read my article and complimented me on the quality of my Star Destroyer replicas. I must say, direct compliments from the 'Captain' himself would have been utterly fantastic if that's all he was taking the time to write to me about.

But, there was more. Scott continued by saying that he had a friend who is a movie director. His friend was making a movie in which there would be a scene that had to do with the making of the original *Star Wars*. Scott was helping his friend find decent replicas of the original *Star Wars* filming models specifically for that scene. He asked if I would be interested in lending my remaining Star Destroyer to the film production.

Words could not express how incredible Scott's

proposal was for me! When Scott Alexander asked if I would be interested in lending my model to the movie production, a door opened that would allow the wishes of a lifetime to come true. And that was only the beginning.

Shortly after receiving his e-mail, Scott and I had a phone conversation that lasted a few hours. He told me that his friend was writer/director Patrick Read Johnson, another familiar name to me from movies I had seen such as *Dragonheart, Spaced Invaders,* and *Baby's Day Out.* He said the movie in production was called *5-25-77.* The title is actually a date most fans of *Star Wars* will never forget, as it was the day the film opened in theaters.

Scott explained that *5-25-77* will be a funny and dramatic film, a heartwarming, coming-of-age and mostly true story of how Patrick Johnson became a filmmaker. The script, he said, involves a scene when Patrick was on a specially arranged tour of Hollywood when both *Star Wars* and Steven Spielberg's *Close Encounters of the Third Kind* were being made. *5-25-77* would recreate those experiences based on Patrick's memories and how it affected him as a young filmmaker.

Scott said that the film had a few producers, one of them Gary Kurtz of *Star Wars.* He said the filmmakers planned to populate the ILM tour scene with studio-scale replicas of as many of the filming miniatures as they could find. He told me how he himself was supplying the production with some of his now famous X-wing Fighter models, which would include one hero and three break-away versions. The breakaway models were needed because the script called for the character of John Dykstra (visual effects supervisor at ILM in 1977) to demonstrate their "breakawayness" by smashing one against a table—something that happened in real life.

I heard much about the movie from Scott that day. I was captivated by the stories and thought this would make a great movie. He said that if I was interested in lending my Star Destroyer that Patrick might even allow me to be on set during shooting. Naturally, I told Scott that I was very interested in lending my model to the production. I would have to take time off work to do it. I jokingly said to Scott, "I guess this is one of those opportunities that when it comes along, if the boss says 'I'm sorry, I can't let you go,' I should respond with, 'Okay, would you like me to be here to train my replacement?'."

He replied in a serious tone, "That's right!"

Scott would inform Patrick Read Johnson. He said I would be hearing from Patrick soon. Everything had to happen quickly because filming was scheduled for the end of July, that same month.

After my conversation with Scott Alexander, I anxiously anticipated the call from the writer and director of *5-25-77*. Then, a few days later I was on the phone with Patrick Read Johnson. Scott tracked Patrick down on vacation so he could contact me personally to confirm the loan of my Star Destroyer. Patrick greeted me with a huge, "HOW ARE YOU?!"

I would describe that first conversation as short, yet intense. At an energetic pace, he went into more detail about the movie and the scene for which he needed my Star Destroyer. Then he told me there were other sci-fi aspects of the script that involved *Close Encounters of the Third Kind, 2001: A Space Odyssey, Jaws, Space 1999,* and *Planet of the Apes* to name a few. He spoke about the film with an enthusiasm that was contagious!

Patrick described the images for his film in such a colorful and animated way, you didn't need any movie experience to believe that there was something extra special about this production. Talking with Patrick, I sensed that *5-25-77* was not just another movie for him and those who were involved with it. When he asked if I would be interested, I told him that he could certainly use my destroyer model in *5-25-77*.

"That's AWESOME! Thank you so much!" he said.

We began to discuss how I would ship the model to him when I remembered the chance to be on the set. Hoping I wasn't being too audacious (but thinking, "When am I ever going to get this chance again?") I asked Patrick if it would be all right for me to bring my Star Destroyer personally.

"That would be great!" he said, adding that if I would like to come early, I could even help set up the shot. He even asked if I would like to be an extra portraying an ILM crew member in the scene. To have the right look, he asked me to let my hair grow as long as I could before the shoot.

When I told him that he could count me in, he genuinely seemed more excited about me being a part of his movie than I was, if that were possible. As he spoke about filming the scenes he kept emphasizing how much fun it was going to be on set. He said it would be like a big sci-fi party... and I just received an exclusive invitation!

Then, near the end of our conversation, Patrick said that they were still looking for other *Star Wars* replica models. He listed what they had and what they needed. They didn't have much at all. He asked if I knew of anyone who might have the needed replica models. Although I did not (due to my being so new to the hobby), I said I would certainly keep my eyes open. Before we hung up, he thanked me again for being a part of his film and said we would be in touch.

Wow! I tried to put what just happened into perspective. Everything was happening so fast that my mind was racing to catch up! The phone call was merely to confirm that I would lend him my Star Destroyer. Before I knew it, I went from lending a model, to helping set up, to being an extra! And not just any kind of extra, but an ILM extra! How many people get to portray one of their childhood heroes in a movie?

I kept thinking this was all too good to be true! It seemed that the best thing I ever decided to do as an artist was to try scratch-building that first Star Destroyer model. What started as merely something to do while I was briefly unemployed (just to see if I could even do it), had snowballed into something bigger than I ever imagined! One thing was for sure, though... a once-in-a-lifetime opportunity just fell in my lap, and I was determined to make the absolute most of it!

CHAPTER THREE

Making Movie Models

When Patrick listed the models he still needed, I took that as an opportunity to do more than just lend a single model to the production. I wanted to build more than the Star Destroyers anyway. The problem was that shooting was tentatively scheduled to take place at the end of that same month (July 2005). There was not much time!

One of the models he needed was an Escape Pod. Even as he listed it, I immediately thought I could build one in time. However, I decided not to tell Patrick. I had such limited experience as a scratch-builder. Instead, I would start one, and if I didn't like how it was turning out, I just wouldn't tell him about it. Yet, I really wanted to surprise him with an additional model.

Scratch-builders usually research a subject down to the smallest detail, tracking down every last piece that was used to make the original and spending months or years building a quality replica. In contrast, I had two weeks to come up with an Escape Pod that, if acceptable to the director, would actually appear in his movie. Perfection down to the smallest detail just would not be possible.

In fact, I found that I could not even think like a

studio-scale hobbyist. Rather, I had to think like a movie model-maker. Most movie models are actually thrown together by several builders in what can be considered record time. If I wanted another model ready for this movie, I had to get busy!

Having said that, I had to replicate an existing subject, so my model had to be recognizable as such. I tried to find as many photos of the Escape Pod as I could. After studying them, I found it to be a bit confusing at first glance because it has features that are one-sided, two-sided, three-sided, and four-sided.

Being unfamiliar with the details, getting them all in the proper position proved tricky at times working only from photos. I found it very helpful to get the toy version to use as a study model. The overall shape of the Escape Pod had to be addressed. I knew that the original was built using paint buckets. If that was good enough for ILM, it was good enough for me.

By scouring the shelves of the local hardware store, I found perfect disposable paper buckets that were the right shape and size. After studying the available reference materials, I began to create patterns for all the plastic panels that would cover the paint buckets. These would form the base structure to be covered in kitbashed detail parts later.

Once the paint buckets were cut to size, I created a frame using foam core circles on an aluminum tube running through the middle. After I glued the buckets to this frame, I then created the conical shapes at the top and the bottom. I attached these to sub-frames (also made of foam core). The Escape Pod was now taking shape.

I had a particular concern when it came to the nose at the top of the model. I was wondering how I could accomplish the compound curve of this surface. A big fan of the 'found objects' approach to model-making, I tried to remember if I had ever seen anything that would match the size and shape I was needing. Nothing came to mind. That same day, my wife who supports me in all I decide to do, came home with a brand new bird feeder that she'd bought for our backyard. I showed her my Escape Pod progress and explained my dilemma. Just as I was describing the shape of the piece I needed, she pulled out a piece of her new bird feeder from the carton and said, "You mean something like this?" There it was!

With a slight alteration it was just what I needed, just when I needed it! I looked at her, and she gave up the piece. As for the bird feeder, without that crucial part, it made a very nice vase filled with roses from a very grateful husband.

With that problem solved, the pod was ready for detailing. Although I had no clue as to what kit pieces were actually used on the real model (I still don't), I did have an idea of what I could use that would look just as good. I used parts from moon rocket models, tanks, and battleships. Many details came from left over kits I bought for detailing my Star Destroyer replicas.

Once the detailing was done, I puttied any small gaps to finish the construction. With the entire model now assembled, I was very much looking forward to painting it. Besides the fact that I would have built one of these replicas sooner or later anyway, the main reason I chose to build the Escape Pod for this movie was because I wanted

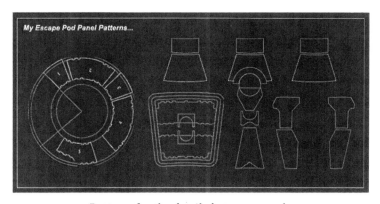

Patterns for the detailed styrene panels.

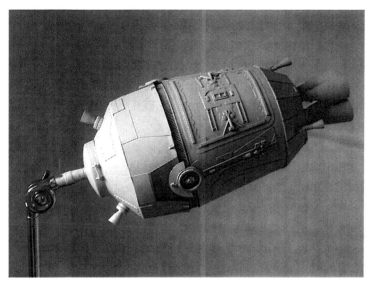

The model before final painting.

An "action" shot of my Escape Pod sent to Patrick for his approval.

The finished model.

to tackle a paint job with heavy weathering—rust, grime, scrapes and burns. I didn't have a chance to do this with my two Star Destroyers since they were mostly all white.

So, I had some fun with this new model. The paint scheme started with a base coat of flat gray. Then I 'beat it up' using a mix of pastels and airbrushing. I tried to match the more noticeable streaks and spots on the real Escape Pod miniature, but I also did my own thing. After a week and a half of building and painting, the model was finally done.

I built my Escape Pod so that it could be mounted on a stand just like my Star Destroyer replicas. After setting it up, I took several pictures of the finished model and sent four of them to Patrick. I have to admit that I nervously awaited his response. With little model-building experience and no movie experience, I didn't know what to expect. I never intended to build an actual movie prop with my Star Destroyer. Even though Patrick saw photos of it and accepted it, I knew it could have been better. Later I would greatly enhance the detail and rebuild portions of it for its on-set movie debut.

The Escape Pod, however, was different. This one was meant to be a movie prop. In the end, Patrick took away any doubts I had due to my lack of experience. His e-mail response simply read, "WOW! FANTASTIC!!!!"

Just like that, it was in.

CHAPTER FOUR

Welcome To Movie-Making

Having traded several e-mails early on, Patrick Johnson and I easily developed a rapport. In one e-mail he spoke of his urgent need for two specific replicas that would be featured prominently in the ILM scene—a studio-scale Landspeeder and a 2-foot square Death Star surface panel. I told him that I would do my best to find these items.

I knew of no one who had built these, but I did know someone who just might be able to point me in the right direction. In an earlier e-mail to Charles Adams, I had told him of this awesome opportunity. Now I asked him if he could help me find people who had built some of the important studio-scale models Patrick needed. Charles knew more people, and I thought if anyone could help, he could.

Although he knew of no one who actually had a studio-scale replica of the Landspeeder, Charles did know of someone who might be interested in building one. It wasn't long before I received an e-mail from Wasili Angelopoulos. A professional model-maker from Amsterdam, Wasili told me that he had known about the 5-25-77 production for about a year. He wanted very much to be involved and said he would be happy to build a Landspeeder replica for the movie. He gave me his website address and, from what I saw, I knew that he would do a great job.

I immediately notified Patrick of Wasili's interest and talent and told him I thought Wasili could make a fantastic Landspeeder. Patrick was very happy to hear this "amazing news!"

He was equally impressed by Wasili's website, saying that we should let him "go for it!" With that, I had the pleasure of telling Wasili that Patrick was giving him the green light to build the Landspeeder.

In several subsequent e-mails, Wasili and I got to know each other. We discussed our enthusiasm for the *5-25-77* project and model-building. To my surprise, Wasili already knew who I was before I first contacted him—though it took a few e-mails before either of us realized it.

"Hey, you're that Star Destroyer guy!" was his response when I told him that I was contributing my replica to the film.

One of the issues Wasili and I discussed was that the replica Landspeeder should have screen-accurate characters 'riding' in it. Patrick had sent me a photo of an original Landspeeder model under construction at ILM, and in this photo, an action figure of *The Six Million Dollar Man* is in the cockpit. Wasili searched for vintage figures from this '70s TV show to stand in for characters Luke and Ben, just as they did in *Star Wars*.

Meanwhile, Wasili was also concerned about how to costume the figures appropriately. To save time, I suggested dressing them with clothing from currently available 12-inch *Star Wars* action figures of Luke Skywalker and Ben Kenobi. As for the droids, I already had a 12-inch vinyl model of C-3PO I was working on, and I found a toy replica of R2-D2.

In the photos of the original Landspeeder model, however, we noticed that the scale droid models used in *Star Wars* looked very crude. Obviously, these models were never meant to be filmed close up. As a result, we were concerned that my robot figures were way too detailed for the scene. To solve this problem, we felt the droid figures needed a 'reverse make-over' in order to give them the right look.

I would have to trim off a portion of C-3PO's legs to change him from a standing to a sitting position. I would then have to putty over much of the detail in his face and chest. That all had to wait, however, until I had Wasili's Landspeeder on the set to get the positioning just right to make it fit the model correctly.

I was prepared to give R2-D2 the same makeover when the time came. When we were on the set, though, Patrick didn't want me to destroy what could become a valuable collectable in the future. Thus, the R2-D2 was left intact, and the movie debut of this little toy droid was short-lived.

Ironically, as I thought about all this later, I realized it could be possible that the intentionally damaged C-3PO figure could end up being worth more than the R2-D2 just because it had appeared in *5-25-77*!

With the Landspeeder in good hands, I turned my attention to finding some Death Star surface panels.

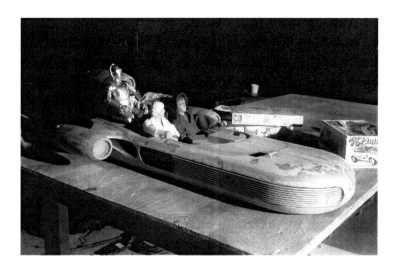

Wasili's Landspeeder replica above.
Below are the action figures we put in the model for 5-25-77.

This beautifully built T.I.E. Fighter model would get a nice closeup in 5-25-77.

This is how Patrick first saw my Death Star panels.

Charles knew of someone who had made a base for a studio-scale T.I.E. Fighter model that replicated the look of an original Death Star surface panel. He sent me a photo of this base with the T.I.E. model mounted on it that he had received from the person who built the model. I then sent this photo to Patrick asking if the Death Star base would work for the scene in question.

Unfortunately, he felt that the scale of the panel was too small. However, Patrick was much more interested in the T.I.E. Fighter model in that photo. He said they did not have one of these yet and asked if I could find out if this one might be available.

At this point I was already acting as an official representative of the *5-25-77* production. As such, I wrote several letters to prospective contributors that began with: *"Hello! My name is Rick Ingalsbe. I am writing to you on behalf of Patrick Read Johnson, writer/director of the movie 5-25-77, currently in production. . ."*

In these letters I talked a bit about the movie, the ILM scene and followed up with a request for the loan of the particular model for use in the film. As a result of this process I was able to procure the T.I.E. Fighter along with other models needed for this scene.

Over a period of several weeks I was constantly reaching out to people who might possibly be interested in providing models for the production. I even tried (unsuccessfully) to get Master Replicas—a company that produced limited edition, high-end Hollywood prop replicas—to lend the prototype of their studio-scale Y-Wing Fighter to the production. Not long before, I had noticed that a Master Replicas *Star Trek* Communicator prop was used on an episode of *Enterprise.*

I thought they might be equally enthusiastic about seeing one of their studio-scale replicas appear in a motion picture. But the Y-Wing was not yet ready for production, so they had no finished pieces to give. (My thanks, however, go out to all those who tried to help me in that endeavor.)

Meanwhile, Patrick put me in touch with one of the movie's producers, Leigh Jones. One of Leigh's duties was keeping track of what was on loan to the production. I, in turn, had to keep her informed about what I was doing. When I was able to procure a model for the shoot, I had to provide Leigh with all the necessary information. This included things such as the name of the owner, what was being lent, the approximate size and weight of the item, where it was coming from and what it was worth. All this had to be taken into account for shipping and insurance purposes, and Leigh had to make sure everything remained within budget.

Over a period of months I put in a lot of hours trying to populate the upcoming ILM scene with some high quality replicas. Patrick was always very appreciative of my efforts and he thanked me for my determination and resourcefulness. Yet, the more I was able to do for the production, the more I wanted to do.

With very little time left before shooting was scheduled to commence in July, I was still having difficulty finding an acceptable representation of a Death Star surface panel. So far, everything I had sent to Patrick was not right.

Then one day, Leigh sent around an e-mail to all

those involved in the production to say that the shooting schedule would be changed from July to the end of August. I was a little disappointed, yet relieved at the same time because there was plenty more to be done.

Patrick told me that the shifting of shooting schedules was normal in the world of movie-making. He said that it would give us all more time to be prepared. Besides that, he said it would give my hair a chance to grow longer for the scene. I began to think that it would also give me a chance to do something else. Now I just might be able to do even more for the production as I had hoped.

Not satisfied with my inability to find an acceptable Death Star panel—and also not satisfied with having just two models in the movie—I told Patrick that I would use the extra month to go ahead and build replicas of the 2-foot square Death Star surface panels myself. He said he would be "eternally grateful" if I could accomplish this.

With that settled, I began planning how I might actually construct these new models. The ILM scene only required one surface panel to be on set for shooting since the rest of the Death Star surface would be added later during post production using a Computer Graphic (CG) special visual effect. Still, I felt the more we actually had on set for filming the better. I went through all my ILM books and found plan drawings of four of the six original surface panel designs. I chose what I thought was the most interesting looking one to build. If I had time, I would build a second when the first panel was done.

I started by tracing the plan drawings from my reference book in the computer. I then created patterns for all the individual structures and printed everything out.

Construction went smoothly and, as it turned out, I did have time to start work on a second panel. The design of that one came from excellent photos of an actual screen-used piece that Wasili found for me on the internet. Both of my panels were made the same way. I began with a 2-foot square plywood base panel. Following the plans I had printed, I built up a frame of 1/4-inch thick wood strips cut to the correct size and assembled with Liquid Nails construction adhesive. This would make the surface of the panels about 2-inches high (or higher in some areas).

Once the glue holding it all together was dry, I then covered the tops of the wooden frames with sheets of styrene to represent the 'floor' or base of each panel. This had to be built up first since there were canyons and other areas that would be recessed into each surface. With the base of each panel complete, various structures were then built out of wood or plastic depending on the simplicity or complexity of each shape. Detailing involved a mix of model kit parts, cut-up sheets of plastic, found objects, and resin castings. As with every scratch-built project, it was very rewarding to see all the various pieces come together to form a finished model.

I resisted the temptation to go overboard with the detailing, however, since what I was making represented the original pieces that were seen in *Star Wars*. As a result, I painted my Death Star surface a simple flat grey with little or no weathering.

While I was in the process of building them, Patrick told me that he couldn't wait to see my Death Star surface panels. When I sent pictures of the completed models, I made sure to photograph them with dramatic lighting to accentuate the features. I even touched up one picture in Photoshop by making copies of the two panels and stretching them into infinity to make the models look like the real Death Star trench miniature.

Patrick's response was more than favorable as usual. He commented in jest that with all the work I had been doing he would have to give me a special title or film credit—something like "model supervisor extraordinaire!" I told him that had a nice ring to it. The very thought of actually having a credit in the film was exciting, but unexpected. I was beginning to wonder if he was actually considering it.

CHAPTER FIVE

An Official Position

Eventually, the tentative August schedule was pushed back yet again. This time no new date was given. It was just until further notice. I knew by now there were many factors that can cause a shooting schedule to change. It was clear, however, that the shoot would not happen before the end of 2005.

In the months that followed I kept myself busy. Now I had the time to go back to my first Star Destroyer model and improve it where I could. I also tried to contact others in the continuing search for the few remaining studio model replicas needed for the shoot. In the process, I met a lot of great people, and I was very grateful to all those who helped. The extra time would also assure that I had the 'hippie' look perfected, which was beginning to drive me crazy!

Then in February 2006 I got the long-awaited e-mail from producer Leigh Jones. The shoot was now definitely scheduled for March! Indeed, it was the real deal this time.

All along I figured that since I was going to be there on set during filming, I could keep an eye on all the models, making sure they were safe, and that they were ready for shooting, etc. This was what I had assured those who were lending models to the production so they would know their property would be in good hands. I also had planned to bring a model repair kit with me, full of all kinds of modeling supplies just in case.

Then, to my surprise, I received a follow up e-mail from Leigh asking if I wanted to do these things 'officially.' My desire to do more for the production was being fulfilled yet again! Patrick and Leigh had talked things over and thought I deserved a screen credit for all the work I had been doing building models for the film and securing the loan of studio model replicas. They asked if I wanted to be the official, on-set "point man" or "go-to guy" for all the models and props on loan to the production for scenes involving the making of *Star Wars* and *Close Encounters*. I would be given the title of "model-making supervisor/ coordinator" or something similar that would be determined later.

Patrick and Leigh also decided they needed someone outside the production's art department who had practical knowledge and experience with studio-scale models to look after these valuable items. Naturally, I accepted. I was quite happy to have an actual job on set. It may have seemed small at this point, yet, as I would discover later, it would actually turn out to be more work, and a much bigger responsibility than I first thought!

In the days before I was to travel to the Chicago area where filming would take place, I received copies of the shooting schedule, call sheets and the *5-25-77* script. The most important of the items sent to me for my now official position as "model guy" was a list of all those who were lending items to the production. This list recorded each item that was on loan, how it was to be delivered to the set, and for how much it was to be insured. My name was listed along with all of those I had contacted. There were also several other very familiar names from the movie industry such as Douglas Trumbull, Gary Kurtz and Greg Jein, to name just a few.

In the script, as in real life, young Patrick Read Johnson visits Douglas Trumbull's Future General shop back in 1977 where Steven Spielberg was making *Close Encounters of the Third Kind*. The following day he would drop in on the folks at ILM as they were finishing up work on George Lucas' *Star Wars*. In recreating these events we had to populate the set of the ILM scene with *replicas* of various *Star Wars* shooting miniatures. For the Future General scene, however, we were fortunate enough to have *actual* props and production items from *Close Encounters*, courtesy of Greg Jein and Douglas Trumbull who are both Patrick's friends.

I was really looking forward to seeing the screen-used Devil's Tower model from *Close Encounters* from Greg Jein, as well as a piece of the Mother Ship miniature, and some unused parts from the Flying Saucer models built for the film. Also on the list was Greg's study model of the Mother Ship itself. This item was to remain in Patrick's possession for the duration of the shoot. It was very delicate and only about 6-inches tall, yet it was worth a small fortune. I was glad that Patrick decided to hold on to that himself.

The items on loan from Douglas Trumbull were not actually models and so I did not expect that I would be responsible for them, so I didn't give them much thought. In addition, Gary Kurtz, producer of *Star Wars* and *The Empire Strikes Back*, sent an original (and valuable) Mylar *Star Wars* "coming soon" poster to the production, but I would not be responsible for this either.

An interesting item to note, however—also listed under Kurtz's name—was a scale model of the Millennium Falcon. I found out from Patrick later that this model was actually a store-bought MPC kit that had been built and painted by ILM for a portion of the asteroid scene in *The Empire Strikes Back*.

By accepting the position of "model guy," I now found myself responsible not only for some high quality studio model replicas, but also some real movie icons as well. From my perspective, I was beginning to think I had the best job in the production!

ARRIVING ON SET

After driving in my packed car for 10 hours, I arrived at the soundstage with great anticipation. I couldn't wait to see the sets and I was also looking forward to meeting people in person that I had been trading e-mails and having phone conversations with for nine months. The first person I met was producer Leigh Jones. She took me on a brief tour of the huge warehouse, showing me where all the various sets were going to be positioned. Leigh showed me what would eventually be 'Steven Spielberg's office' and the 'Future General model shop.' Both sets were incomplete at this point.

In the area where the model shop would be set up I

saw a large landscape miniature on a custom made table-top. This forced-perspective landscape was a recreation of one made by Greg Jein for *Close Encounters* and had been built by Patrick Read Johnson himself. Leigh then showed me other sets like the ILM screening room and what looked like a huge water tank where, later in the week, we would recreate the swirling cloud effects used in *Close Encounters*. A few other minor sets would be erected temporarily for certain scenes here and there and then torn down to make room for others.

I then asked Leigh about the ILM set. She pointed to double doors on the far wall which led to another portion of the colossal building. A recreation of ILM would eventually be built there and filmed later in the schedule. As of yet, little had been completed on this set.

Leigh then introduced me to assistant directors Mike McNerney and Dan Suhart. Right away I knew I would enjoy working with them. They seemed equally glad to be working with me. Another person I met that first night was Rob Proce, a skilled carpenter who had worked as the construction coordinator on the film before I came on board. Rob is a high energy fellow with a lot of enthusiasm for this project. He and I would end up working together for much of the shooting schedule.

I did not get to meet Patrick that first night since the shoot scheduled for the following day was to take place on location, and he was there finalizing preparations. After Leigh finished showing me around, she needed to head out to that location herself. After my tour, I needed to unload my models and put them in the model room where all the other items on loan would be kept securely under lock and

*The warehouse-turned-soundstage near Chicago where
the ILM and Future General scenes were filmed.*

The forced perspective landscape model with a photo of Greg Jein.

Nando, Rob, Chris and Dan.

Me with producer Leigh Jones on the ILM Set.

key. Very few people had access to this model room. Besides myself, Rob was one of the few who did and he showed me around what I would consider my "office" for the duration of the production.

There, still in the boxes they had been shipped in, were all the *Star Wars* shooting miniature replicas, Greg Jein's property and some large, antique cases that contained what was being called the *Star Wars* camera. I was told this was the actual VistaVision camera head used to film the special effects shots in *Star Wars*. All these items were to be in my care and under my supervision. You can imagine how much I was looking forward to unpacking everything!

I have to admit, though, that I was a bit puzzled that first night. When I arrived at the warehouse I fully expected to see finished (or at least mostly finished) sets. I knew a set for something like the ILM scene would be very large and complex. With such a tight shooting schedule, I was really surprised that this set was not already built. What had been started, however, was an impressive replica of the Dykstraflex motion control rig and track. But this, too, was incomplete.

As it turns out, a huge portion of the warehouse-turned-soundstage where the recreation of ILM was to be built was the storage area of the otherwise empty building. It was full of junk accumulated over what appeared to be a very long time. This area was absolutely full of very large, heavy equipment and bulky objects that took up much of the space. All this would have to be moved before ILM could be recreated there. I seriously began to wonder if this set would be ready in time for shooting.

Still, I couldn't worry about it too much. I figured this sort of thing must be a normal part of the world of movie-making. One way or another it would probably get done. I had my own job tending to the models and props, and getting them ready for filming was my primary concern.

So, after meeting people and touring the facility, I checked into my hotel room. I wanted to be well rested for my first full day of movie-making.

CHAPTER SIX

On Location

On my first day it was decided I would spend the morning at the shooting location to get to know more of the movie crew. In the afternoon I would leave that location and begin the process of unpacking models back at the warehouse.

By the time I arrived on location, scenes were already being shot. There were many people on hand for this, so I did my best not to get in the way. As these scenes had little to do with studio-scale models, it was difficult to resist feeling like a fifth wheel... at least at first.

It seemed like a long time before there was a break between scenes when producer Leigh Jones was finally able to introduce me to the director, Patrick Read Johnson. She did so simply by asking, "Patrick, do you know who this is?" Patrick looked at me as though he should know, but did not. He had seen pictures of me before I had my new 'hippie' look, but with all the new hair I had cultivated; my own mother wouldn't recognize me!

"This is Rick Ingalsbe," Leigh said. Then, with a smile he gave me a big bear hug and told me how glad he was that I was there.

Throughout the morning I did my best to continue staying out of everyone's way, the 'fifth wheel' thoughts still in effect. Patrick did give me small tasks to do here and there, which I appreciated very much. Leigh then introduced me to the art department crew. I was glad that they had some things I could help out with as well.

For the most part I spent the morning observing take after take of the day's scheduled shoot. The biggest problem for the production that first day was the weather. The day began with a thick fog. When the fog cleared the wind picked up—a lot! After a while the wind caused the power to go out temporarily. The shooting schedule was very tight, so production had to move along. The scheduled shots to be made indoors at this location simply had to wait. In their place, some outdoor shots not affected by the power outage were immediately set up, powered by a generator.

Later that morning while helping Patrick set up for a shot, I had a chance to tell him that I had received and read my copy of the *5-25-77* script just days before. I mentioned that after reading it, I believed his movie was going to be a big hit. I wasn't just saying that, either—this film has something for everyone. You don't have to be a sci-fi geek or even a *Star Wars* fan to appreciate the heartwarming, funny and very human story that Patrick is telling. Knowing that I truly meant what I said, he thanked me, adding that he really needed to hear some encouragement, given the obstacles to shooting.

After lunch, I left the shooting location to begin my real job. I arrived at the warehouse where set builders were busy working on projects that would be needed for the following day. Since the scene at ILM was last on the shooting schedule, no further work had been done on this set. Again, I wondered if it was going to be ready—but I had no time to think about that. Instead, I needed to focus on the painstaking task before me.

I set up a couple of long tables by the double doors leading to what would become the ILM area. One by one I brought the large boxes out of the model room to begin unpacking them. Sure I would have to repack all these items once filming was complete, I brought out my camera so I could take detailed photos of how everything had been packed. I had to stay organized, so I kept a folder full of my photos, notes, a contact sheet as well as production call sheets, a shooting schedule and the script. This folder proved more valuable to me as time went on.

My first official duty as "model guy" was setting up Scott Alexander's X-Wing models. Earlier he had sent me detailed notes on how to unpack and assemble these studio-scale fighter replicas. For shipping purposes, Scott had left some parts unassembled. I was supposed to attach the wings to the fuselages, for example, and complete the cockpit detail by adding the pilots, canopies and R2 units. This was simple enough—or so I thought!

Because three of the four X-Wing fighters were breakaway models, I thought it best to start with those and then move on to the remaining hero version. The breakaway models came in two boxes. When I opened the box containing the wings I found, to my horror, that these breakaway models had arrived *broken away!* Out of the 12 separate wings (four wings per fighter), only one was still intact. All the rest were broken, some in very small pieces.

Filming actress Emmie Chen.

Patrick sets up an outdoor shot after wind blew the power out.

I spent hours fixing broken X-wings... so they can be smashed to bits!

The models and all the other items on loan to us were locked in this room (my "office") every night.

Clearly, I could see that Scott had taken great care in packing these brittle resin parts as best he could. But it was no use—they had still been damaged during shipping. It looked like these boxes must have been handled with anything *but* care while en route to the set!

Fortunately, I was able to reach Scott by phone and I explained to him what had happened. Disappointed but optimistic, he talked me through the process of fixing and correctly repositioning the broken pieces. With all these repairs now needed, unpacking anything else would have to wait until morning.

YOU DON'T KNOW WHAT YOU'VE GOT THERE?

My plan for the next day was to continue unpacking and readying the models. I had managed to finish fixing the wings of Scott's X-Wing fighter models late the previous night. I was then able to complete work on all the X-Wing replicas during the morning. I had it in mind I would be working with the models all day while the shooting schedule took the cast and crew to their next filming location at the Genesee Theater in Waukegan, Illinois. There, filming of actors and extras was to take up the entire day. As much as I wanted to be there, however, I felt I just had too much to do.

Then Rob, who was busy at the warehouse as well, came to me and said that he just got off the phone with Leigh. He said she needed me to take a "box of stuff" over to the theater where Patrick would go through the contents to choose what he needed for a scene the next day. Rob showed me where to find this box and said I should head over to the location right away. So, taking a break from the models, I put this box full of large envelopes in my car and off I went.

The Genesee Theater wasn't far away. So, before long, I was carrying the box of envelopes around the shooting location looking for Leigh. I found Dan who was one of the assistant directors I met when I first arrived. He was on stage coordinating the flood of extras that had filled the theater. Dan used his headset to track down Leigh for me, who, as producer, was moving here and there all over the building seeing to the smooth operation of every aspect of the production.

When Leigh finally caught up with me she explained that Patrick needed to go through the contents in the box. She said I should be ready to organize the items into groups according to what was *in* and what was *out*. This sounded simple enough. But, she added, we had to wait for Patrick in order to get started. At that time he was filming a scene backstage in which he was not only directing but was also in front of the camera. Not only was Patrick the writer and director of *5-25-77*, he also played parts in it. He was playing director Stanley Kubrick of *2001: A Space Odyssey*, and he would also play the part of his own father in the film.

When Patrick's scenes as Kubrick were complete Leigh and I planned to catch him in the makeup room where he would be getting a shave and hair cut in preparation for playing the part of his father that same day. Every single minute of the movie-making process had to be utilized, so Leigh would arrange for Patrick to sift through the stuff in the box I had brought while he would

The Genesee Theater (photo by Jay William Stephen).

Some Close Encounters *production items on loan from Douglas Trumbull.*

Actor Kevin Stephens (Steven Spielberg) with just a few of the many Close Encounters *storyboards on loan from Douglas Trumbull.*

A closeup of a Close Encounters *storyboard.*

be having his hair cut. In the meantime, I had to wait.

While Leigh was off making these plans, I was near a table where there were snacks and drinks available for the cast and crew. I decided to get a cup of orange juice while I waited. I barely had a sip from this cup when Leigh arrived to hurriedly usher me to the makeup room. As I picked up the box I had brought, she took the orange juice cup from my hand. We then had to wait for an elevator to take us down below the stage to the dressing room. While we were waiting I reached for my cup with one hand while balancing the large box in the other. Leigh indicated she would rather hold on to it. After all, she didn't want anything to accidentally spill into the box.

It was then that I finally decided to ask what it was I'd been hauling around all this time.

"You don't know what you've got there?" she asked.

Looking down at the large envelopes like I should know, but did not, I said, "No."

"Those are the actual *Close Encounters* storyboards and production photos on loan to us from Douglas Trumbull," was her response.

When Leigh said this all I could picture in my mind was Steven Spielberg himself shuffling through every last piece of the 'fortune' that was now in my hands. With my eyes wide and my jaw open, I suddenly found I had a tighter grip on the box than before. All I could say was, "Oh...right...you hold the orange juice."

In the makeup room I had a chance to take the photos and storyboards out of the envelopes. It was then I realized that Patrick would be choosing which pieces to use as set dressing for the scene that would take place in

'Steven Spielberg's' office at Future General. Concealing my ignorance-turned-excitement over what I was now holding in my hands, I familiarized myself with these icons of cinematic history to be better prepared when the director made his choices.

Patrick came in feeling good about the shots he just completed as Stanley Kubrick. He greeted me and we got right down to business. With a smooth nonchalance, I tried not to let on that I hadn't known what I'd been carrying all this time. As far as Patrick was concerned, I knew the importance of what I had all along!

As he was getting a buzz cut from the hair stylist, I handed him groups of storyboards. He handed them back to me one at a time saying, "Yes...yes...no...yes...Hey, that's a good one! Yes...yes...no...no...yes..."

I then organized his choices. After that, I headed back to the soundstage, once again convinced I really did have the best job in the production!

CHAPTER SEVEN

The Soundstage

UNLOADING MODELS
AND A BIT OF MOVIE HISTORY

Back at the soundstage, I continued unloading the *Star Wars* shooting miniature replicas. The X-Wings were now done, so I moved on to the 6-foot model of the Rebel Blockade Runner spaceship. This was one of the few replicas I had not procured, so this was the first time I saw it. Rob and Dan cautioned me about it. They were hesitant to even touch it. Handling this miniature was a task they gladly left to me as the official "model guy."

After examining the ship closely I could understand why they were so reluctant to touch it. Big models like this are difficult to work with. It is even worse when they are big, heavy, and very fragile. I have to give the builder a lot of credit, though—the Rebel Blockade Runner is not an easy subject to replicate. I recognized that it was built with the same just-for-the-love-of-it care that I put into my Star Destroyer models.

The rebel ship arrived in two parts with the huge engines detached from the rest of the model. Immediately I could see that this miniature could only be handled in certain places. The real problem was there were very few points from which it could be safely lifted. This made the ship difficult to assemble and even more difficult to mount on a stand for filming. A half-inch thick metal rod about a yard long had been supplied and this was the only means of mounting it. There was just no safe way I was going to get it all together by myself so I asked Rob for help.

Between the two of us, we managed to figure out a setup that eventually worked. We quickly found that the engines made the model tail heavy when mounted on the supplied rod, so I drew up a quick sketch of a padded pedestal that would hold up the back end and Rob fabricated this in no time. When we finally propped the huge beast of a model on the rod and pedestal, I must say it looked very impressive.

I had been looking forward to seeing the T.I.E. Fighter replica for months since I first contacted the owner. It was in a huge box buried in packing peanuts. Like every other model, some assembly was required. Made of solid resin, this model was also heavy and quite delicate. Once it was together, however, the assembled miniature was an amazing sight. Like Scott Alexander's X-Wing fighters, the T.I.E. fighter recreation was about as close as you could get to seeing the real thing. It was a big hit with the *Star Wars* fans in the cast and crew.

The same person who supplied this miniature also provided parts of un-built T.I.E. Fighter models and pieces from replica Y-Wing Fighters. When it came to a Y-Wing, I was glad we at least had some pieces of a few of them to show. In addition to the Master Replicas version that I had been unable to procure, I did manage to find one other well-built Y-Wing replica. Unfortunately, the owner was not interested in lending it to the production. I can't say I blame anyone who turned us down. After all, it is a big risk to loan out something that expensive and special. Even with insurance, many of these items are irreplaceable.

As I unpacked the *Star Wars* models, I arranged them on a large table. With my Star Destroyer, Escape Pod, and Death Star panels added to the mix, it was finally beginning to look like the ILM archives there on the set. I made sure to take plenty of photos for posterity. No question about it, I really loved my job!

After the *Star Wars* models had been unpacked, next up were Greg Jein's items. I started with what was called a "detail ring" on my list of items. It was a detailed miniature section from the *Close Encounters* Mother Ship. If you hadn't known what this was, you wouldn't have looked at it twice. Most people who saw it on set didn't, but I knew what I was holding! This was the ring-shaped portion of the Mother Ship just below the 'lip' of the large dome. It was highly detailed with rectangular shapes. This portion of the Mother Ship model could be seen in the film when the character of Gillian looks up at the ship as it first appears over Devil's Tower.

I never found out whether this was a spare part or a section from the filming model itself. I guessed it was probably a spare because I haven't heard of anyone saying there were pieces missing from the filming model (which is currently on display at the National Air and Space Museum's Dulles facility). It was certainly an original artifact from the film, though, because it looked as if it had

Me in my element. I can honestly say I appeared in a movie with a bunch of gorgeous models.

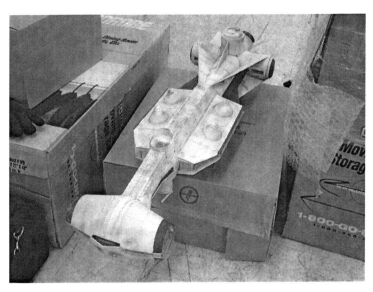

Unpacking the huge Blockade runner replica, minus the engines.

I was in charge of this camera head, which shot the effects for my favorite movie, Star Wars.

With Greg Jein's Devil's Tower model made for Close Encounters.

30 years worth of dust on it! I would have to clean it up before filming.

Next I opened the box containing unused parts from the Flying Saucer miniatures also built for *Close Encounters*. Like the Mother Ship ring, they also had a thick layer of dust. They looked as though they must have been stored and ignored in Greg's garage for the three decades. As I unpacked them, I received an unexpected surprise when I found that these flying saucers had actually transported 'life forms' on their journey to me as two live spiders crawled out of them!

Moving along, we came to what I really wanted to see next—the Devil's Tower miniature. Rob came over to help unpack this since we were both very interested in it. From what I understood, this was the model used in the final scenes with the Mother Ship. We carefully unwrapped it like surgeons performing a delicate operation. Once unwrapped, I set it on the table and I could suddenly hear John Williams' score in my mind. This was more like it! Now I felt like I was dealing with a cinematic icon. Having my first all out 'geek moment,' I had Rob take pictures of me posing with it.

PRODUCTION WOES
AND AN UNEXPECTED OPPORTUNITY

More than anything else, the two things most movies have working against them are time and money. There's always a need for more of both, and the *5-25-77* production was feeling the effects of those needs. The schedule was being pushed back for various reasons and sets were not being finished on time. Patrick said it best when he explained that the budget was "somewhere between insane and implausible." It was not exactly ultra-low; it was just that the film was ultra-ambitious for its budget.

Despite these problems, however, everyone was working very hard to keep up. I continued having my doubts that the ILM set would be ready on schedule. Recreating ILM on a single soundstage was ultra-ambitious in and of itself. In a conversation I had with Leigh, she admitted that she was also concerned. After talking about it further, I told her that if I could help out in any way they could count on me.

I put everything I had into what I was doing because I really believed in this movie. One of the reasons I wanted to be a part of it—even if only a small part—was because I wanted to see that the ILM scenes would be done right. I thought it would be a shame if these scenes were not everything they could be due to production woes.

The Future General set was also of concern since the *Close Encounters* scenes were scheduled to be filmed prior to the ILM sequence. Rob took the initiative and started putting the Future General set together on his own while I was unpacking the models. By the time I finished, he called me over to have a look at his recreation of the Future General model shop. It looked great!

Since I was a model-maker, Rob asked me to help 'dress' the set. I gladly agreed to help him out, though I felt he'd already gotten pretty far on his own. There were several workstations on which we arranged glues, paints, knives, brushes, model kits—all the stuff you would expect to see in a model shop. We arranged the supplies to look like they had been well used. We had things like spilled paint, filthy rags, kit parts scattered everywhere, and small bulletin boards with notes stuck on them.

Before long, it was after midnight. There was still more to do, so we expected to pick up where we had left off the next morning. I locked the models in my "office" for the night and went back to the hotel.

The next morning I had the digital photos I'd taken the previous day printed out before heading to the sound-stage. Leigh had informed us that she and Patrick were going to be there early that morning, so Rob and I planned to arrive early to meet them. When Patrick and Leigh arrived they began to discuss the production difficulties.

After a while, I felt that Patrick needed something to smile about, so I decided to show him my photos.

As he looked at one after the other, I could see a twinkle in his eye. The 'sci-fi geek,' the adolescent subject of this movie, was alive and well in this now adult film-maker. It gave him comfort to know that my portion of the ILM scene would be ready for the camera. After gazing at the pictures, he wanted to see the Future General set where he was equally pleased with the progress Rob had been making. Our extra efforts gave Patrick a much needed lift.

After all, *5-25-77* was more than just another movie to him, it was his dream project. I was pleased that Patrick was pleased. I was immensely grateful to him for inviting me to be a part of this project, so I wanted it to be the best it could possibly be. Of course, it was also my dream-come-true opportunity to be working on a movie, and doubly so since *5-25-77* is a movie which involves

Star Wars and ILM.

At that moment, Patrick decided to do something none of us saw coming. He was so impressed with our progress that he made the decision to give both Rob and me a 'field promotion' right there on the spot. From that point on, all the other departments would answer to us. The Future General set would now be Rob's responsibility, and turning to me, he said I would be in charge of the ILM set.

"You will be responsible for everything that happens beyond those double doors," Patrick said to me, pointing in the direction of the area reserved for the *Star Wars* scenes.

He would come up with new titles for us. Rob would be "Visual Consultant for the Future General Set," while I would now be the "Visual Consultant for the Industrial Light & Magic Set"—or something like that. The exact wording would be decided later.

To say I was stunned would be a major understatement. After all, Rob had experience working on sets, but I had none. Patrick said he knew I wasn't expecting this, and I could turn it down if I felt I wasn't up to it. "Still," he said, "the job is yours if you want the responsibility."
To put all this in perspective, Patrick had just taken the largest, most complicated set in the entire film and handed it to a guy with absolutely no movie experience whatsoever. I couldn't believe it!

Like everything that had happened to me since I first decided to build a studio-scale model, just when I thought the situation couldn't get any better, it did. The magnitude of this opportunity was too great. There was no way I was going to turn it down. ILM was now mine!

[Years later I asked Patrick about this. He told me that he knew that I would 'freak out' at first, yet, even though he gave me the option to turn it down, he knew I would do it. He said he watched me on set, and I reminded him of himself when he first got involved in movie-making. He also knew that I had more knowledge about ILM than everyone else on set besides him, and I understood what he was trying to accomplish.]

Later that day I got a call from Scott Alexander. He wanted to find out how the shoot was progressing. As I tried to remember the fancy title I had just been given, I told Scott what Patrick had done. Laughing with surprise at this news, Scott congratulated me by exclaiming that, in just two days, I had gone from an art intern to an art director on my first movie! That's when it all really started to sink in.

With the models now ready for the camera, I turned my attention to this next great challenge. I was looking forward with great anticipation to this awesome new responsibility—the recreation of Industrial Light & Magic as it was in 1977!

CHAPTER EIGHT

Recreating Industrial Light & Magic

Industrial Light & Magic as it was in 1977 was a far cry from the huge, multi-divisional movie-making empire it is today. ILM, as most know, was founded by George Lucas in 1975 to develop new optical-effects techniques unlike anything that was done before *Star Wars*. To accomplish this, Lucas assembled a team of young experts and set them up in a warehouse in Van Nuys, California.

Twentieth Century Fox funded the *Star Wars* special-effects house with $2 million. With most of the budget going for the development of new technology and miniatures, there was very little money for anything else. Thus, they made the most of what they had while working long hours in, at times, extreme heat. Fans have all heard stories about the first ILM crew with the unorthodox working environment, the hippie attitude, the unenforced schedules, the goofing off, the makeshift 'dunking' tub in the parking lot, and the panic-stricken studio executives at Fox. Yet, in the end their efforts would blow audiences away and revolutionize the movie industry.

It is important to remember that for *5-25-77*, ILM of

1977 is first and foremost a plot element in the story that Patrick Read Johnson as writer and director was telling. Recreating ILM on the soundstage had to be done in a way that best tells that story. Yet, at the same time both Patrick and I wanted to truthfully tell something of the extraordinary people who worked on *Star Wars* in a way that celebrates their achievement.

Because my new position was unexpected, I did not bring my large collection of books, videos and DVDs with me to use as references for creating the original ILM. The best reference I had, of course, was Patrick's first hand account. But, Patrick also had his own collection similar to mine, and he supplied me with some of his books to refer to. I was happy to see that most of them were the same books I had back home. Because mine weren't personally autographed by Gary Kurtz like his, I tried to be extra careful with them.

From the moment I first walked in the building I could see why Patrick chose this warehouse to represent ILM. It closely resembled the Van Nuys facility according to the photos and documentaries I had seen of it. The first thing we did was discuss the overall layout. With the notes Patrick made I drew a floor plan of the stage area mapping out all the major set elements, model placement, and how the camera would be tracked through the scene.

To turn that drawing into a functional movie set required a lot of ingenuity and a lot of hard work. I would enlist the talent and skills of the crew to make it happen. Leigh had put together a team assigned to assist me in anything I needed. Since this part of the soundstage was used for storage, little could be done until the huge, heavy items were relocated. I had the unhappy job of giving my team the unpleasant task of moving all that heavy stuff. The dedication those guys put into clearing that area was nothing less than inspirational! All together it took more hours than I care to count, but they tackled the problem head on and got it done.

Meanwhile, I began focusing my attention on finishing the Dykstraflex motion-control replica. In every reference I saw of this pre-home computer contraption, one detail stood out more than others that I had to mimic... cables, cables and more cables! There were tons of cables taped all over the thing! As computers of the period go, the real thing must have been a nightmare to engineer.

For props and set dressing, I had what looked like a large pile of junk at my disposal. In there I found spools of cables in varying thicknesses. Trying to make it look like the reference photos, I attached cable after cable to the motion-control rig. I got to a point where I thought I just might have enough of these cables on it, but to ensure the right look I added even more. I'm sure I must've put between 150 and 200 yards of cables on it in several layers. I then found interesting looking objects to double as electronic and mechanical gizmos. In a way, this was like kitbashing on a large scale using old discarded objects and junk.

Much of what I had to do to create ILM was what ILM had to do to create *Star Wars*. To me, this was actually a good thing, as it added to the authenticity of the set. It had to have that thrown together look. All of ILM's budget went into effects and not furnishings. This can be seen in photos of ILM at the time. Work benches were nothing more than pieces of plywood or doors placed on sawhorses. For our model shop, I would collect as many sawhorses not in use that I could find and asked the crew to create several more.

To save time, I had the tabletops of the Future General model shop set, shot earlier in the week, separated from their legs (model supplies and all) and transferred to the ILM set where the sawhorses were positioned and ready to receive them. The Future General set also had a huge metal shelf full of supplies and model kits. That had to be disassembled and relocated to the ILM model shop set, where it was reassembled and restocked. For additional set dressing, we put copies of *Star Wars* storyboards on the walls of the model shop. Some of that heavy equipment that had previously been stored in the building actually made it into the scene, posing as model-making machinery.

We had ordered two bluescreens that were, of course, very important to the ILM set. One of them was used for actual bluescreen shots for other scenes in *5-25-77*. That one—the larger of the two—covered much of the back wall where the Dykstraflex motion-control rig was positioned. The smaller one was used purely as set dressing, and was positioned in an area closer to the 'entrance' to our ILM facility.

Patrick reserved an area of the set where he wanted me to set up my Death Star surface panel models. I had three of them at 2-feet square. I described the first two, which I made out of wood and other materials. The original Death Star surface was made out of hundreds of foam castings.

Patrick's script called for one foam panel to be

picked up and tossed. I didn't know this when I built my first two, so I had to quickly create a foam panel on the spot. I had Rob build me a 6 x 2-foot table at about 3-feet high where I set the panels. In an open space in front of this table, Patrick asked me to position fluorescent ping pong balls on pedestals. John Knoll of ILM and visual effects supervisor for *Star Wars: Episodes I-III* would fill in that space with computer generated Death Star surfacing. I measured an area that was 16 x 10-feet, and set the ping pong balls at each corner on pedestals. Again, Rob came through with the pedestals, which, in the final scene, will be the actual legs of imaginary tables with the Death Star surface added later in post production.

Another element needed was a 6-foot square crate to house the 5-foot Millennium Falcon model (added later in post production, courtesy of John Knoll). Once again, I asked Rob and he built one for me in record time.

With these and other set elements in place, it was time for me to bring out the rest of the *Star Wars* replica models. One by one I put them in position around the set. I had the un-built models fill the model shop work benches. Each table was designated as the X-wing table, the T.I.E. table, Y-wing and so on. I reserved two tables for the Breakaway X-wings; One on which they would be standing in a row where the actor playing John Dykstra would snatch one up as he walks by, and the other where he would smash the model to pieces against it. That second table I nailed to the saw horses so that it would stay in place when the X-wings met their doom.

I had the Star Destroyer, Escape Pod, T.I.E. Fighter and Hero X-wing all mounted on stands and positioned in

Setting up my Star Destroyer for the shoot. Building this model was one of the best decisions I ever made.
(photo by Jay William Stephen)

Recreating ILM of 1977 for 5-25-77 was the most difficult, most rewarding, and most FUN job I've ever had in my career!
(photo by Jay William Stephen)

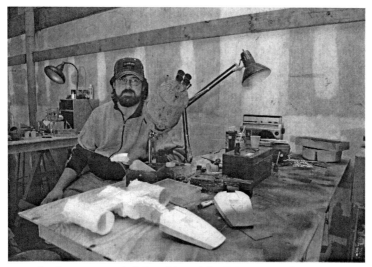

Setting up one of eight tables of the ILM set 'model shop.'
(photo by Jay William Stephen)

John Francis Daley (Pat), Patrick and me with the Landspeeder.
(photo by Jay William Stephen)

specific areas of the set. The yard-long mounting rod for the huge Blockade runner was much too low for filming, so we had to improvise to raise it nearly twice as high. As I mentioned before, the size and weight of this fragile model made such a task very difficult.

I don't know if it was luck or planned, but Wasili's Landspeeder arrived from Amsterdam with no time to spare to take its place on the set. I was looking forward to seeing it since the day Wasili first contacted me about building it. Believe me, I was not disappointed! The word around the set when I brought it out was, "Wasili rocks!"

I set it on a table in an area of the set reserved for it. As set dressing for the ILM model shop, I had several model kits of all kinds that I positioned at every station. As an inside joke, I placed a model kit of a Ford Pinto next to this replica of Luke Skywalker's worn-out hot-rod, since a real Ford Pinto was the beat-up ride of *5-25-77's* main character, 'Pat Johnson.'

Finally, after days and nights of long hours, little sleep and a lot of hard work, the Industrial Light & Magic set was complete. I felt a sense of relief and great accomplishment. Making the best of what limited time and resources I had, I tried to be as accurate as possible, and yet, I felt it equally, or even more important to capture the 'essence' of ILM for the sake of the *5-25-77* story. In the end, as one who wanted to see this project done right, I was quite happy with the result.

With great pride in what was accomplished, I went to find Patrick to tell him that ILM was ready. He'd been waiting a long time to hear those words. Even though I was happy with it, ultimately I knew it was Patrick who needed to be satisfied, and I could tell right away that he was. As he walked into the set he had a look on his face that showed why he wanted to make this movie in the first place.

Together we walked through the set. Ideas for shooting the scene seemed to come to him spontaneously—ideas that would enhance his original plan. As we came to specific models, Patrick would say, "Wouldn't it be really cool if the camera came through like this..." With laughter and high fives we couldn't wait to shoot the scene based on these new ideas! He was like a kid in a candy store; someone who was in his element. The enthusiasm he displayed when he first shared his vision for this scene with me many months before was reprised as he could now see and walk through this finished set. It was 'creativity in action' for Patrick, it was fulfilling as an artist for me, and it was a whole lot of fun for both of us! It was what I imagined movie-making should be all about.

SHOOTING THE SCENE

With as much as has been written about *Star Wars* by fans and film critics, I believe it all can be boiled down to one word... FUN! *Star Wars* was meant to be an enjoyable movie experience. For those of us fortunate enough to be around when the film first opened in 1977, the fun and magic of seeing *Star Wars* for the first time was a unique experience that has never quite been duplicated by any other movie. No one had ever seen anything like it before. It was fresh, it was positive and it took the nation, and the world, totally by surprise, going on to become a world-wide cultural phenomenon.

For those younger *Star Wars* fans not around back in 1977 who wonder what it was like for those of us who were, *5-25-77* should give them a good idea. As a movie-maker, Patrick's goal was to shoot the ILM scene in such a way as to capture a portion of that 'original' fun that *Star Wars* instilled so audiences today can experience, or re-live it in a fresh, new way. He would do this through the eyes of *5-25-77's* main character played by actor John Francis Daley, who did a magnificent job throughout the entire film as young 'Pat Johnson.'

In the story, young Pat tours the ILM facility with a sense of awe and wonder. He sees the models and a rough cut of the film. He realizes he is the first to learn just how special, and how much fun this new *Star Wars* movie will be before anyone else—before it is even in theaters. Being an enthusiastic teenage sci-fi geek, Pat can't wait to share his life-changing experience with his family, friends and classmates.

But, how do you explain what a *T.I.E. Fighter,* *Millennium Falcon*, or a *Wookie* is to people who have never heard of such 'nonsense?' Such is Pat's dilemma, one that further isolates him as the town weirdo. That is, until *Star Wars* is finally released.

That is the story behind the scene. Now we were about to shoot it. All the months of building models and recruiting model-makers, and the long days of hard work putting the ILM set together came down to this—this was finally the moment for which I was introduced to the world of movie-making.

I looked forward to being an ILM extra. Earlier in

the week I had already appeared in the Future General scene as one of Steven Spielberg's *Close Encounters* model-makers. In the Future General scene I worked with actor, David Shin, who was wonderful as Greg Jein. Now I was going to play an ILM crew member and work with actor Dan Behrendt, who did a fantastic job as John Dyskstra.

I was very impressed with both David and Dan, as they were only on hand for their scenes and that's all, while the rest of us had been continuously on set day after day. I thought how hard it must be for these actors to arrive on set for a single day and jump into character cold like that. I especially felt that way about Dan who, as Dykstra, had to spew out nonstop techno-babble few people are meant to understand as the camera rolled. On *Star Wars*, it is said that George Lucas' one direction was, "Faster and more intense." Dan would have to proceed under similar direction from Patrick for this scene.

I talked with Dan before rehearsals to fill him in on what Patrick was looking for from the Dykstra character. I told him to just think "caffeine." This gave him time to mentally prepare. He said it took him a lot of practice to memorize his difficult lines before coming to work that day. I only had to correct him once when referring to the Escape Pod as an Escape 'Capsule.' Not that it was necessarily wrong to call it that, but I could see *Star Wars* fans everywhere nitpicking over it.

In the end, though, Dan pulled off his lines brilliantly. Because of the pacing of the scene, several rehearsals were necessary to ensure every mark was hit at just the right time. After rehearsals, when John Daley and Dan

Patrick demonstrates for the crew how the camera should pass by the hero X-wing model.

Lighting the models on set.

Rehearsing the camera moves around the large ILM set.

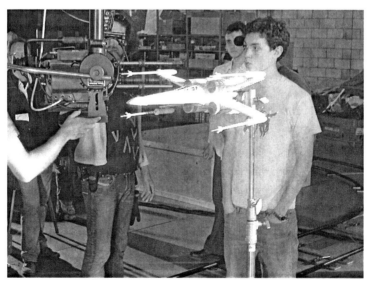

John Francis Daley with the hero X-wing model between rehearsals.

were finished in hair and wardrobe, we were ready to shoot. All the actors and extras took their places around the set. There were "model-makers" at the work stations, "filming crew" at the motion-control unit and people ready to carry props here and there, all of which brought life to our tribute to Industrial Light & Magic.

I also took my place as an ILM technician. As the camera and actors pass by, I am supposed to be removing my Escape Pod from a stand. It may not win me an Oscar, but I couldn't have been happier about what I was doing. Of course, I was still on the job as the "model guy," so I had supplies on hand ready to repair the foam Death Star panel that Dan would toss take after take. I was glad that I only needed to do minor repairs once or twice, as it held up pretty well. I also had to go around the huge set to reposition models that get moved during the scene. The scene also involved Scott Alexander's breakaway X-wing Fighters, which were now poised and ready to be smashed to bits. Between takes, someone asked me if I cringed every time one was destroyed, especially after all the hours I put into repairing them. It really didn't bother me because, like the foam panel, that is what they were there for.

True, the X-wings were expertly crafted and beautifully painted by Scott, and would have been a valuable addition to anyone's collection. But, they had been created as props that served as tools to tell a story (although, I must confess, I did keep the pieces of one of them as a souvenir, and even rebuilt it).

One by one, take after take the X-wings were utterly destroyed. Like shattering a champagne bottle against a new vessel in a christening ceremony, the last X-wing came crashing against the table signifying the end of the scene, and with it, the end of principal photography on 5-25-77. I can honestly say that if the final scene is anything like the fun we experienced shooting it, then audiences will thoroughly enjoy it, and Patrick will have accomplished his goal!

[In 2008, 5-25-77 was screened as '77 at the Hamptons International Film Festival. When the audiences saw the ILM scene, a collective gasp of excitement could be heard throughout the sold-out theater. Upon hearing that—and with a big smile on my face—I leaned over to whisper in my wife's ear, "I did that."]

The day after the ILM scene was shot, I spent many hours packing all the models on loan to us for the return trip back to their owners. In the midst of this, Patrick came to the set with the one model he'd kept with him the entire time—Greg Jein's priceless study model of the Mother Ship.

Patrick asked me to pack it with some additional support for the trip home to Greg. I told him I would take care of it for him. It seemed fitting that he handed over to me this object of great value, so carefully guarded, and was then able to walk away confident that it was in capable hands. It sort of typified what had happened to me those nine months on a larger scale.

For Patrick, the ILM experience was an important, pivotal moment in the movie and in his real life. He handed the ILM set over to me with the same confidence and trust,

Don't blink or you'll miss me! Here I am with my Escape Pod as John Daley as 'Pat' walks past me in the ILM scene.

My Star Destroyer behind the Blockade Runner in the ILM scene.

John picks up the pieces of the smashed X-wing model in the ILM model shop.

The Close Encounters *Mother Ship study model built by Greg Jein.*

and I did my very best to take care of it for him. At first I wondered how Patrick could take such an important set for such an important scene and entrust it to someone with no movie experience. But when I think about it, he'd only ever asked for a single model. And, seeing a once-in-a-lifetime opportunity before me, I refused to settle for just that.

As a result, in the nine months he had known me, Patrick could see that I was someone who could get things done. And I usually got things done quickly and inexpensively while maintaining a high quality standard. I said at the beginning that I was determined to make the most of this opportunity. By working hard and giving it everything I had I did just that. I got way more out of this than I could have ever imagined.

At the wrap party Patrick and I took turns thanking each other. He thanked me for helping make his dream of *5-25-77* come true, I thanked him for my movie-making dream come true.

As the film moved into post production, I expected that my work on *5-25-77* was finished... but it wasn't.

CHAPTER NINE

Post Production

Just when I thought my work on *5-25-77* was complete, my incredible movie-making experience took an unexpected twist. In November 2006, I received an e-mail from Patrick Read Johnson. He was faced with a dilemma concerning the portion of the ILM scene where the camera point of view 'flies' over the surface of the Death Star.

As I stated before, our plan on set was to begin the shot with the three surface panel models I created. Beyond them, in an open 16 x 10-foot area, there would be a computer generated model to complete the Death Star flyover. Patrick had asked me to position ping pong balls on set to mark this area so the CG model could be added in post production. Originally, John Knoll of Industrial Light & Magic was going to supply the computer generated Death Star model.

John Knoll has become something of a giant in visual effects in the last decade. He attributes much of his breakthrough successes to his friend, Patrick Read Johnson. Early in his career, John was given an opportunity to show what he could do when Patrick asked him to handle a difficult effect on a film Patrick was directing. After proving himself, John would later become the visual effects supervisor on *Star Wars: Episodes I-III*.

It was during the making of that second *Star Wars* trilogy that John told Patrick there had been computer Death Star surfacing done as fill-ins here and there for areas of the planet Coruscant. Those fill-ins might be just what we needed. However, like the proverbial needle in the haystack, that particular CG rendering could not be located in time amongst the huge archive of files. Therefore, he would try to find the time to construct one for us.

THE DILEMMA

John's role on *5-25-77* would be visual effects consultant. It is a much more limited role than visual effects supervisor, which John had already been assigned to on another film that was moving into post production at the same time as *5-25-77*. John wanted to be there for Patrick in any way he could despite his busy schedule, and he had made many valuable contributions to *5-25-77* already.

Movie-making is a rigid, deadline-oriented business requiring 100% and more from those who work on them. Eventually John's other projects required his full attention. As a result, John had no time to construct the CG Death Star model. Patrick is no stranger to the demands of movie-making deadlines. Understanding John's position, Patrick had to do what I believe is one of the things he does best—take a setback and turn it into an advantage. Where there is a need, Patrick will find a way.

First, Patrick had to assess the situation with his

effects crew. Post production was moving along steadily on *5-25-77*. The visual effects supervisor on the film is Mike Pawlak. Mike is very capable, and would've jumped at the opportunity to create the much needed CG Death Star surface. But, he and all the effects personnel had a full plate already with no spare time to create a CG Death Star surface.

THE SOLUTION

While all this was happening, I was back home thinking my contributions to *5-25-77* were behind me. I so much enjoyed my work on the movie that I wished there was more I could do.

One weekend I was thinking about the scene with the Death Star surface. I had two photos taken on set of the open area where the CG model would eventually be—one taken by me, the other by photographer Jay William Stephen. I began to wonder what it would look like with the CG model in place. Then I thought, maybe I didn't have to wait. I began to construct a much smaller scale version of the Death Star surface as a model that covered a 4 x 2-foot board using copies of tiny, fan-made resin Death Star panels I bought at a convention.

After assembling and painting it, I photographed it to match the position and lighting of each photo. I then composited the model into those photos. When I finished, I thought Patrick might like to see them. So, I e-mailed them to him with a short note saying something about, "What the scene might look like when finished..."

His response was more than I expected. He told me

about his problem. We traded a few more e-mails about it in the following weeks. At one point, he even considered using the model I built to fill the scene. But, we both knew that a CG model would be the best way to do it.

Then suddenly, once again, he surprised me with another "proposal." With all his effects crew tied up with other tasks, he told me that he was thinking about the composite photos I had sent him. With as much confidence in me as he had during production, he told me that if any-one could do it, I could. He then asked me if I would like to take a crack at creating the CG Death Star surface—and now the trench as well.

I learned early on that when Patrick asks me if I would like to take a crack at something, there is only one answer—just say "yes" and figure it out as you go. When I read his e-mail, I knew I couldn't turn this opportunity down any more than when he asked me to art direct the very set for which he needed this CG model. My only problems were I hadn't done anything 3-D on the comput-er in 10 years, and I had no software to do it with.

I decided to put the e-mail aside and call. Patrick answered, and I eagerly told him I would do it. I also told him that I needed the software to do it with. He then put me in touch with Mike Pawlak who helped me get the ball rolling.

Of course, the finished model was needed ASAP. Because of this, I had to learn the 3-D program as I built the model. The software was actually a free, downloadable program off the internet. The software I had used years earlier was called Form-Z, a very complex program with tools upon tools located all around the interface. I was very glad that the program I would be building the Death Star surface with was much easier to learn.

I would work a full day at my graphic design job, then come home and immediately spend each night working on the model. The first night I was able to complete one full panel of the surface in about four hours. That meant one down, 52 panels to go!

As most *Star Wars* fans know, there were only six panels designed for the Death Star surface that were built and copied in foam hundreds of times, then cut and arranged like a huge puzzle. My CG Death Star surface would be built the same way. After I completed the sixth panel, it was then a matter of copying and arranging them to construct a trench and surface.

Even though I marked off the area on set where the Death Star would be, I really didn't know exactly what Patrick had in mind. So, I checked with Mike to make sure what I was building in the computer was correct for the scene. I didn't know, for example that Patrick wanted the trench in the surface, or how that trench would be aligned. Once Mike explained it to me, I was able to build the computer model appropriately.

I sent JPG images of my progress to Mike and Patrick almost daily. I knew that from the pacing of the scene that the Death Star surface would be in motion on screen, and not for a very long time. This meant that I had an advantage in the small amount of detailing needed for the panels. Ironically, when I sent one of my progress images to Patrick, he pointed out that I probably had too much detail for what the actual crude panels really looked like. I guess I was having too much fun with it, and in CG

This is one of the composite photos I sent to Patrick that made him decide to ask me to create the CG model.

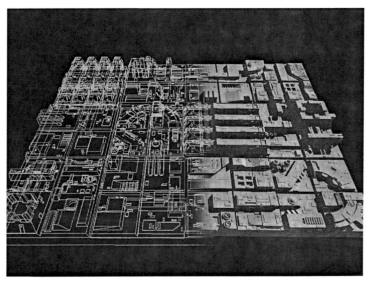

the CG model in progress.

The finished model.

The CG Death Star in the ILM scene.

there is so much you can do that it is difficult to know where to stop. After a week, I had the surface with trench completed. Because in the scene it was to represent a real, physical model for a make-believe special effects shot, I then had to build in the computer the 'wooden' tables the panels would sit on in our scene. The tables were modeled after the ones used at ILM back in 1977. Mike had sent me reference photos to make sure I got the right look.

They informed me that just before Thanksgiving, producer Gary Kurtz (*Star Wars, The Empire Strikes Back*) would be in town for a preliminary screening of *5-25-77*.

Naturally, and if at all possible, they wanted to have the Death Star surface in the scene for the screening. This left me less than a week to finish, but I was confident that it could be done. The final element Patrick wanted me to create was the Gun Towers that appear here and there around the surface. Once everything was complete I delivered it all to Mike.

5-25-77 gave me several opportunities, several firsts for me—my first movie experience, my first models/props built for a film, my first time art directing a set on a film, etc. Now I was delivering my first CG model. Both Patrick and Mike were very supportive of my efforts, knowing that I had very little time to complete the task they asked me to do. In the end, they were very satisfied with my work.

What's more, when I sent my final JPG image of the completed Death Star trench, Mike responded with an e-mail that read, "You should know that Gary Kurtz is here. When he saw your Death Star you got a HUGE smile out of him!"

When I read that I can guarantee that there was an even bigger smile on my face! I wrote back to Mike asking him to say hello to Mr. Kurtz for me, and to thank him (as the producer of *Star Wars*) for my awesome childhood memories!

CHAPTER TEN

Designing The Website

Even though the film was not quite finished, Patrick decided that he wanted to show his movie on the 30th anniversary of *Star Wars*. What better place than at *Star Wars* Celebration IV in LA in 2007? With the film deep in post production, plans for the screening of *5-25-77* on 5-25-07 were being made by director Patrick Read Johnson and producer Gary Kurtz.

To announce this screening, Patrick took down the initial movie website at www.5-25-77.com and replaced it with a one page ad that started with, "Even after 30 years, you never forget your first time: *5-25-77* on 5-25-07."

Patrick and I hadn't spoken about it, but, when the screening in LA was over I expected the website to be back up and running again. As it turned out, months went by, and that screening announcement still substituted for a full website. In my mind, the movie needed to have a continued web presence. Of course, this got me thinking.

Ideas would cross my mind about what the website could look like. I decided to come up with a few samples that defined a new look and style. I then offered my ideas to Patrick to use if he so chose for whenever he was ready to relaunch the site.

When Patrick is excited or happy about something, it is reflected in his e-mails in capital letters. There was no question that he felt I was going in the right direction when he wrote, "THAT IS BEAUTIFUL!" He then told me that he had been wondering for a long time what to do for the website, and that my take on it was, "SPECTACU-LAR!" It was then that he asked me if I wouldn't mind redesigning the entire site.

I already had some thoughts on what it could look like, and now I had the chance to go for it. I wanted the look of the site to revolve around the main character, Pat Johnson's love of movies. There is a line about Pat in the film, which can also be heard in the trailer which says, "To everybody else movies are something you do when you are tired of real life. To you real life is something you do when you are tired of watching movies." I thought that best describes Pat, and I wanted the website to reflect this thought.

Being in a movie theater is like being in a safe haven for the Pat Johnson character in the film. Right away I knew I wanted the website trailer to appear as though it were playing in a movie theater. I did the same thing for the gallery page. Keeping with the movie theater theme, I scanned old tickets found in a drawer to represent buttons to advance the gallery of photos and for 'getting into' the theater to see the trailer.

Patrick had given me the entire rough cut of the movie months earlier. I used that to extract any images I would need for characters and the gallery of photos. I spent countless hours going through the movie, over and over again to choose images at just the right moments.

Since the Pat character spends all his spare time making movies with a Super-8 movie camera in his backyard, I thought it appropriate to have the website menus appear as strips of Super-8 film.

I made good use of the movie poster art created by artist Mike Pawlak, who also served as the visual effects supervisor on the film. Coming up with variations of this poster, I was able to create the home page, synopsis, and production pages.

Originally Patrick asked me if I could have the site finished and online in a week. Considering my other commitments, I told him that wouldn't be possible. Instead I did my best to have it done in two weeks. But ideas inevitably kept coming. Before we knew it, two weeks turned into two months of what Patrick called a "productive period of gestation."

In that time Patrick came up with the idea of a map page that would further explain Pat's feelings about growing up on "the edge of the edge of nowhere," but would also show clips of the various places that are important to the story. Calling it "Pat's World," I submitted several designs before we got it just right.

Character descriptions were a team effort with ideas coming from myself, Patrick, producers, and even some of the actors.

Then at the beginning of October 2007, the new official *5-25-77* movie website was launched. And, like the movie itself, it went public as a work in progress.

For the premiere of the film at the 2008 Hamptons International Film Festival, the title of the film changed from *5-25-77* to just '*77*. This change required that I update the site in time for the festival.

Creating the movie website proved to be a challenge, as I was so new to website design and development at that time. But I got through it, and again, in yet another way, I was glad to be able to contribute to the progress of this film.

[In 2013, it was necessary to relaunch the updated website with a new URL: www.5-25-77themovie.com]

CHAPTER ELEVEN

The Visitor

By early June 2008, Patrick Read Johnson was making progress trying to finish *5-25-77*. He was putting the finishing touches in the editing process while John Knoll was working his magic on scenes that required very complex special effects.

At this same time, marketing of the film was in the hands of the William Morris Agency. That was exciting because Patrick was looking forward to the much needed financial backing from the agency necessary to finish the film. One of the decisions I was not in favor of, though, was that they changed the title of the film to just '77.

During all of this, I was again contacted by Patrick to build yet another model for the movie. Patrick had cut into the film a temporary animatic which included the 'Visitor' ship. In the *5-25-77* script (as in Patrick's real life story), the character of young Pat Johnson makes his Super-8 movies in his backyard and his garage-turned-soundstage. One of his homemade epics is called "The Visitor," about an alien being coming to Earth and trying to experience life as an earthling.

To create the footage of character Pat Johnson's

Super-8 film, Patrick needed a model of the Visitor's spaceship. As the film's model-making coordinator for the ILM scene of *5-25-77* ('77), he asked me if I would build the model for this scene.

Patrick had designed the ship in the same 3-D software I made the Death Star surface model with. It was a one-man (alien) spaceship with a diamond-like shape and a small cockpit. He sent me the file, which I dissected to make plans for a 17-inch long model. Unlike the *Star Wars* filming models, which had to look as though they were built by the ILM crew, this model had to look as though it were built by a teenage amateur. Therefore, I built it out of sheet styrene, leaving some rough edges. Patrick asked me to paint it using fluorescent orange and blue to match the full-size cockpit built for actor John Francis Daley to sit inside for closeups.

I found an alien figure on eBay that could fit inside the Visitor ship model, which resembled the alien mask worn by John as Pat Johnson in the film.

In less than a week I had the model finished. Patrick was going to come to my home to personally pick up the model. Patrick and I stayed in contact through e-mails and phone conversations, but I hadn't seen him since we shot all our scenes on set two years earlier. I was looking forward to his visit. He was coming from another visit to his friend and visual effects legend, Douglas Trumbull, who had been kind enough to lend us all the actual storyboards from *Close Encounters of the Third Kind* for scenes in *5-25-77*.

I always love to see Patrick's reactions to the work I do for him, and I couldn't wait to show him the model.

Before he arrived, I couldn't decide where and how I was going to present it to him, presentation being everything. Finally, I simply set it on the coffee table for him to see as he walked in the room. When he did, his eyes were immediately attracted to the bright, neon orange and blue of the Visitor ship. As usual, his reaction was very positive, like a kid at Christmas with a new toy! He was about to reach for it when he stopped suddenly to look up and ask, "May I?"

"Of course. It's yours!" I responded.

We had a great time during our visit. He showed me the amazing things John Knoll was doing for the movie and talked about some of the changes since the last cut of the film I saw. One of those changes involved the model I had just presented to him. It would be part of a very creative transition scene, a daydream sequence with this new model flying through the mind of the main character's imagination.

CHAPTER TWELVE

Promotional Opportunities

When I was working on creating the ILM set for *5-25-77*, I received a call from Scott Alexander, who was calling from California. He called frequently during the course of shooting to see how I was doing, since it was he who recruited me for my first movie experience.

As we talked, he asked me if I was going to be at WonderFest that year (2006). Still new to the world of model-making, I didn't know what WonderFest was. He explained that it is an annual sci-fi convention held in Louisville, Kentucky. It is a "Weekend of Fun for Movie and Model Fans," as WonderFest.com puts it. Scott tries to go every year, and encouraged me to go, saying that I would love it. Besides, it would give us a chance to finally meet face-to-face.

My wife and I decided it would be something fun and different to do, so we made plans to meet Scott there in May of that year.

We thoroughly enjoyed all that the convention had to offer. I was in model 'heaven' in the dealer room, my wife enjoyed the presentations that were given by the Hollywood guest speakers, and we both were enthralled with Scott's fascinating stories of his movie-making experiences and knowledge. We made plans to return the following year.

WonderFest gave me ideas for promoting *5-25-77*. Back home there was an annual IPMS (International Plastic Modelers' Society) model contest held locally in my area. In the contest back in 2003, my first scratch-built Star Destroyer won two awards, the only time I ever entered anything. This was before the museum or movie experiences happened. Now I had arranged with the IPMS organizers to have a table reserved for a display of all the models I made for *5-25-77*, plus one of Scott's smashed X-wing Fighter models that I salvaged from the set. I made several posters out of the on-set photographs and mounted them on the wall behind my table. Guests would come by and ask about the models, and I talked to them about our up-coming movie. It was very successful as a promotion, as the models and my story were very well received by the attendees.

This led to my decision to contact the people who organize WonderFest. The convention staff answered my letter and invited me to come, as they said my experiences with the Chicago Museum of Science and Industry and my work with the movie are just the kinds of things WonderFest attendees would want to hear about. On the weekend of May 26 and 27, I would have the great honor of being a guest speaker at WonderFest 2007.

With great excitement, I got to work on my presentation. Along with PowerPoint slides of several photos, I brought three of the models I'd built for the film that would be exhibited in a display room. My display was featured right next to an impressive collection of classic horror movie props brought to the festival by the legendary Bob Burns, world renowned archivist and film historian of props, costumes, and other paraphernalia used on the screen. Bob and I had a very nice chat away from the crowds one morning. A highlight experience for me was when he allowed me to touch the original 1933 King Kong stop-motion puppet armature!

The night before my presentation I went through all my notes and slides, not wanting to forget any details. I saw on the schedule that my talk was at the same time as actor Robert Picardo (the doctor from *Star Trek: Voyager*). I told Tina that I wondered how many people would actually show up to mine. As it turned out, I had a good size audience. A big reason why I wanted to do WonderFest was not only to promote *5-25-77*. I also wanted to meet model and sci-fi fans who, like me, are dreamers.

The theme of my message was that dreams can come true. If it could happen to me it could happen to anyone!

After my talk there were a lot of questions I enjoyed answering. Even Tina was asked a few unexpected questions on how she felt about all that had happened to me. Thinking of the prayer she said on my behalf from the beginning, and all that took place since, she told those attending of her pride in my accomplishments, and that she was always ready to support me in all my endeavors.

Afterward, many people came to me to say how inspired they were by my story, that it gave them hope. That is why I wanted to do it, because following a dream is what it's all about!

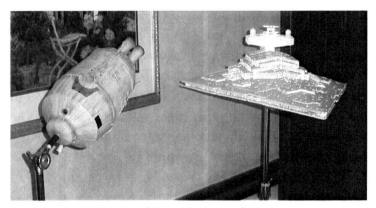

My 5-25-77 models on display at the convention.

My WonderFest presentation.

CHAPTER THIRTEEN

The Hamptons Film Festival

In October 2008 *'77 (5-25-77)* would premiere at the Hamptons International Film Festival. I received an e-mail from Patrick that went out to all the cast and crew. This was our first chance to see the film on the big screen in a theater. Naturally, Tina and I had to go!

The Hamptons may be in our home state, but being on the other end made for a very long and beautiful drive. We love New York State in the fall, and the scenery of multi-colored hills was breathtaking.

Early in the morning we left our motel to find a place to eat. While we dined, Patrick called me to make plans to meet later in the day. It was then that he surprised me with yet another promotion. Because of all I had taken upon myself to do for the film, I had just been officially given the title of *'77's* associate producer. This was to be added to model-maker, model-making supervisor/coordinator, and ILM set realization. These are all on the Internet Movie Database (IMDb) along with others for the film that include visual effects digital artist and the extras I played in the Hollywood scenes.

It was good to see Patrick again. I was also looking

forward to seeing producer Leigh Jones, whom I had not seen since the scenes were filmed more than two years earlier.

As a special guest, Patrick had Herb Lightman flown to the film festival to see *'77*. Patrick met Herb in 1977 when Mr. Lightman was the editor of American Cinematographer magazine. It was Herb who took a teenage Patrick on the tour of Hollywood that is shown in our movie. As a character in the film, he is played by veteran actor, Austin Pendleton. Because Patrick and Leigh needed to attend publicity engagements, Tina and I had the great honor and pleasure of spending the entire weekend with Herb. We met him in the filmmaker's lounge at the festival headquarters... a funny little man with plaid pants and a bright red fishing hat.

I walked up to him as he sat in a chair that seemed to swallow his tiny frame... "Hello, Mr. Lightman, I am Rick Ingalsbe. I am a friend of Patrick Johnson."

A deep voice came from the small man as he reached for my hand, "Well, any friend of Patrick's is a friend of mine."

With a background in filmmaking, Herb had us spellbound with many stories of his life's adventures. We heard all about his younger days as an apprentice to the likes of Alfred Hitchcock, Samuel L. Goldwyn, and other giants of the Golden Age of movie-making. At 88 years old, Herb Lightman instantly became one of the top names on my list of most interesting and influential people I've ever met.

Also at the festival was visual effects supervisor, Mike Pawlak, actresses Emmie Chen who played Linda in the film, and Katie Jeep who played Robin. There were other crew members there that I did not get to work with, so it was nice to meet them and talk a bit about our work. We all gathered at the theater as the crowds filed in.

The film was a near sellout the first night, and thanks to word-of-mouth publicity, was a complete sellout the next day. Tina and I sat with Herb for both showings. It was the first time I'd seen my work on the big screen. When it was over, and the credits began to scroll, right at the beginning, there was my name as the associate producer. Then I was in the company of my now good friend, Scott Alexander and the people I recruited as model-makers, and together with movie-makers I had admired for decades. Four times my name appeared. A dream that came true. It brought tears to my eyes.

Before each screening Patrick was introduced to say a few words. After the film he was called up again to take questions and introduce the members of the cast and crew in attendance.

Also in the crowd was Patrick's other very special guest, the legendary visual effects master, Mr. Douglas Trumbull *(2001: A Space Odyssey, Close Encounters of the Third Kind, Star Trek: The Motion Picture, Blade Runner, Silent Running)* with members of his family. Like Herb, Mr. Trumbull is also portrayed as a character in the film.

Patrick asked Herb to come forward. All in attendance were treated to Mr. Lightman's firsthand account of the events played out on screen by actors John Francis Daley as Patrick, and Austin Pendleton as Herb Lightman. It was a very touching moment when a choked up Mr. Lightman expressed how proud he is of Patrick.

The program, schedule, button and ticket from the festival.

With Herb Lightman above, and Patrick below
at the 2008 Hamptons International Film Festival.

Douglas Trumbull also came forward to tell his account of how he'd met Patrick back then.

At the award ceremony, we were all happy to learn that '77 was presented with The Hamptons International Film Festival's Heineken Red Star Award. This award represents innovation, originality, and vision in filmmaking.

After the screening of the film, cast, crew and guests celebrated at a nearby restaurant. We dined on a private terrace behind the facility. There I had the chance to thank Patrick for my latest promotion. The highlight of my evening (and perhaps my career) came when Patrick introduced me to Douglas Trumbull. He explained to Mr. Trumbull how I got involved with the movie and all the work I put into it. Mr. Trumbull told me about how his father worked at ILM during *Star Wars*. He then told me what a great job I had done on the film. Coming from him, you could give me an Academy Award, and I don't think I could have been happier!

When the festival was over, and we all had to leave the next day, Tina and I made plans to take Herb Lightman out for breakfast before we got on the road. We had many filmmaking conversations over the weekend, and they continued through our meal. We talked about everything from editing to the importance of choosing a proper title—something he learned from Alfred Hitchcock. I'll always cherish the time we spent with him. He's a small man with a huge heart, a humble man who has lived an adventurous and interesting life.

CHAPTER FOURTEEN

The Third Replica

By the end of my involvement in *5-25-77* my model-making knowledge and skills had rapidly increased. I went from making models as a hobby to doing it on a professional level almost overnight. Charles Adams decided to discontinue Starshipbuilder.com. So, I joined other online communities devoted to studio-scale model-making.

Many like-minded people from all over the world became my friends. I was delighted when some of them told me that they were inspired by my Star Destroyers, and decided to take on that subject themselves. The work they produced was absolutely fantastic! So fantastic that the very people I had inspired were inspiring me. I accomplished so much in such a short time with my two Star Destroyers, yet was never satisfied with their inaccuracies.

Those inaccuracies were becoming more and more apparent, as I saw the outstanding work my new friends were doing. Ironically, after all I had experienced, I still had not seen the real Star Destroyer in person. Yet, as envious as I was of those who had, their good fortune was my good fortune. Because of the generosity of people sharing their pictures online, countless high-resolution photos of the filming model taken from every conceivable angle were made available.

By then I had also learned much about the kitbashed details needed to make a more accurate replica. I decided it was time to build a third Star Destroyer... and to do it right this time.

My goal was to build this new replica as much like ILM built the real one as I could, using similar techniques to achieve a similar outcome. This model would be entirely hand-made. If I had chosen to fabricate and laser cut all the parts with computer precision and perfect symmetry, as models are made today, it would lose some of the pre-computer age craftsmanship that made the original so appealing to me.

A make or break issue with a Star Destroyer replica is proportions. They are more important than details, and very hard to achieve. You can have every last kitbashed part used on the original, but if your proportions are off, the entire model will not look right. However, if you have the correct proportions, even with most of the original's details, the model can pass as a credible representation.

One of the reasons a Star Destroyer proportions are so difficult to replicate are all the angles upon angles. An error in one area can cascade throughout the entire ship. My first two models are good examples of this. I wanted to avoid those errors this time. The best way is to thoroughly know your subject. I never saw the real thing for myself in a museum, but I did have so many great photos. A collection so large they filled the pages of four binders.

Another unique reference I had was a video of the ship taken for me in a museum by friends; I specifically asked them to do a slow walk around the model. Four binders of stills is great, but they don't show depth, and perspective distortion can lead to errors. By seeing the model as the videographer walked around it, I could see how the perspective changed from each angle. It made it much easier to guess the length of the model, which had been somewhat of a mystery. It turned out not to be 3-feet long at all, but closer to 4-feet.

Finding all the right kits for detail parts, with their increasing prices and rarity, is becoming more and more a challenge in scratch-building studio-scale models. There are those who feel that a replica is less than credible if not dressed with all original kit parts. I've learned through experience that this is not necessarily true. It all comes down to what is important and satisfactory in the eyes of the individual. It takes an enormous amount of time, energy, and money to build these models. These factors can be the difference between finishing a model and continuing a perpetual project that goes on indefinitely.

Most of the details on a Star Destroyer can be thought of as impressionistic, so making them up as you go is acceptable. Having said that, there are areas on my third replica where accurate details are a must. They are what I consider the 'focal points' of the ship—the bridge, the bottom hull and docking bay, the engines—those areas are where the eyes go first, the key elements highlighted in scenes of the film for which the model was built.

On the original Star Destroyer, the starboard side of the ship was never seen on screen, and some areas were even left void of detail. On my new replica I used those areas (as well as others where the original parts are very hard to find) as a blank canvas to make up the details.

An early stage of construction on my third Star Destroyer replica.

The 4-foot long bottom hull before detailing.

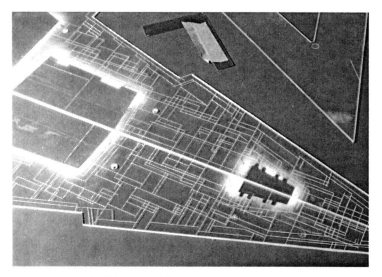

Scribing panel lines... a tedious process.

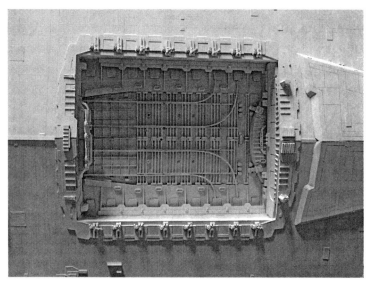

The nearly completed docking bay.

Doing this is more creative for the hobbyist and more of what it was like for the builders of the original filming model, since the ILM crew did not have to research and track down parts as we 'replicators' do.

In 2011, it was announced that Lorne Peterson, retired ILM model-maker and author of the book Sculpting a Galaxy: Inside the Star Wars Model Shop, would be a guest speaker at WonderFest. I had spoken there in 2007 about *5-25-77*. Now I had the opportunity to go back as a fan to meet one of my childhood heroes, the man who was in charge of building the original Imperial Cruiser himself.

I was invited to be part of a small group of model-makers who would have the honor of spending the week-end with Mr. Peterson. The group assembled a display of their studio-scale models—replicas mostly of *Star Wars* subjects—for the convention as a tribute to Lorne. I brought what I had of my third Star Destroyer, which was only the bridge and superstructure. I had yet to start on the huge, 4-foot wedge-shaped hull and engines. I actually had no intention of displaying my unfinished piece pub-licly, so for the first day of the convention Lorne did not see my work. But the guys within the group saw what I had brought and graciously insisted that it be included in their display the second day.

That was the day Lorne saw it. Since it hadn't been there the day before, he took special notice. He asked the group, "Whose is this?"

"That's Rick's," they replied. Lorne turned to me, "Rick, is this yours?"

At that point, going through my mind was the very first, crude wooden replica I made in art class and all attempts that followed. Now here I was with the man who built my favorite filming model as he was looking at my latest rendition in progress. "This is very impressive work," he said.

There are moments in my career which I consider highlights I will always cherish. Seeing my second replica in the museum exhibit was certainly one. Meeting Douglas Trumbull and receiving his compliments on my work was another. Talking with Lorne Peterson about my third Star Destroyer replica was yet another one of these moments.

As he examined my work in progress, he began telling me stories of how they built the original Star Destroyer at ILM. He pointed at areas of my model to show me who at ILM did each part and how. Also, my decision to make up some details rather than copy the original piece for piece was a good one, as Lorne made a positive comment on that. Through a dinner, a breakfast, and another dinner, Lorne was kind enough to answer all our questions about how the *Star Wars* filming models were made. He also shared many stories about the making of *Star Wars*, some we got to hear twice as they were part of his presentation.

I was so impressed with how patient and gracious he was with our endless questions. He really enjoyed sharing his numerous insights and experiences as much as we enjoyed listening to them.

I took the opportunity to tell Lorne of my involvement in *5-25-77*. I brought a small photo album full of

My third Star Destroyer replica.

With Lorne Peterson at WonderFest 2011.

photos of the ILM set I created for the film and all the models that were made for it. I explained that in addition to all my work behind the scenes, I even appeared in the film, too. Patrick asked me to grow lots of hair and a beard so I could look like one of the ILM guys as they made *Star Wars*. Although I was not given a specific character to portray, in my mind I was trying to look like Lorne Peterson. I showed him a photo of me on set as him.

When I asked if we could have a picture taken together, he put on glasses and a baseball cap to look like me. Of course, I also have a photo of us with Lorne as himself. When I saw how that picture turned out, I cringed because I don't think I ever looked more like a fanboy in my life.

Because I had much more work ahead of me on my Star Destroyer, Lorne was kind enough to stay in contact with me in the months following to answer more questions as they came up during the rest of the build. My hope was to have the model finished before WonderFest 2012 the following year. That may sound like enough time, but I would need that whole year to finish, and then some. Some kitbashed parts that were near impossible to find happened to be the ones I wanted for my model. I decided I would glue on temporary parts, then replace them if the right parts ever turned up. The online communities exist for these kinds of dilemmas.

My third replica would not be all I wanted it to be without the help of my new friends. The hard-to-find parts came from all over the world from people who were lucky enough to have them, and kind enough to come to the rescue. Enough of the ship was done in time for the convention in 2012.

I got permission from the WonderFest crew to display it near where Lorne Peterson saw it the previous year. I needed to consider how I would display this now full Star Destroyer model. I thought of how my second replica was in a booth in the museums. It was on a mirrored base with the mounting rod coming out of the mirror. The base of the booth doubled as a crate that carried the model in transit to the next location. I built a similar traveling crate that would act as the base for my display. I even had a mirror so people could see the under-side of the ship just like at the museum.

The fun for me at conventions is watching the looks on peoples' faces when they see my work. Whenever possible, I like to hang out and talk with people as they photograph the model and ask me questions about it. Since I still have never seen the original Star Destroyer in person, I was hoping to meet someone who had.

That didn't happen until the show was over and I was in the process of packing up the model for the long trip home. I was approached by someone who told me that the real filming model used to be in an exhibit in the muse-um where he was working. He would spend his lunch breaks looking at it, day after day for the length of its stay. He then gave me the best compliment I could have received, saying my replica so closely resembled the real thing that it made him feel like he got to see it one more time.

I had finally built the replica model of my dreams. I still had not had the chance to see the real thing in a museum, though. If I ever do, it would make this 'journey' of mine complete.

Some model-makers think of me as some kind of an 'authority' on Star Destroyers. Until I see it for myself; how my latest replica compares to the original, I can't call myself that. But, as Scott Alexander said to me in a recent conversation, "Rick, you've built three of these. Face it, you're an expert!"

My completed third replica at WonderFest 2012.

CHAPTER FIFTEEN

Hearts of Dorkness

In the last half of 2012, Patrick Read Johnson set out to take his film on the road. I first learned of this when he sent me an e-mail stating that on May 25th, 2012, he and a small group would depart from a famous railroad crossing in Wadsworth, IL. on what they had planned to be a 30 day odyssey, driving in the same 1975 Ford Pinto that appeared in *5-25-77*. With support vehicles following, they would make their way across the country, stopping at roadside attractions, drive-in movie theaters, small town cinemas, sci-fi conventions, classic car meets, etc.— all of it uploaded to their web page as they attempt to raise the remaining funds needed to finish the film.

As part of this, they would be creating featurettes about the making of the film that would be played in small episodes during the trip. Patrick wrote to me to say that, "YOU are ONE of those episodes, if you'd like to be... So, let me know if you want guests with cameras in your home any time soon and we'll set it up!"

Tina and I thought it would be exciting and fun to be a part of this documentary, and so we made arrangements. We invited him to stay with us to do the interview. Filmmaker Morgan Flores, who is making this documentary called *Hearts of Dorkness: The Road to 5-25-77*, would join us, and conduct the interview.

They first went to Douglas Trumbull's home to interview him and tour his studio, after which they headed toward our home. En route I received a follow up e-mail saying that they were on their way and had lots to tell us.

Tina prepared guest rooms, which we've affectionately dubbed the 'Moonwatcher' suites, while I put together a small filming set in our living room for the interview. I hung a black backdrop on the wall. Behind the chair I would be sitting in, I arranged some models as set dressing with my newest Star Destroyer replica and other models that were used in *5-25-77*.

When they arrived, Patrick introduced us to Morgan, and we liked her instantly. The four of us did a lot of talking that night. During our discussion, the fact came up that the William Morris Agency (WMA), which was representing *5-25-77*, was no longer in business. They were responsible for changing the title from *5-25-77* to just *'77*.

Patrick asked my advice about changing it back. I told him that I thought changing it to just *'77* was a mistake, and that I never liked it. I was all in favor of changing it back to its original title. He was happy to hear that and whole-heartedly agreed. After receiving the same opinion from many others, *5-25-77* was once again the official, permanent, unchangeable title of the movie.

We heard more about the trip they were about to embark on. Patrick wanted to accomplish a few things, most importantly raising money to finish the movie. The William Morris Agency was going to put up the funds needed; however, that never happened because of WMA going out of business.

I had been asked many times by fans why the film is taking so long to finish, and this was one of the main reasons. Patrick had told me that there were always distributors interested in releasing the film once it was finished. But the days of a studio putting up money to finish an indy film are pretty much gone. They won't do it if they don't have to.

This left Patrick looking for new and creative ways to raise the funds. Taking the film to audiences himself, showing it to them and asking for their help seemed the best way to do it. The plan was a month-long road trip that would start in Wadsworth, Illinois, head southwest through Texas, out through Nevada and on to California making several stops along the way to screen different cuts of *5-25-77* as a work-in-progress.

This would raise awareness of the film, enough to hopefully raise the money to finish it once and for all. Patrick also took the opportunity to screen different versions of the film to get reactions and feedback from these test audiences that would help determine the final cut of *5-25-77*.

After hearing about this plan, and a bit of catching up, Patrick treated us with videos he had just taken while at Douglas Trumbull's place. We got to see his incredibly impressive studio, as well as parts of the interview they did with him. This gave me an insight on what they were looking to accomplish, and what to expect when they interviewed me.

We decided that my interview would take place in the morning, since it was getting late and they were tired from the long drive. In the morning Tina made breakfast for everyone, and we talked a bit more about other movies both done and in the works. After our meal, we all got ready for the interview. Morgan and Patrick set up the camera and lights while I prepared.

It was a bit awkward for me at first since I had not yet done an interview like this before. Morgan fed me the questions, and after a few I began to loosen up. Tina was watching Patrick's reactions to my answers, and now and then she said he looked up at her with a smile when he especially liked what I said.

With the interview done, we all went out for lunch. Then, they had to head back to Chicago to make final preparations for the trip.

Soon after, the *Hearts of Dorkness* website was online. I would follow their progress often through the site and through the writeups and video interviews that appeared on other sites at each location. It seemed the film was getting very positive reactions from audiences. At one stop in Texas they had two screenings scheduled. The fans loved the film so much, they paid for a third screening the following day.

What was meant to be a one month trip turned into six. On such a long journey, things did not always go smoothly. They ran into difficulties along the way—the motor home broke down in South Dakota, their computer was damaged, costing a lot to fix, which meant extra days in hotels. Near the end of the trip the Pinto's brakes gave out.

Now and then during those months I would send my greetings and well-wishes to him. One reply listed some of these difficulties, and asked me to help get the word out. I did what I could, making announcements on various websites. I had a *Hearts of Dorkness* advertising banner on my own site from the beginning, which had an enormous amount of hits from the link Patrick and Morgan had set up from their website.

After six months the trip was summed up on the Hearts of Dorkness website in this way...

On May 25th, 2012, the 35th Anniversary of the release of the original *Star Wars*, Patrick Read Johnson, departed Wadsworth, Illinois, in the film's 1975 Ford Pinto, and began a 30-day cross-country/road-trip/fundraising campaign odyssey designed to finally bring his long-awaited film to the screen.

His goal? To raise the funds needed to finish *5-25-77* with a multi-media adventure which was documented, and made available, here on this website, (in addition to/through all the other *HOD* social network avenues). The best moments of the adventure will finally be compiled and sculpted into a documentary: *Hearts of Dorkness*, to be released in conjunction with the DVD of *5-25-77*.

PRJ and the *Hearts of Dorkness* team visited places that have inspired the dreams of sci-fi fans and filmmakers alike. Devil's Tower, Wyoming-- Meteor Crater, Arizona-- Roswell,

New Mexico...

Along the way, Patrick test screened a working cut of the *5-25-77* in small-town theaters, living rooms, on a hand-strung screen under the stars—going directly to the source—the film's target audience—to find out what they think about *5-25-77*, and to get their opinions about how to land at the best final cut of the film.

What was intended to be a 30-day road trip during the summer became a 143-day odyssey stretching into the fall, and was ultimately brought to a close in the middle of October 2012 when the call of dreams colliding with reality causing Patrick to switch gears once he reached Los Angeles.

Though at the end of the road trip, Patrick did not reach the funding goals for *5-25-77*— Patrick did succeed in raising awareness about his film, breathing new life into *5-25-77's* want-to-see factor, and energizing longtime and new fans... All of this building more momentum every day toward a bright fate for *5-25-77...*

CHAPTER SIXTEEN

The Next Wave Film Festival

Even though the ultimate goal of the road trip was not reached, there was a growing fan base, and the word was spreading about this amazing indy film.

Then Patrick received a bit of good news. In January 2013, he sent an e-mail saying, "Hey! Just thought you'd like to know..." This was followed by a link to the TIFF Theater website where this announcement was made, "The Toronto International Film Festival's Next Wave Festival has invited Patrick Read Johnson to show *5-25-77* February 16, 2013."

Patrick ended his e-mail with, "PLEASE COME!"

I received this news with both excitement and a sense of irony. That's because in 2008, when the film was being marketed to the film festivals, we tried a last-minute attempt to get into Toronto.

Patrick would have sent the movie directly to Toronto, but there was no rush delivery service over the U.S.–Canadian border that could deliver it in time to meet the festival's submission deadline. Because this was a last minute attempt and because Tina and I only live about 90 minutes from Toronto, I told Patrick we would take the film to the festival staff personally.

Patrick overnighted copies of the film to us, and the

very minute we received them, Tina and I were in the car heading to Canada. We arrived in Toronto with not a moment to spare. We delivered the film, and after having lunch in the CN Tower's rotating restaurant high above the city, we headed back home where we waited to hear if *5-25-77* would be added to the festival's lineup.

After much waiting and anticipation, we finally received the disappointing news that *5-25-77* did not fit the overall theme of movies Toronto was showing for that year.

However, *5-25-77* is told from a teen's point of view, and the Next Wave festival of 2013 was for movies of that genre. So, after five years, we would finally be screened in Toronto.

Tina and I went to the festival with friends who would finally get their chance to see *5-25-77* after hearing my stories about this movie for years. We met up with Patrick at the TIFF theater. He was constantly being rushed here and there in preparation for the show. Morgan Flores was also there, as a trailer for her *Hearts of Dorkness* documentary would be screened after the film.

Patrick had arranged for VIP seating for Tina, myself and our friends. When the theater was filled to capacity, the festival staff introduced Patrick. He explained to the audience that this cut of *5-25-77* was one of a few that he had in the works, each based on particular feedback from the road trip screenings all over the United States. He also explained that the film was still a work in progress, so some portions of it were going to appear a bit rough around the edges.

As the film played, I noticed all the scenes that were

in, out, rearranged, or redone—different from any other version I had seen before. No matter how many cuts of the film I've seen, I still love this movie, and it was great to see it on the big screen again. I was especially pleased to see *"5-25-77"* as the title of the film, no longer just *"'77."*

After the movie, the audience stayed for Q&A with Patrick. During this session, he introduced me to the audience and plugged my website, which had received the largest amount of hits in its existence because of the Toronto festival and the link they set up on the *HOD* site. Then Patrick introduced Morgan. She came up front to say some things about *HOD*, and we got to see the trailer she put together for the documentary.

We were happy to see Morgan again. We caught up a bit as she told us more about the road trip, and the documentary still in progress. She was, in fact, filming much of the festival events taking place around us for her film.

When the night was over, we parted ways again, waiting for the next chapter in this story, which will lead to the long-awaited official release of *5-25-77*.

CHAPTER SEVENTEEN

Reflections

As I write this book, I received word that two major studios have expressed interest in releasing *5-25-77*. So many audiences have already seen it, either at one of the film festivals, or as part of the *Hearts of Dorkness* tour. The responses have been overwhelmingly positive. I believe in this film's ability to touch hearts, and I also believe it will eventually play in theaters everywhere.

Now, another film festival has shown interest in screening the film; Cinetopia International Film Festival in Ann Arbor, Michigan, June 2013 brings *5-25-77* another step closer to that release.

I can't help but look back at these last 10 years with wonder at all the amazing things that happened, and all the fascinating people I've met, many of whom I am pleased to call my friends. All of this because I decided one day to try something I had never done before—scratch-build a studio-scale model. Some call it fate; others would say it was an amazing coincidence that I happened to build two Star Destroyer replicas at exactly the time when two major productions needed them (and no one else was building them).

I believe everything happens for a reason; that all

things come together for a higher purpose. I've learned that people should go for their dreams, no matter how 'impossible' anyone might say the dream might be. I wasted too many years convinced that my dreams could not happen.

Then suddenly it all changed, and with a little faith and some much needed support and encouragement from a loving wife, these remarkable events took place which thrust me into the world of movie-making... and lifelong dreams came true.

When I was interviewed by Morgan Flores about this, she asked me what I would say to other model-making hobbyists with similar dreams. I answered, "I'm just a fan like everyone else. If this can happen to me, it can happen to anyone!

"Keep on doing what you are doing. Keep on building and don't stop dreaming... because you just never know!"

So, what was making *5-25-77* like? To sum it up from my point of view, it meant long 18-20 hour days on set, day after day with about 3-4 hours of sleep per night. I lost 10 pounds in one week, as I hardly thought about food. My feet were killing me from being on them all day, and my hands always seemed to be chapped and bleeding as a result of the cold weather combined with the rough work I was doing. I never worked harder on anything in my career and I was completely exhausted when it was over.

Yet, as hard as it was, I can honestly say that I thoroughly enjoyed every minute of it! When you get the chance to do something you've always wanted to do, but never thought you would, and when your heart and soul are so passionate about something that time seems to stand still, then nothing else seems to matter... *you are where you belong!* I was at home on the set. I've never felt so alive in my career doing anything else.

I used to think, "If I only had a chance." Well, Patrick Read Johnson gave me that chance, for which I will always be grateful. I can honestly say I gave it everything I had and made the absolute most of it. I was told by people in the business that you either have what it takes or you don't, that you either love it or hate it. For me, I can't wait to do it again, and again, and again!

So, when *5-25-77* makes it to a theater near you, look for a guy in the background of the model shops of Future General and ILM wearing '70s duds, sporting long black hair and a thick beard, on set with actors John Francis Daley and Austin Pendleton. That would be me... *having the time of my life!*

Patrick Read Johnson and me. This photo was taken just after the final scene was shot for 5-25-77.

CPSIA information can be obtained at www.ICGtesting.com
Printed in the USA
LVOW05s1451111213

364858LV00001B/60/P